AF624297

Professor M. Hiriyanna (1871–1950) is recognized in learned circles both in India and abroad as an outstanding authority on traditional Indian philosophy. This monograph attempts to bring his contribution to Indian philosophy to the notice of a wider circle of readers. Deeply versed in Sanskrit classics and equally proficient in English literature, Hiriyanna worked with single-minded devotion to the cause of Indian philosophy and literary studies. This volume brings together the cream of Hiriyanna's contribution, spread over his numerous articles and books, in one conspectus and evaluates his place among the builders of Indian philosophy. Though Hiriyanna did not claim anything like a philosophy of his own, he had a distinctive perception of both the general spirit and the specific concepts and doctrines of Indian philosophy. This book seeks to highlight Hiriyanna's characteristic approach to Indian philosophy in all its aspects. It starts from the general standpoint of Hiriyanna in regard to Indian philosophy and takes the reader through the details of his interpretation of Indian metaphysics and value investigation. Brief, significant quotations from Hiriyanna are given at appropriate places to bring the reader's attention directly to Hiriyanna. The numerous references given to Hiriyanna's works will also be helpful in the study of Hiriyanna in the original.

T.P. Ramachandran took his M.A. from the University of Travancore in 1952, Ph.D. from the University of Madras in 1962, and D.Litt. from the same university in 1981. He started career in 1952 as a Lecturer in Philosophy in the National College at Tiruchirapalli. Moving on to the Department of Philosophy in the University of Madras in 1964, when it was upgraded into a Centre for Advanced Study, he served as Senior Research Fellow, Lecturer, Reader, and Professor, and retired in 1987. His publications include *The Concept of the Vyāvahārika in Advaita Vedānta* and *The Indian Philosophy of Beauty* (in two parts). His main interest is in Indian philosophy with special reference to Values and Meta-philosophy. For many years he has made a close study of Hiriyanna's works, to which he is particularly drawn, and the present book is a product of that study.

M. Hiriyanna

The Builders of Indian Philosophy Series

General Editor: R. BALASUBRAMANIAN

B.G. TILAK
S.H. Dixit

J. KRISHNAMURTI
Ravi Ravindra

KALIDAS BHATTACHARYYA
Debabrata Sinha

K.C. BHATTACHARYYA
K. Bagchi

P.N. SRINIVASACHARI
K.R. Sundararajan

P.T. RAJU
K. Srinivas

RABINDRANATH TAGORE
P.K. Roy

R.D. RANADE
S.S. Antarkar and *Shubhada A. Joshi*

SRI AUROBINDO
M.P. Pandit

T.M.P. MAHADEVAN
R. Balasubramanian

T.V. KAPALI SASTRI
Prema Nandakumar

M. Hiriyanna

THE BUILDERS OF INDIAN PHILOSOPHY SERIES

M. Hiriyanna

T.P. Ramachandran

Munshiram Manoharlal
Publishers Pvt Ltd

ISBN 81-215-0943-2
First published 2001

Typeset, printed and published by
Munshiram Manoharlal Publishers Pvt. Ltd.,
Post Box 5715, 54 Rani Jhansi Road, New Delhi 110 055.

Humbly dedicated
to the sacred memory of my preceptor
JAGADGURU ŚRĪ CANDRAŚEKHARENDRA SARASVATĪ
ŚRĪ ŚAṄKARĀCĀRYA ŚRĪCARAṆĀḤ
of Śrī Kāmakoṭi Pīṭha at Kāñcī
whose eternal grace guides me ever

Contents

The Builders of Indian Philosophy Series

The philosophical concepts and categories associated with Sāṅkhya, Vaiśeṣika, Cārvāka, Jaina and other systems are as old as the Vedas. However, the formulation of different systems should have taken place later on. Unfortunately, we do not know about the historical development of these ideas prior to the systematic presentation of them in the form of *sūtras* (aphorisms) which serve as the basic text for each of these schools. Because of the brevity of the *sūtras*, it is difficult to understand the *sūtra*-work without the help of a commentary. Then came the commentaries and sub-commentaries of various kinds called *bhāṣyas, vārtikas, vṛttis, kārikās*, and *ṭīkās* explaining the various texts which were interconnected starting from the basic *sūtra*-text. Texts, both expository and polemical, were written defending the basic doctrines of each system and also criticizing the views of other systems; and these texts are also commentaries.

It must be borne in mind that a commentary is much more than an exegesis. It is also creative while doing the work of interpretation. One should first of all "understand" the text before interpreting it. The "understanding" that serves as the basis for interpretation is a preliminary interpretation. The choice of a text as well as its identification as such-and-such involves interpretation; and the method one adopts in the analysis of the text also involves interpretation. Object and method are inseparable. The text taken up for interpretation has a context or horizon of its own; the interpreter, too, has a horizon of his/her own. The interaction between the two horizons is a basic element in every kind of interpretation. This interaction between the two horizons, which goes on whenever a text is explained, "enriches" the text and makes it both purportful and purposive. So a commentary is as much original as the text it is commenting on. The *bhāṣyas* of Śabara and Śaṅkara, the *vārtikas* of Kumārila Bhaṭṭa and Uddyotakara—works such as these are first-rate philosophical texts noted for their originality and creativity. In short, Indian philosophy was built and developed, strengthened and shaped by the commentarial tradition.

Contemporary Indian scholars, academic as well as non-academic, have enriched the tradition in several ways. Like classical commentators, they are "builders" of Indian philosophy in the two areas of pure and applied philosophy. The monographs in this series called "The Builders of Indian Philosophy" are intended to elucidate and highlight their contribution to Indian philosophy.

R. Balasubramanian
General Editor

Preface

Five years after retirement, when I had begun to withdraw from academic activities, my old friend, classmate and colleague, Dr. R. Balasubramanian, invited me to contribute a monograph on Hiriyanna to a series on Builders of Indian Philosophy. The invitation was too strong to resist, notwithstanding domestic difficulties, as I have always loved and admired Hiriyanna. The work has taken double the time offered to me. I owe its completion to the substantial support and suggestions and the constant urge given to me by Dr. Balasubramanian at every stage. And for the immense trouble he has taken in going through the matter from manuscript to print, I am grateful to him.

Being one generation removed from Hiriyanna, I cannot claim the privilege of having sat at his feet. But Dr. Balasubramanian and I had the good fortune of listening to glowing accounts of Hiriyanna's character and learning from one of our own teachers, the late Professor M.K. Venkatarama Iyer of the National College at Tiruchirapalli, who was a student of Hiriyanna. I have scrupulously sought not to allow my personal regard for Hiriyanna to influence my treatment of the subject, but to bring to bear on it the same objectivity which Hiriyanna observed in his treatment of Indian philosophy. When I started the work, another old friend and colleague, Dr. N. Veezhinathan, cautioned me on a special difficulty regarding the subject—that its angle was to be, not Indian philosophy as such gathered from Hiriyanna, but the way Hiriyanna understood and interpreted Indian philosophy. Indeed, I often found it difficult to sustain my eye on that point of view in the course of my writing especially because of Hiriyanna's self-effacing style. But I hope, I have fairly succeeded in fulfilling this requirement and dispassionately estimating the place of Hiriyanna among the builders of Indian philosophy. This book brings together the key ideas spread over Hiriyanna's various writings. And I hope that this will stimulate interest in the study of Hiriyanna in the original and provide some lead in following his thoughts. As Hiriyanna is universally recognized as a safe and certain guide to

Indian philosophy, I also hope that this book will incidentally serve as an invitation to the study of Indian philosophy.

T.P. RAMACHANDRAN

Namakkal, Tamil Nadu
1 January 2001

Abbreviations

AE	*Art Experience*
EIP	*The Essentials of Indian Philosophy*
ICV	*The Indian Conception of Values*
IPS—I	*Indian Philosophical Studies—I*
IPS—II	*Indian Philosophical Studies—II*
MP	*The Mission of Philosophy*
OIP	*Outlines of Indian Philosophy*
PEIP	*Popular Essays in Indian Philosophy*
QAP	*The Quest After Perfection*
R	*Reviews*

1
Introduction

1. PROFESSOR HIRIYANNA: HIS LIFE AND PERSONALITY

Life

Mysore Hiriyanna was born in 1871. His early education was in Mysore. His teacher, Sri Periaswamy Tirumalachariar, to whom he was greatly devoted, was his early inspiration in Sanskrit. Hiriyanna took his B.A. and M.A. degrees through the Madras Christian College. After a few years in government service, which included the Librarianship of the Government Oriental Library in Mysore for a year, he took his L.T. degree in 1895 through the Teacher's College in Saidapet, Madras, as a government scholar on deputation. His teaching career began in 1896. For sixteen years he taught in the Government Normal School at Mysore, first as Assistant Master for eleven years and then as Head Master for five years. It was in 1912 that Hiriyanna was appointed Lecturer in Sanskrit in Maharaja's College, Mysore. He became Assistant Professor in 1914 and Officiating Professor in 1917. From 1918 till he retired in 1927 he served as Professor of Sanskrit in the University of Mysore. In 1921 for a brief period he was also Curator in the Government Oriental Library in Mysore.

After retirement, Hiriyanna was more actively engaged in writing. He was also connected with the activities of learned societies. In the 1935 session of the All-India Oriental Conference held at Mysore he presided over its Indian Philosophy section. He was General President of the Indian Philosophical Congress at its Hyderabad session in 1939. The All-India Oriental Conference elected him as the General President for its 1951 session to be held at Lucknow, but Hiriyanna had to decline the offer for his failing health. In appreciation of his services to Sanskrit, the Madras Sanskrit Academy honoured him with the title of *Saṁskṛta-sevā-dhurīṇa*. He passed away in 1950. A volume of studies dedicated to the memory of the great Professor was brought out from Mysore by his students, friends, and admirers. The birth centenary of

Hiriyanna was celebrated under the auspices of the University of Mysore from December 15 to 17, 1971.

Hiriyanna as a Teacher and a Scholar

Hiriyanna had a high sense of the vocation of a teacher. His dedication to teaching was complete. He prepared for his own use extensive notes based on his intimate and continuous study of original sources. Sometimes he dictated his notes to his students in subjects which had no suitable text-books. He revised his notes every year. He was so conscientious in the discharge of his duties that he had hardly any time to think of publishing his writings. It was only after he retired and was relieved of teaching duties that he took seriously to publishing them. As a teacher full of learning and imbued with a high sense of duty and rectitude, he naturally commanded the confidence, love, and reverence of his students and colleagues. He had already become a legend by the time he entered the Maharaja's College after serving in the Normal school.

Hiriyanna's learning was deep and thorough. As a master of Sanskrit he was an authority on both Alaṅkāraśāstra and Darśana in Indian thought. Among the schools of Indian philosophy Advaita was his *forte*. But his grasp of all the other schools was no less, he having mastered each of them from its own authoritative sources. In fact, whatever he wrote in Indian philosophy bore the stamp of authority of one who had closely studied the original sources in every branch and school of philosophy. He was equally read in Western philosophy and could not easily be taken for a ride in the field, though he was not inclined to write on Western philosophy as such. He was well read in English literature as he was in Sanskrit literature.

For all his learning, Hiriyanna was invincibly modest. Learning did not sit heavily on him. Devoted entirely to his studies and shunning publicity, he did not seek recognition and felt embarrassed when it came. Even by temperament, he was a quiet scholar. He did not take part in organizational work in the cause of philosophy and Sanskrit, but devoted all his time and energy to literary pursuits. It is said that he avoided public and social functions.

Hiriyanna was no dry and rigid scholar. He was equally endowed with a fine sensibility and love for art. He brought to bear on his aesthetic writings not only his scholarly talent, but also his personal taste as an aesthete (*sahṛdaya*). He had a special love for South Indian music.

Hiriyanna lived a perfectly ordered and disciplined life. He was simple to the point of austerity. As in his life, so in his writings there was a neat way of doing things. In spite of close reading, he handled books with care. He carefully and neatly arranged and preserved all his records. Papers already published in various journals, unpublished papers, reviews which he wrote on books over long years, and finally the manuscript of his last great work, the *Indian Conception of Values*—all became available to an eager clientele in book form because of this lovely habit.

His Intellectual Honesty

Both in personal life and in scholarship Hiriyanna was absolutely true to himself. In his writings he never forgot to acknowledge in a handsome manner even a small help received from anyone, however humble or young he was among scholars. It is usual to come across a footnote here and there that he owed a particular reference or an idea to somebody.

Hiriyanna always checked his material with the original sources, and whenever there was a doubt, he would rather omit the material rigorously than venture any provisional opinion or vague surmise. He was absolutely candid in admitting the shortcomings of his earlier findings whenever new material came to light. When he wrote out his material, he was so fastidious that he was never quite satisfied with what he had written. He revised his draft several times, even allowing some time to lapse, until it came up to his exacting standards. His desire for thoroughness was so demanding that he would never rush to print his production. If he found that someone had written on the subject in the meantime, he would rather withhold his work than duplicate what was already done. Only when he felt that he had something distinctive to say, did he care to publish his work. A striking instance of this attitude was his *Outlines of Indian Philosophy*, which came out after the works of Dasgupta and Radhakrishnan had appeared.

Another respect in which his intellectual honesty showed itself was his dislike of haste whether in appreciating or criticizing another's views. Both appreciation and criticism should be preceded by thorough understanding of the point of view and ideas put forth by the writer. In all fairness to someone with whom he could not agree, Hiriyanna would take pains to study his view thoroughly before venturing his opinion. Equally so, his appreciation of the agreeable was restrained and informed. This was in the best Indian philosophical tradition where full and faithful exposition of the rival position always preceded its refutation and the establishment of the position held by oneself. Himself a great exponent of Advaita, Hiriyanna is noted for his objective representation of other schools

His Academic Generosity and Fairness

Hiriyanna was always willing and eager to help his juniors in scholarship. Though he did not spare himself, he was tolerant of those who could not come up to his high standards. He was noted for his kindness and consideration and unfailing courtesy. He gave suggestions, read and revised manuscripts, and wrote out opinions of books at great sacrifice to his own time and energy.

Hiriyanna's generosity to future scholars comes out in his writings. He was himself a researcher *par excellence*. He had an uncanny insight into unexplored areas in Indian thought. While he had himself worked on some of these and published his finding in his own inimitable way, he was equally aware that it was humanly impossible for him to pursue all his leading ideas in his own lifetime. But far from keeping these ideas to himself, through his writings he eagerly shared even his distant thoughts with future students in the hope that they may find his suggestions fruitful.

Hiriyanna was fair to all scholars, whether they were old or young, and whether they were already known to the scholarly world or yet to make their mark. Nothing goes to immortalize this quality more than the reviews he wrote on books over a number of years. It is said that Hiriyanna's academic generosity had its complement in his personal generosity, which he took care to conceal. Though himself of modest means, he readily responded to students and pandits who sought his aid. His help, being free from a sense of condescension, never humbled the receiver. Himself a pandit of pandits, he had great respect for their traditional learning.

Temperamentally, Hiriyanna was incapable of giving offence to anyone. He would not even answer unfair criticism. He would bear it patiently in the firm conviction that truth would ultimately triumph and silence his detractors.

His Ideal of Life

Hiriyanna's ideal of life was a perfect harmony of *pravṛtti* and *nivṛtti* as taught in the *Bhagavad-gītā*. He lived a balanced and full life—a life in this world, but not of it, a life which was active and useful, but without expectation and desire and without either exultation or bitterness.

His fondness for this ideal is not only testified to by those who were close to him, but also comes out clearly in his writings. It would be no exaggeration to say that his account of the *Bhagavad-gītā* is his own testament of faith.

Hiriyanna's Language and Style

This aspect deserves to be taken up last as it provides an important key to Hiriyanna's writings, which are to be considered later. Hiriyanna was a master of English prose. He wrote in a diction that won the admiration of the English-speaking world. It was grammatical without being pedantic. It was direct and plain and at the same time pleasingly idiomatic. "The style is the man." And Hiriyanna's style of writing bears out his qualities of head and heart.

Hiriyanna's style, in the first instance, was brief, crisp and to the point. He never indulged in verbosity and flamboyance—a weakness which only obscures the subject and confounds the reader. Hiriyanna regarded more words than are necessary to convey a point as a patent distraction. Well has it been said of him that he never wrote a useless word. An offshoot of this brevity was that his manner of putting across an idea was unique. It was strikingly fresh and epigrammatic in such a way as to fix the idea intended in the mind of the reader. At the same time, by virtue of their laconic style, Hiriyanna's writings could not be expected to accommodate and oblige the casual and cursory reader. They were meant for the serious student, whether he was a specialist in the subject or a general reader. They required close and careful study, often more than once. In fact, a second reading would often yield deeper meaning than the first.

Brevity and hard reading, however, did not leave the reader of Hiriyanna in doubt or confusion. Hiriyanna was clear in expression and logical in exposition. He had the knack of using the right word for an idea. The sequence of ideas was also natural and logical so that a whole argument unfolded itself step by step. His arrangement of sentences and paragraphs was fully geared to this end. He never lost himself in sentimental over-statements and exaggerations. His writing was strictly rational and controlled.

The intellectual regimen of Hiriyanna's writing did not render it cold and dry. There was a felicity about it suggesting that in the higher reaches of thought truth and beauty tend to coincide. What is lucidly logical becomes for that very reason pleasant also. He made a fine art of technical writing. The result was that even the most complicated problems of philosophy became in his hands quite intelligible and interesting.

Hiriyanna never strayed from the subject on hand. Irrelevant ideas were mercilessly excluded. Points which were relevant to the subject but of secondary importance received attention only proportionate to the main topic. He never allowed them to overshadow the latter. Whether in relegating these points to notes or in incorporating them in the text, his decision was accurate. His notes are few. He did not clutter his writing with too many of them. Only those points which were of additional value received notation. Others which were of a clarificatory nature were artfully incorporated into the text. He would smoothly change track from the main idea to a subsidiary point of clarification and explanation, and without tarrying for too long in it, return to the main topic without producing any sense of jolt.

Above all, Hiriyanna's style was not only formal but courteous. He never hurt even those with whom he differed however strongly. He had the gift of being critical without being caustic. Strong language was foreign to his repertoire. While he set for himself the most rigorous standards of scholarship and hated all sham and pretence, he had a delicate and good-humoured way of pulling up anyone for shallowness of equipment. When he was convinced that somebody was wrong, whether out of ignorance or carelessness or presumption, he expressed his disfavour firmly, but politely. Nothing brings out these qualities more vividly than his reviews of books, a good collection of which was published in book form by Kavyalaya Publishers in 1970. Raghavan says in his Foreword to the book as follows:

> While reviewing helps a scholar to keep in touch with the flow of books, and to contribute to the advancement of learning with his constructive criticism and guidance, it also, unfortunately, brings him into some tension with fellow-authors of whose writings he is obliged to be critical. That this latter is not unavoidable is a lesson which all reviewers may learn from Hiriyanna who, in his writings, main or subsidiary, was an *Ajātaśatru*, as indeed he was in his life.[1]

2. HIRIYANNA'S PHILOSOPHICAL PERSPECTIVE

Indian Philosophy

Hiriyanna was personally committed to Indian philosophy. He regarded his service to the cause of Indian philosophy as a matter of patriotic duty. In fact he envisaged two types of patriots. Speaking at a Śrī Śaṅkara Jayantī celebration in 1917, he said:

> It appears to me that at the present juncture in the history of our country, we require two classes of patriots to work for our amelioration—one chiefly looking forward and bent upon restructuring the future; the other mainly engaged in studying and interpreting the past so as to throw light on the right manner in which that reconstruction should proceed.[2]

It was a time when reformers and builders of a high order were emerging to carry the country forward on the social, economic and political plane. While recognizing the importance of their service, Hiriyanna felt that there was equal need for patriotic work at the less conspicuous but equally important plane of culture and learning—of studying and interpreting the past for guiding the future.

> Without a full and proper cooperation between these two classes of workers there will be no continuity in our progress. We shall be tearing ourselves away from the past and shall lose what is precious in our heritage instead of preserving and developing it.[3]

Relation with Western Philosophy

For all his love and knowledge of Indian philosophy, Hiriyanna was far from being a chauvinist and isolationist. Though he did not believe in the possibility of constructing a uniform philosophy for East and West, he was always keenly aware that East and West have much to learn from each other. "Parochialism is as indefensible in philosophy, as it is anywhere else."[4]

In comparing Indian philosophy with the Western, Hiriyanna was never tired of cautioning against the temptation to see only agreements. Such a temptation may even result in the Indian scholar trying to square his philosophy with the terms of the West, taking Western thought as the standard, and thereby misrepresenting Indian philosophy. He strongly felt that each tradition had its own genius, and barring certain points of resemblance, there were significant differences among them. And the recognition of differences was more important to him than the perception of agreements in the proper understanding of the two traditions.

> It seems to us that if the two are to be compared at all, it should be, first and foremost, for pointing out the differences between them; for if Indian thought is worth study, it is so on account of the special contribution, it has made to the sum of human knowledge and not on account of its coincidences with European thought, however striking or curious they may be.[5]

While making this caution, Hiriyanna also denounced the prejudice against comparison arising, though it might be, from the legitimate fear that Indian philosophy might lose its identity thereby. He felt that there was really no harm in a comparative study provided (i) the writer was properly equipped for it and was impartial in assessing the merits of the two philosophies and (ii) he was intent on pointing out the differences between the two instead of merely getting lost in similarities. He observes that, far from being undesirable, such a study seems to be necessary now in the interests of philosophy itself. Otherwise, the relative worth of Indian philosophy may remain unknown to those Indians who owe their allegiance to Western thought and who, in their ignorance of the value of Indian philosophy, may grow antipathetic to it.[6]

Thus, Hiriyanna struck a balance in his attitude to Western philosophy. For his own part, while writing on Indian philosophy, he did not indulge in comparisons with the West for the sake of such comparisons. He entered into a comparison only when he felt that it would help directly or indirectly in understanding a point in Indian philosophy. While he interpreted Indian philosophy to the West in modern (Western) terminology, he never allowed himself to be distracted from his concern for Indian philosophy by superfluous comparisons, however attractive they may in themselves be. In short, he was not a comparative philosopher as such, but an Indian philosopher who was receptive to the West.

Tradition and Modernity

It is impossible to speak of anything like a "Hiriyanna school of philosophy." This is precisely because Hiriyanna was not eager to set up a philosophical system of his own. He was not an "original" philosopher in the sense that he had something different to say from what the traditional schools held. He was wedded to the Indian tradition in philosophy and called for investigation into its various branches. However, respect for tradition did not mean for him literally reproducing what has been discovered in it in modern terms. According to him, if the results of the investigation have to be made intelligible to the modern reader, they have also necessarily to be interpreted—without of course distorting the essential spirit of the original. It was "modernism in expression, not modernism in spirit"[7] that he called for. Such an interpretative expression of old thought in modern terminology is no doubt difficult, but, given knowledge and care, it is not impossible as he himself has demonstrated in his writings. On the importance of thorough knowledge of the tradition the following observation is apt.

> ...however necessary it may be to reinterpret the teaching of the past, if its significance to the present is to be well brought out, it is essential that the

new interpretation should be based upon a right and precise understanding of that teaching.[8]

Hiriyanna had no weakness or fancy for being original in the sense of importing any new meaning into the tradition just for the sake of being new. He took pains to do justice even to the schools with whose views he did not agree. All this does not mean that Hiriyanna had no original contribution to make to systematic philosophy. He was a researcher and thinker *par excellence*. He discovered many a new idea or import in the old systems which lay hidden from general recognition. Even familiar concepts in the systems yielded to his analysis their unsuspected implications.

Value Standpoint of Indian Philosophy

Hiriyanna was convinced that Indian philosophy is endowed with a high mission. Though an academician to the core, he did not look upon Indian philosophy as a mere academic exercise or intellectual pastime. He had a living conviction that Indian philosophy has a subtle abiding significance in shaping the lives of peoples and individuals. It is true that the pragmatic spirit of Indian philosophy is bound to be recognized by anyone who correctly understands it. But what is distinctive about Hiriyanna is that he highlighted this significance more than any other modern writer on Indian philosophy. It was his eagerness to emphasize the practical significance of Indian philosophy that led him to devote special attention to values.

> Philosophy was never an arm-chair study in ancient India, and what turned great minds to it was not a desire merely 'to advance knowledge', as the phrase now goes, but an intense interest in the problems of practical life. Accordingly Indian philosophers kept their theory in closest touch with life and did not tolerate the slightest divorce of practice from precept.[9]

Value as the Culmination of Indian Philosophy

Hiriyanna took every opportunity to show that epistemology is only the necessary auxiliary to metaphysics and that even metaphysics is but a means to axiology. It is true that no philosopher can afford to do without a metaphysics, without some conception of reality. Even materialism is a type of metaphysics. But Hiriyanna was keen to point out that philosophy cannot stop with metaphysics. The theory of reality has to pass over into value inquiry if philosophy is to find a human appeal. And this is what Indian philosophers have seen to.

> ...the pursuit of theory is, in one sense, the life and soul of philosophy. Without a proper basis in it, there can be no clear idea of what our purpose in life is, and therefore of what right living should be. The fact is that theoretical investigations are not unnecessary; only the results reached through them require to be related deliberately to the needs of practical life. This is a truth which has always been recognized in India....[10]

On the traditional classification of the subject-matter of philosophy into *prameya, pramāṇa* and *prayojana,* Hiriyanna observes that it brings out two distinctive features of Indian philosophy. One is its *critical spirit.* Early speculation was on facts falling under the head *prameya.* But under the stress of growing disagreement among the inquiring, it was realized that it was unsatisfactory to talk of facts before examining the means for ascertaining and verifying them. Hence, attention came to be transferred to the nature and scope of *pramāṇas,* or means of knowledge. The other distinguishing feature of Indian philosophy that this triple classification brings out is its *pragmatic spirit.* According to the ancient Indian view, even *pramāṇas* are not the goal of true philosophic quest. They may lead to the discovery of truth and thus satisfy the intellect. But unless and until the truth discovered is realized in one's own life, philosophy cannot be said to have fulfilled itself. Hence, Indian thinkers insisted on the need for following up speculative truth by a course of self-discipline calculated to bring about such realization. It is this pragmatic spirit that is illustrated in the section on *prayojana.* It only shows that "philosophy, as understood in India, was essentially concerned with values."[11] The following passage is significant.

> ...we may draw attention to what is a common feature of all the Indian systems. They are not motived by the purpose merely of discovering truth, but also by that of realizing it in life. It is such realization that marks the attainment of truth, in the proper sense of the term, and not merely arriving at a speculative notion of it. In other words, Indian philosophy regards truth as not merely a fact but also as a value. To give our intellectual assent to a doctrine, however vital that may be, is therefore not all; we must see that it inaugurates a new life. This is the significance of the personal discipline prescribed in all the systems as the necessary accompaniment of philosophic study.[12]

Value as the Motivation behind Indian Philosophy

That epistemological and metaphysical inquiries must ultimately lead to value inquiry, is a feature to be expected in any tradition of philosophy. In the West this truth was put forward with great force by such eminent thinkers as Plato in ancient, and Spinoza in modern, times. But Hiriyanna points out that what is distinctive about the Indian tradition is that the consideration of value was not just the consequence of its metaphysics and epistemology; it stood behind these inquiries as their motivation and aim. Theoretical inquiry not merely results in being applied to values, but is even undertaken for the sake of being so applied. Hence, axiology becomes the dominant concern of the Indian philosopher to which metaphysics and epistemology become subordinated as means. In this sense Hiriyanna describes Indian philosophy as "essentially a philosophy of values."[13] It is this deep conviction that runs through all his writings.

> One of the distinguishing features of Indian philosophy is that, throughout its long history, it has consistently given the foremost place to values.... The recognition of its importance by Indian thinkers does not mean that they treat of value as the subject-matter of only a particular branch of philosophy; rather it inspires their investigation as a whole, and its influence is seen in every department of philosophic thought. Indian philosophy may, on this account, be described as essentially a philosophy of values.[14]

Mokṣa as the Ultimate Inspiration for Indian Philosophy

The reason for the primacy of values in Indian philosophy is not far to seek. It lies in the kind of urge which Indian philosophers felt for embarking on their quest. It is usual to say that in the West philosophy had its origin in wonder and curiosity and that Indian philosophy arose out of the perception of evil and suffering in life. Hiriyanna feels that the distinction is not so neat as it is made out. The intellectual urge of wonder and curiosity is not without a practical significance, and the practical urge to overcome evil and suffering is not bereft of wonder and curiosity. Without entering into the details of this relation at the moment, it requires to be noted that Indian philosophy is *primarily* the outcome of the human predicament. Life involves suffering. And it is natural for man to yearn for complete and permanent freedom from suffering, which is what *mokṣa* basically means for all schools of Indian philosophy. It is this innate longing for liberation, as Hiriyanna points out, that has been the central motivation for philosophy in India. In every school epistemology subserves metaphysics, and metaphysics itself is oriented to *mokṣa*. We do not know why we suffer, and we search for the nature of reality so that we may find a solution to the problem of misery. As a class, Indian philosophers did not waste their effort on such problems of knowing and being as had no bearing, direct or indirect, on liberation.

> Philosophy is not therefore 'a game of speculation', as it has been described, meant only to afford intellectual satisfaction by dispelling doubts, but a practical study which should issue in the right mode of life. Its aim is not merely to unravel the mystery of existence but to discover a way out of the misery of life....[15]

Thus the ideal of *mokṣa* informs and directs the course of epistemology and metaphysics in India. Such a dispensation implies that *mokṣa* is the highest ideal of life. Hence, it becomes the task of axiology not only to show how *mokṣa* is the ultimate value, but also to assess the worth of every other value in relation to *mokṣa*. The conclusion reached by the majority of thinkers is that *artha* and *kāma* are lower values and that *dharma*, though higher than these two, is itself a means to *mokṣa*. Philosophy thus becomes a trans-valuation of values.

> ...we may define philosophy, as conceived in India, as a *criticism of values*. Other branches of learning also deal with select values; but the idea of preference or of better and worse is not, strictly speaking, involved in them.[16]

Philosophy and Religion in India

The orientation of Indian philosophy towards *mokṣa* brings it into close alliance with religion. Religion in the broadest sense, whether it involves the idea of God or not, is man's quest for liberation. It involves both belief and practice—the belief in the possibility of absolute freedom from suffering and the practice of the disciplines leading to the realization of that freedom. Philosophy in India has never been divorced from religion taken in this sense. It has supplied the theoretical background to the practical quest of religion. We have already referred to Hiriyanna's view that Indian philosophy is essentially a philosophy of values, as the consideration of value dominates epistemology and metaphysics. Now, in so far as *mokṣa* comes to be regarded as the highest value, the Indian philosophy of values itself may well be described as essentially "a philosophy of religion." Though Hiriyanna does not use such an expression, the implication is clear when he shows the unity of philosophy and religion in India.

The close alliance of philosophy and religion in India has been to mutual advantage. Philosophy acquires a practical significance, and religion ceases to be dogmatic. Hiriyanna is never tired of stressing this advantage to both. At the same time, a word of caution is also discernible in several places in his writings against mixing up the standpoints of religion and philosophy. According to him, the two are distinct, though related. Therefore, in the treatment of Indian philosophy he calls for an intellectual approach—whatever may be one's personal commitment to religious belief and practice—if we are to make our philosophy heard by the modern world.

> The intermixture of religion and philosophy is a prominent feature of ancient Indian speculation. It has no doubt its own advantages, for religion thereby becomes rationalized and philosophy ceases merely to gratify theoretic curiosity. But, however useful this intermixture may be in life, for purposes of presentation, the two should be separated. Otherwise, our philosophy will not appeal to the modern mind with sufficient force and its work will ever remain underrated. One of the first duties of the student of Indian philosophy is accordingly to turn his attention to an independent exposition of what is strictly philosophical in Indian thought.[17]

Hiriyanna's Special Interests

Though Hiriyanna did not leave any aspect of Indian philosophy untouched, he set his heart on some areas of it. We may cite with confidence two such areas. One was Advaita, and the other, Aesthetics.

Advaita: In his assessment of the schools of Indian philosophy, Hiriyanna's standpoint was Advaita, about the satisfactoriness of which he was firmly convinced. He looked upon Vedānta as the culmination of Indian philosophy and upon Advaita as the fulfilment of Vedānta. He saw in Advaita not a school among schools, but the wholeness and completion of all the partial points of view represented by other schools. At the same time, he was not dogmatic about Advaita, nor blind to its own difficulties in meeting the criticism of other schools. His support for Advaita was thoroughly rational. He was never carried away by emotional fervour for the school. In his criticism of other schools, the standpoint of Advaita is clearly discernible. But the criticism was never superficial and groundless. His criticism was based on clear understanding of the schools, for he always took pains to go to the original sources of every school or position. His fairness to the schools which he expounded and evaluated was, thus, unmistakable. And while being plain in stating his views, his language was also restrained.

Aesthetics: Among value studies, aesthetics occupies a special place in the mind of Hiriyanna. Hiriyanna felt that it was a neglected field in any philosophy as compared to logic and ethics. But he was more irked by the criticism offered by some Western scholars that Indian philosophy is oblivious of the aesthetic value. In meeting this charge, Hiriyanna first drew a distinction between the treatment of beauty in nature and the treatment of beauty in art. He pointed out that in Indian philosophical works there was enough material on beauty in nature, though it lay scattered. And as for beauty in art, though Indian philosophical works appeared to side-step this aspect of the value, they could not have really ignored or neglected it, seeing that there was a rich heritage of art and art criticism in the country. Hiriyanna felt that the impact of this heritage on philosophy in India and the reaction of philosophy to it was exactly the matter of investigation. Therefore, Hiriyanna was the first writer in modern times to initiate an organized study of the philosophical treatment of the concept of beauty in India. He saw in this unexplored area resources for the benefit of universal philosophy and laid the foundations of this study in his papers, most of which are collected and published in that wonderful little book, *Art Experience*. In this task he drew richly on his profound knowledge of Sanskrit literature and literary criticism as well as on his grasp of philosophical systems.

3. HIRIYANNA'S WORKS AND THEIR CONTRIBUTION

Hiriyanna's works may be classified under four heads: (1) textual studies, (2) independent works, (3) collected papers, and (4) reviews. We shall identify the works under these heads and observe the nature of the contribution which Hiriyanna makes to knowledge through them.

Textual Studies

This group comprises translations of four Upaniṣads, viz., *Īśāvāsya, Kena, Kaṭha,* and *Bṛhadāraṇyaka*, and critical editions of three later Vedānta works, viz., the *Naiṣkarmyasiddhi* of Sureśvarācārya (with the *Candrikā* of Jñānottama), the *Vedāntasāra* of Sadānanda, and the *Iṣṭa-siddhi* of Vimuktātman (with extracts from the *Vivaraṇa* of Jñānottama).

(i) *Translation of Upaniṣads*: It was between 1911 and 1919 that Hiriyanna produced English translations of these four Upaniṣads together with his translation of Śrī Śaṅkarācārya's commentary on each. The last work comprised only Part I, Sections 1-3 of the *Bṛhadāraṇyaka Upaniṣad*. The *Īśa* and *Kena* translations carried also an Introduction and Notes. Years later, Kavyalaya Publishers, Mysore, reprinted the *Īśa* and *Kena* translations after including the text of the Upaniṣads and the commentary in each case in the Devanāgarī script.

Hiriyanna's skill as a translator becomes evident early in these works. The rendering into English of any Sanskrit work is itself difficult, for, in Hiriyanna's own words, "the very moulds in which thoughts are shaped in the two languages are often different."[18] Over and above this, an Upaniṣad presents its own difficulties in translation. The language of the Upaniṣads is not only archaic Sanskrit, but often ambiguous as well, open to difference in rendering and interpretation, as demonstrated by the existence of different commentaries. The use of one or other commentary as a guide to a line of rendering and translation is inevitable in the case of an Upaniṣadic text. Hiriyanna's translation closely follows the commentary of Śrī Śaṅkara. The Ṭīkā on this commentary, usually ascribed to Ānandagiri, has been used for further clarification of subtle points, and such clarification has been included in the form of footnotes.

(ii) *Critical editions of later Vedānta works*: The aim of critical edition, or textual criticism, is the restoration of a text, as far as possible, to its original form, the form intended by the author. About Hiriyanna's powers as a critical editor of classical Sanskrit texts, K. Kunjunni Raja writes:

> Professor Hiriyanna did not claim to have had any special training in modern Western methods of manuscriptology and textual criticism; his aim was to give an authentic and correct text with all necessary and useful information to help serious students; and the thorough and deep knowledge which he had in the fields of his studies enabled him to arrive at the correct solutions intuitively.[19]

Critical editors often rest satisfied with what is called lower criticism, i.e., restoring a correct text. But to Hiriyanna this was not an end in itself. It is preliminary to higher criticism, which consists of analysing and interpreting the meaning and significance of the contents of the work. With this end in view, Hiriyanna edited the three important Advaita works noted above. All the three editions carry an Introduction, which is a brilliant exposition of the main topic of the work set in a wider perspective to enable the reader to enter into the spirit of the work and assess its true contribution to Advaita. There are also extensive notes to all the three editions explaining subtle points of detail in the text. Hiriyanna is an adept in notes-writing. His notes not only form excellent guides to the understanding of the text, but, even when taken by themselves, they enlighten the reader on small doubts and problems in the relevant or connected fields. Among the three editions, the *Vedāntasāra* carries, besides the text, an English translation of it. The translation, while closely following the text, is natural and free from strain. Of the three works edited, the edition of the *Iṣṭasiddhi* is generally regarded as Hiriyanna's monumental achievement in the field of textual criticism.

The product of textual criticism is a definitive edition. By collating manuscripts of different readings, a "final" reading of the text concerned is arrived at. Hiriyanna exercised meticulous care and caution in examining and collating manuscripts. It is admitted that the reading arrived at is "final" only with reference to the manuscripts available at the time of the edition. There is no guarantee that the edition will not call for revision in the future. If a new manuscript comes to light later on with a reading different from the ones already consulted, the extent and nature of the difference will have to be considered before deciding whether the existent edition requires correction or not. That Hiriyanna was fully conscious of this contingency speaks of his high intellectual honesty. He could even anticipate the possibility of a fresh edition and give hints to subsequent scholars for further investigation. But while granting that no edition is "final" in the strict sense of the term, it should be acknowledged that an earlier edition, with all its limitations, is of invaluable help to a subsequent editor. It is a stepping stone to further approximation to the original text in the light of later research. Even in this sense Hiriyanna's editions are a valuable contribution to research in Sanskrit philosophical literature. Writing on the *Iṣṭasiddhi* edition, Kunjunni Raja observes:

> Later research in the field by Professor V. Raghavan has shown that what was taken to be a third manuscipt of Jñānottama's commentary, containing several differences in reading, is actually the original commentary of Anubhūtisvarūpācārya and that Jñānottama is a second-hand commentator, profusely incorporating Anubhūtisvarūpa's commentary in this case, and Citsukha's commentary in the case of his *Naiṣkarmyasiddhi* commentary. But that does not affect the value of Professor Hiriyanna's edition of the *Iṣṭasiddhi*.[20]

Independent Works

Hiriyanna wrote the following independent works: *Outlines of Indian Philosophy, The Essentials of Indian Philosophy*, and *The Indian Conception of Values*. Of these three works, the first two may be considered together as both deal with the history of Indian philosophy. The *Outlines* was modestly described by the author as primarily intended to serve as "a text-book for use in colleges where Indian philosophy is taught."[21] But it was actually the product of his painstaking research over a number of years in the history of Indian philosophy and was thus much more than a text-book. *The Essentials* is a simpler and shorter account of the subject ostensibly to meet the requirement of the general reader.[22] But this was as scholarly as the previous work. *The Essentials* bears a general likeness to the *Outlines*, but there is also some variation in the treatment of some topics. Though less detailed, it contains two important additions, namely, Buddhism as originally taught by the Buddha apart from early or canonical Buddhism and the Dvaita school of Vedānta. It is remarkable that even unconsciously no portion of the earlier volume has been verbally reproduced in *The Essentials*.

The general plan of the two books is to start from the early sources of Indian philosophy in the Veda and trace the development of the schools of philosophy through the long ages upto about a century or two ago. The history of the Indian philosophical schools cannot be dealt within the same manner as schools or thinkers of European philosophy. In Europe we find a succession of philosophical positions taken up by successive thinkers, each succeeding position refuting and nearly replacing the earlier one. But in India, although all the schools did not originate exactly at the same time, each of them developed alongside the other schools. The different thought patterns, Vedic and non-Vedic, took shape on parallel lines through mutual impact down the centuries. The reason was that in Indian philosophy was closely connected with religion. Each school of philosophy produced its own followers, who advocated its doctrines and passed on its tradition to the succeeding generation. The historical succession is not strictly among the systems, but within each system. In the course of this parallel movement, however, some schools ceased to be living philosophies partly because of the dominant appeal of other schools and partly because their own better elements were absorbed by others. Still, since the growth of Indian philosophical schools is largely not successive, but simultaneous, a chronological arrangement of the schools is out of question for a historian.

The historian of Indian philosophy has to follow his own arrangement. Hiriyanna follows an order which is evidently based on his personal commitment to Vedānta. After dealing with the Veda and the early post-Vedic sources and tendencies, he deals with the non-Vedic schools: Cārvāka, Jainism, and Buddhism. Coming to the Vedic schools, he starts with Nyāya-Vaiśeṣika, and passing through Sāṅkhya-Yoga and Mīmāṁsā, culminates in Vedānta. He represents Vedānta in its two main forms, absolutistic and theistic. In each of the two volumes, Hiriyanna, while giving a connected and comprehensive account of the subject, also puts it to interpretation and criticism. The *Outlines* carries a valuable Introduction on the main features of Indian philosophy.

The Indian Conception of Values is considered to be the *magnum opus* of all the writings of Hiriyanna. It is understood that this was also the last of his scholarly efforts. It was published posthumously in 1975. The publisher's note to the volume makes one somewhat pensive. The work, we learn, was undertaken in the last years of Hiriyanna, fighting against ill-health. The manuscript as left by the author, though marked "final," contained copious marginal notes and quotations, which the author might have desired to organize further. Readers of Hiriyanna should be grateful to the publisher and to all those connected with the work for saving and making available in print as much of these notes and quotes as possible. The book begins with an Introduction on value in general. The distinction between fact and value, the locus and content of value, and kinds and orders of value are dealt with. The Introduction is followed by a detailed discussion of the logical, the ethical, the absolute, and the aesthetic values in four substantial parts of the book.

Collected Papers

Hiriyanna's contributions to learned journals, his addresses to learned bodies, and independent papers, spread over a number of years, cover a wide spectrum of subjects. After his death they were painstakingly collected and published in the following seven volumes, each of which, though small in size, contains gems of thought: *Popular Essays in Indian Philosophy, The Quest After Perfection, Art Experience, Sanskrit Studies, Indian Philosophical Studies—I, The Mission of Philosophy*, and *Indian Philosophical Studies—II*. It may be noted that some of the independent papers included in these volumes appear in print for the first time.

The titles follow a certain broad categorization of subjects. The articles included in *Popular Essays in Indian Philosophy* are largely on general topics in Indian philosophy. *The Quest After Perfection* is mainly on values. *The Mission of Philosophy* contains essays on the nature of philosophy besides other subjects. *Art Experience* exclusively deals with aesthetics, and *Sanskrit Studies,* with Sanskrit literature. *Indian Philosophical Studies—I* and *II* cover epistemology and metaphysics, together with studies in the history of Indian philosophy.

Reviews

The reviews written by Hiriyanna from time to time on books published have themselves an enduring value such that they call for inclusion among his works. Naturally these reviews have been collected and published in book form. One hundred and twenty-two reviews have been compiled in this volume. The works reviewed here cover almost all the schools of Indian philosophy, many of them dealing with Advaita. There are also works dealing with the Upaniṣads, the *Bhagavad-gītā*, the *Brahmasūtra*, and Aurobindo's thought. The rest are on religion and philosophy in general and Indian philosophy in particular. In addition to the reviews included in this volume, six reviews find a place in the collection *Art Experience* (10-15) and two in *Sanskrit Studies* (VII and VIII). And these additional reviews are of books bearing on the themes of these two collections, namely, aesthetics and Sanskrit literature respectively.

What makes Hiriyanna's reviews a contribution to knowledge is well explained by V. Raghavan in his Foreword to the *Reviews*. Hiriyanna, it is noted here, consistently followed a plan whenever he wrote a review. His review consisted of two parts. In the first part he gave a general account of the branch of knowledge to which the book belonged, its problems and the contributions already made to the subject. His object in doing this was to set the book concerned in its relevant background so as to assess its exact worth. Against this background he proceeded in the second part to describe and examine the contents of the book.

The general account of the relevant branch of knowledge in the first part taken by itself forms a good introduction to the fundamentals of that branch, its problems, and the demands those problems make on a scholar. It is written in such a neat and precise manner as to help correct prevailing misconceptions about the subject and put it in the proper perspective. Even the second part of the review, which is particularly directed at the book in question, becomes a contribution to knowledge. Before offering his approval or disapproval of the position taken by the author on any question, Hiriyanna takes care to elucidate the nature of the question involved. Thus, the review as a whole transcends the limited purpose for which it is ostensibly made. It helps to enlighten the reader on the character of the subject besides evaluating the book under review. So Hiriyanna's reviews actually supplement the service done by his other contributions.

There is another significance to Hiriyanna's reviews. They bring out an important aspect of his character—his attitude to other scholars. The attention that he pays to the books reviewed is uniformly serious and considered irrespective of the personality of the author or the nature of the subject. His judgement is objective and free from prejudice and predilection. He weighs each book by its own declared purpose—whether it is meant for introductory general reading or as a text-book for students or as a research contribution. He does not find fault with the book for omitting what the author himself does not intend to convey, but judges it purely by its adequacy to meet the task it has set before itself. But whatever be the object of the book, he applies exacting standards in regard to its material, organization, and presentation. Failure to consult the relevant sources, unsustainable interpretation of relevant material, lack of coherence and consistency in arrangement, perversions, exaggerations and belittlements in expression—these never escape his keen eye. But in setting forth his assessments, Hiriyanna chooses his words carefully. In praising the virtues of a book, he is candidly liberal, but never gives the impression that he is playing them up. In pointing out its errors and shortcomings, he is equally frank, but unhurtful. He does not stop with criticism. He offers suggestions for improving a book without the least show of condescension. No wonder, Hiriyanna won the respect of authors and editors who valued his views even when they were of disapproval. It is no exaggeration to say that Hiriyanna was a model to all reviewers.

4. THE PLAN OF THIS BOOK

Hiriyanna took to Indian philosophy with a deep sense of commitment. He was a master of its details, and he handled them with precision and care. At the same time he had a rare insight into its central message. We find that it is almost a passion with him to impress on students of Indian philosophy that, out of their interest in the rich variety of metaphysics and epistemology, they should never miss the soul of Indian philosophy which is practical. By a practical aim Hiriyanna does not mean mere moral instruction. The practical orientation is towards what is regarded by Indian philosophers as the highest end of life. This message breathes through all his writings whatever be the aspect of philosophy he writes on. In the fresh light he sheds on many a point of detail in Indian philosophy, Hiriyanna makes his own valuable contribution. But his major contribution lies in the uncanny skill with which he gives articulation to the essential spirit of Indian philosophy which is, more than anything else, spiritual. We shall keep this as our background when we deal with Hiriyanna's philosophy in all its aspects.

There must be a method in which we could deal with the leading thoughts of Hiriyanna. It seems convenient to begin with what is of a general nature in his contribution and pass on to what is particular. So, we shall first set forth the nature of philosophy in general and of Indian philosophy in particular as Hiriyanna perceives it. Then we shall deal with the early sources and trends of Indian philosophy as a prelude to the study of its later development. After this we shall take up the major divisions of Indian philosophy for treatment.

The first of these divisions will be metaphysics as it is central to philosophy. The treatment of metaphysics will be by each system of Indian philosophy, the reason being this. The chief problems that usually find a place in any metaphysics are the physical world, the soul, and the ultimate reality. Hence it might be tempting to divide our treatment into three parts, one dealing with the physical world, another with the soul, and the third with the ultimate reality—discussing in each part the views of the several schools on the concerned question. But this is not practicable in view of the fact that Indian philosophy has always recognized the mutual dependence of these questions, such that one of them cannot be discussed without some reference to the other two questions. To avoid such overlapping, we shall follow the systems as such one by one with reference to its metaphysics. There are six systems belonging to the Vedic tradition and three to the non-Vedic.

After metaphysics we pass on to values. We first discuss general problems in value and then deal in detail with each of the higher values, the logical, the ethical, the aesthetic, and the ultimate. The epistemology of each school of philosophy will be, by necessity, referred to in the treatment of its metaphysics. But the fundamental problems of epistemology will be discussed under logical value. Likewise, the nature and means of liberation as conceived in each school will naturally be considered in connection with its metaphysics. But the ultimate value as such will be reviewed and discussed in the last section under values.

The book is divided into seven chapters. The topics discussed within each chapter are, as far as possible, substantially the same as the themes covered in the various writings of Hiriyanna. The contents of his independent works and collected papers have been carefully analysed, arranged according to their inner affinities, faithfully interpreted, and presented under suitable titles. Of Hiriyanna's textual studies, the introductions which he gives in these works have been consulted, as they throw additional light on his approach to Indian philosophy. The texts as such have been omitted from the purview of this book, as they call for separate studies by themselves. In the end we shall evaluate the place of Hiriyanna among the builders of Indian philosophical thought.

REFERENCES

1. *R*, pp. iv and v.
2. *PEIP*, p. 2.
3. Ibid., p. 2.
4. *R*, p. 252.
5. Ibid., p. 27.
6. Ibid., p. 124.
7. *IPS—II*, p. 113.
8. *R*, p. 259.
9. *PEIP*, pp. 2-3
10. *R*, pp. 200-201.
11. Ibid., p. 65.
12. *PEIP*, pp. 59-60.
13. *QAP*, p. 21.
14. *ICV*, p. 1.
15. *QAP*, pp. 28-29.
16. Ibid., p. 24.
17. *R*, pp. 7-8.
18. *Īśa*, translator's note, p. v.
19. *Rājasudhā*, Collected Papers of Dr. K. Kunjunni Raja, Madras, 1982, p. 18.
20. Ibid., pp. 19-20.
21. *OIP*, p. 7.
22. Vide *EIP*, p. 5.

2

Groundwork for Indian Philosophy

1. THE NATURE AND SCOPE OF PHILOSOPHY

Before entering into the details of Indian philosophy as interpreted by Hiriyanna, it is necessary to see his perception, first of the general features of philosophy, and secondly of the special features of Indian philosophy. This is the purpose of this chapter.

An objection commonly raised against philosophy is that it has no individuality of its own and that it can be resolved into science and religion. This is not true. We shall first consider how philosophy stands to religion. The most striking characteristic of religion is that it formulates an ideal which is the highest man can think of. An ideal implies that efforts should be made to realize it in one's own experience. Hence religion is concerned not only with formulating the ideal, but also with determining how the ideal is to be realized. Another characteristic of religion is that it believes in the supernatural. Hence, in support of its doctrine, it takes recourse to direct revelation by some beneficent being. In the train of this basic belief follow other beliefs like the immortality of the soul, its independence from the body and so forth.

Philosophy also seeks after the formulation of the supreme ideal. But for support, it appeals to reason and common human experience instead of to revelation. It attempts to formulate the ideal in one of two ways. It takes for granted certain postulates and deduces conclusions from them. Or it aims at constructing a view of the ideal by analysing human experience. In the former method philosophy resembles religion. And this has been the character of philosophy in the past. The latter method gives only tentative conclusions and seeks universal assent. But philosophy in neither of these forms believes in the supernatural without at the same time rejecting it altogether. It holds its unsettled questions in suspense, and so does not contain any dogma. Thus the very spirit underlying philosophy and religion are different. Only the general aim is common, viz., man's search for the ultimate ideal. The settled views of religion are of great value in influencing the conduct of people, and this is an aim which is very important to religion. Philosophy too is not without an influence on human conduct, but this is only one of the aims of philosophy.

As for science, it proceeds by a purely rational investigation into the data of experience. It is content with tentative conclusions so long as they have not been tested. And it does not make a fetish of the conclusions once reached if subsequent enquiry casts any doubt on them. In this openness of attitude philosophy agrees with science. But there are also differences between the two disciplines. First, no science takes the whole of reality for its subject-matter as philosophy does. Nor can all the sciences put together represent the concrete integral truth of reality, each science being only a partial consideration of reality. Secondly, science is concerned with truth, but not with the value, the truth may have for life. On the contrary, it is value that finally matters for philosophy. The sciences over-emphasize ontology, which is only one phase of philosophy. The applied sciences are no doubt connected with values, but these are only empirical values. They are not concerned with the higher values, which are the special concern of philosophy.

If the identification of philosophy with religion results in its becoming dogmatic, its identification with science makes it a purely theoretical inquiry. Nevertheless, its association with both has saved it from the disadvantage of being identified with either. Its association with religion has been the means of preserving its true aim—the discovery of the nature and means of the highest human value. And its association with science has helped it to maintain its original rational character. Religion is interested in values, but not science. Science is wary of its investigations, but religion calls for faith. It is philosophy, which has the advantage of both, that bridges the gulf between the two.

Philosophy resembles common sense also but only upto a point. In common life we pursue values, but the values are mostly secular. The higher values, which are spiritual, are the concern of philosophy. The common man has only a vague notion of the highest value, and so its influence on his life is not considerable. But philosophy has to envisage the ideal as best as it can and devise suitable means to effect it. In doing these, it defines the relation between secular and spiritual values. It thus rationalizes common sense.[1]

2. PHILOSOPHY AND LIFE

Whether philosophy has any connection with life is an age-long controversy in the West. Plato taught that the two are intimately connected, but Aristotle did not see any relation whatsoever between them. Medieval thought sided with Plato and recognized that philosophy cannot be indifferent to life's problems. Under the influence of science modern thinkers like Bradley and Russell, though differing in other respects, commonly question the legitimacy of relating philosophical theory with practice. But a few still consider that "there can be no better truth about ultimate things than the one that helps us to live rightly."[2] In India only some like the early Mīmāṁsakas repudiated the relation between life and philosophic knowledge. But as a rule Indian thinkers from early times attached little value to mere theory that finds no expression in practice.

Among the practical problems with which the relation of philosophy could be discussed the most important is that of the central ideal of life. It can be shown that there is a mutual dependence between philosophy and this ideal. The determination of the nature of the ideal and the effort for achieving it calls for philosophic knowledge. Conversely, the successful pursuit of philosophy itself presupposes the practical effort for achieving the ideal. We shall first indicate the dependence of the final ideal on philosophy.

The well known higher values are truth, beauty and goodness. Philosophy represents the pursuit of truth. Psychologically and historically, art and morality—which represent beauty and goodness—operate even before the onset of philosophic consciousness. So, can we say that either of them could serve as the final ideal of life? To answer this question, we have to consider the nature of art and morality.

Let us take up morality first. Unselfishness, or disinterestedness, is universally recognized as essential to morality. It is not easy to overcome our inclination to selfishness, but without an effort to do so there can be no moral practice. But merely abandoning natural inclinations does not by itself make a man moral. Active devotion to the good of others is another necessary feature of morality. Mere asceticism is an inverted form of selfishness in that the ascetic is pre-occupied with himself. "Self-mortification is not finally less reprehensible than self-indulgence."[3] Self-denial should take on a positive character. That is, it should be supplemented by altruism. In fact, altruistic deeds should be the real means of achieving self-conquest. Thus morality is "disinterested altruism."

By art we mean here fine art. And we discuss it here from the point of view of one who appreciates it and not from that of the artist who creates it. Art involves disinterestedness in a much deeper sense than morality. In moral life one tries to secure it in a measure through conscious activity for a definite purpose. But in contemplating a work of art, one forgets oneself in the represented object and thereby becomes completely unselfish for the moment. Thus the artistic attitude, unlike the moral, is not only unselfish, but also self-forgetful. Therefore it is marked by a unique delight. It must also be remarked that by describing the art attitude as one of contemplation, what is meant is that the mind concerns itself with the presented object itself, and not with the consequences of a practical activity with reference to the object. If we think of a road as in some way attractive in itself, this is the aesthetic attitude. If we think of it as a means to reach a destination, this is the practical attitude. Morality is such a practical attitude, the attitude of action. It aims at a purpose, whereas aesthetic experience is sought for its own sake.

We have so far explained the nature of art and morality. The question is whether either of them can by itself serve as the ultimate ideal of life. Art and morality signify a contemplative and an active attitude respectively, but life is not either all contemplation or all activity. Aesthetic experience is externally induced. Hence it is transient; and as soon as it is over, selfishness and moral indifference may well reassert themselves. Morality involves conscious struggle against selfishness, and hence the unselfishness secured, though continuous, can only be partial. Thus, though unselfishness is common to both art and morality, it is provisional in the former and incomplete in the latter. To be the ultimate ideal of life, the unselfishness must be such that one can rest forever in it with a feeling of contentment. The need for conscious effort is an index that in mere morality the final ideal has not been reached. Moral action should become spontaneous and self-forgetful like art experience. Judged by its intrinsic character, art experience may suggest the contentment characteristic of the final ideal. But the feeling of contentment in it is too fleeting. To be final, the state must endure. Art experience, moreover, is not only induced from without, but also induced by a stimulus which is outside reality, as it were. Hence, we are forced to conclude that, neither separately nor together, art and morality can serve as the supreme ideal of human life. However, taken together, they are sufficient to indicate to us the nature of the goal, as we shall presently see.

From what has been stated so far, it must be clear that the ideal should contain both the attitudes signified by art and morality. First, disinterestedness should be a constant and necessary feature of it. Secondly, the ideal must have two phases, one active and the other contemplative. Further, the defects of art and morality must be absent while their excellences are combined. Conscious effort should cease, and whatever active service there is in it should be spontaneous and joyous. The joy should endure through the direct contemplation, not of a fictitious situation, but of reality. The presence of such an ideal cannot be logically proved. But the best thought all over the world holds that there is such an ideal. Indian thinkers go farther and maintain that it can be achieved even now in this life.

Is there any means by which such an ideal can be realized? Even this would be suggested if we look into the reasons for the limitations of art and morality. Let us take up morality first. Moral action has to take place in a particular situation. It involves tension, because we understand our relation to that situation only imperfectly. If the reaction to a given situation is to be spontaneous, i.e., free from tension, what is required is a complete knowledge of the situation. And if the same state of spontaneity is to be expected in any and every situation, whatever it be, one needs to know the ultimate truth about the universe. "In other words, ideal conduct presupposes philosophic knowledge."[4] By philosophic knowledge is not meant a mere conceptual view of the ultimate reality, for mere intellectual conviction cannot influence conduct. If philosophic knowledge must effectively express itself in practice, the conceptual view must become a direct experience of the ultimate.

> The person who thus sees reality will infallibly act rightly, and his conduct then, instead of being the result of strife will become the effortless expression of an inner conviction.[5]

In fact, moral activity then becomes not only unselfish, but also, like art contemplation, spontaneously joyful. Thus the analysis of morality inevitably points to the need for experienced truth.

Art also gives us a clue to the need for philosophic knowledge. The attraction of art is the pure delight which accompanies its contemplation. What is this delight due to? Partly it arises from the impersonal attitude induced by the fictitious situation. But it is equally also due to the fact that the situation, though fictitious, is self-complete, "for art deals in wholes."[6] In looking at a painting or in witnessing a drama, we realize "the whole of its universe, as we might term it, in everyone of its parts."[7] If the same attitude could be induced in us towards the actual universe, we can derive the same kind of joyful experience directly from it or from any of its numerous aspects. It is philosophic knowledge, or the direct experience of the ultimate reality, that alone can confer such a synoptic vision. The knower becomes a detached spectator of the universe. "Whatever significance art has, that he discovers in life and the world as a whole."[8] We may, therefore, say that with the onset of philosophic knowledge both art and morality are transformed and transcended. Art fulfils itself in a mystic contemplation of nature, and morality, in spontaneous virtue.

Thus art and morality point not merely to the nature of the ultimate ideal, but also to the means of attaining it. In effecting the transition from themselves to the ultimate ideal, they do not cancel themselves. On the contrary, the excellences of both are conserved and accommodated in the final ideal when it is secured. With the aid of philosophic knowledge they become metamorphosed in it. "... they are both combined in it at a higher power."[9] Beauty and goodness, or art and morality, attain their fulfilment through one and the same means, viz., philosophic knowledge. The defects of each, which we have noted already, are the result of a fragmentary view of the world taken by us in pursuing them. When each is informed by all-comprehensive philosophic vision, they cease to be separate ideals, but become two expressions or phases of one and the same final ideal. This is exemplified in the life of a great sage like Vālmīki. Whether in moments of contemplation or of action, his life is characterized by the same detachment and the same joy.

Thus philosophy aids art and morality to fulfil themselves. Man instinctively pursues them believing that they are themselves the final ends. But neither art nor morality is self-sufficient. If philosophy does not come to their aid, the deepest yearning of man for the final ideal of life will end in frustration. Though philosophy may start from curiosity, it does not, and need not, end with satisfying it. Here it may be objected that an application of philosophy to the aid of art and morality will vitiate the character of philosophy as the disinterested pursuit of truth. But such a prejudice arises from a confusion between two grades of value—one secular and the other spiritual. To pursue truth with a view to securing empirical values like wealth or fame, gain or glory, may vitiate the investigation, but to pursue it for the fruition of spiritual values like beauty and goodness cannot result in any such vitiation, for their essence, like that of truth, is disinterestedness.

We have so far seen how the formulation and accomplishment of the final ideal of life depends on philosophy. The reverse is also true. The successful pursuit of philosophy itself demands in one sense the effort towards the achievement of the ideal. It may be said that curiosity is the origin of philosophy and that its function is to satisfy this instinct in man to know the truth. The role of curiosity in giving rise to philosophy cannot be denied. But if philosophy is not to deviate from truth, the curiosity must necessarily be disinterested. Otherwise, it is sure to lead us astray. Here arises the need to relate philosophy to morality, if not to art, morality being the chief means to the cultivation of disinterestedness. When so related, we have the practical, as distinguished from the merely speculative, approach to philosophy. This is what the Indians have always advocated. One of the reasons for the impression that philosophy is not related to life is the wrong notion that mere curiosity is the origin of philosophy. What is needed, is disinterested, and not mere, curiosity. And the disinterested pursuit of truth presupposes moral preparation. Thus philosophy is related to life in two ways. It formulates the final ideal and directs the course of right living and art contemplation towards that goal. Conversely, it depends on right living for its successful pursuit.

3. THE MISSION OF PHILOSOPHY

The value of philosophy is sometimes called into question for the reason that there is neither finality nor universal acceptance with regard to any system of philosophy so far devised. The charge is valid, but just for this reason philosophy need not be abandoned forever. Only we need to revise our view of what we could expect from philosophy. After all, the tendency to philosophize is natural to man and cannot be suppressed. Even the critic, in denying the worth of philosophy, must be doing so on the basis of some view he takes of life and the world. "Indeed, it seems that we can neither think nor act cogently without holding some view of the universe, either explicitly or implicitly."[10]

The Urge for Philosophy

We may get a hint about the value of philosophy if we look into the tendency to philosophize. Some say that philosophy begins in wonder; others, that it starts from curiosity. Both alike imply ignorance as their background. Ignorance stands for partial knowledge and not for its total absence. Things of which we know nothing excite neither wonder nor curiosity. So wonder and curiosity represent an urge not for knowledge, but for *fuller* and *better* knowledge. Wonder and curiosity accordingly signify partial knowledge, and they prompt us to secure more satisfying information about the object in question. Hence philosophy has its origin in our awareness of our ignorance, and it is meant to remove doubt and imperfection in our knowledge of facts. We cannot, however, stop at mere knowledge of facts. Of course, we are used to abstract and theoretic sciences like formal logic and mathematics. But really the idea of fact cannot thus be divorced from that of value.

> Knowledge is generally a prelude to some action, and the realization thereby of some end; and if curiosity or wonder aim at knowledge, it is only in order to bring about sooner or later an appropriate action.[11]

The value of curiosity and wonder is not fully explained without reference to a practical motive. (To say that fact and value are necessarily related is not, however, to identify the two as pragmatists do.) The dissociation between pure and practical reason is, therefore, artificial. It is such dissociation that is responsible for the modern distrust in philosophy. It has led to the idea that philosophy has no bearing whatsoever on life and does not merit attention. Hence, though philosophy first aims at removing doubt and adding to our knowledge, it is eventually meant to serve some practical end of life. The real question is what this practical end might be.

The Need to know the Final Ideal of Life

The practical goal of philosophy is the determination of the final ideal of life. This will become evident if we compare philosophy with science. Science seeks to remove our ignorance of the physical conditions under which we live. Our common knowledge of the environment is imperfect. Our practical disappointments are the consequence of this imperfect knowledge. Better knowledge will help us in the conduct of life. The pursuit of truth in this sense is the chief, though it may not be the sole, object of the several sciences. By rendering our knowledge of the environment accurate and orderly and by extending its bounds, science helps us to overcome the physical evil to which we are subject. But the knowledge that results from science admits of being utilized in diverse ways, not all of them good or good in the same degree. Science as such does not concern itself with the moral worth of its applications. Thus arises the question of moral evil apart from physical evil.

To eliminate moral evil, we need a criterion to distinguish what is good from what is evil in the consequences of our actions and further to distinguish what is better from what is merely good in them. Such a criterion is not possible until we determine what man's highest end is. To determine that end is the prime aim of pursuing philosophic truth, as distinguished from scientific truth. The principle of moral choice is this: that which aids the attainment of the final ideal or at least does not stand in its way is good, and that which does the opposite is bad. When the good and the bad are thus distinguished, it becomes relatively easy to distinguish between the good and the better, i.e. to institute an order of preference among whatever is good.

> So if the object of science is to dispel the ignorance concerning the *conditions* of life amidst which we live, that of philosophy is to find out the *end* or *ends* for which, in the ultimate sense, we ought to live.[12]

The Nature of the Final Ideal as Implied in Morality

A conception of the ultimate end can be arrived at through an analysis of the moral good. This line of approach is adopted here, because the practice of morality precedes philosophical inquiry. And even in moral practice some conception of the final ideal is implied. Only, this is not adequate. It is the task of philosophy to draw out the implications of the moral ideal and thereby articulate the final ideal.

Moral life as commonly practised represents an unreflective state. It is based on man's awareness of others and their resemblance to himself in motives. The aim of morality at this level is to seek the good of others as well as of oneself. But moral life as thus conceived and practised involves a clash between self-love and benevolence. It shows that the common moral ideal needs to be clarified and analysed. It is the task of ethical philosophy to do this.

Benevolence involves self-sacrifice. What is the significance of this self-sacrifice? Lack of clarity in this respect leads us to see unselfishness where there is really none. A patriot is not really unselfish. He is only less selfish than those who prefer their own interests. The country is an alter-ego pitted against other countries. A mother sacrifices her own comforts for the sake of her child. But she cannot be expected to show the same concern to the children of others. There are thus two forms of selfishness—one, pure self-love, and the other, the love of self which appears in a disguised form.

Genuine detachment, or unselfishness, admits of no limitation, no exclusion of anyone from the sphere of one's concern. It is based on the conviction that all is one's own or that none is so. All exclusion implies preference of one's own self in one form or other, as in the case of a patriot or of a mother. The reason is that selfishness and unselfishness are contradictories. They do not mix. Either one is selfish or unselfish; and no middle course between them is possible. Partial detachment is a contradiction in terms.

As between the two, selfishness and unselfishness, only unselfishness is absolute. It admits of no degrees. But there are degrees of selfishness. Fortunately, the possibility of achieving genuine unselfishness is latent in man. For no man is completely selfish. All so-called selfishness is qualified by some consideration or other which induces a person to put some restraint on it. It is the measure of this restraint that varies, making for more or less selfishness. And the ideal of unselfishness signifies the complete overcoming of selfishness.

Unselfishness, however, is not the whole of the moral good. It is negative, while the moral good represents the achievement of some positive purpose. The moral good implies working for the welfare of others. In fact, detachment cannot be cultivated except through engaging oneself in appropriate altruistic activities. But what is the scope of 'the others' whose good we are to seek? Obviously, in principle, it should not exclude anyone. It should include *all* other selves; for any limitation in the sphere of the good intended will, to that extent, introduce selfishness. Thus though the practice of morality may fall short of the ideal, the ideal to be kept in view in moral life is the good of the whole. Thus the implications of the moral ideal are unselfishness and universal good. But at the level of morality these are only partially realized. To realize them fully is the final ideal.

The Means to the Final Ideal

The task of philosophy is not merely to formulate the final ideal, but also to determine the means to its realization. If the good of the whole is the end, its pursuit requires a knowledge of that whole—as complete a knowledge of it as possible. No doubt, the conception of the whole differs. Some philosophers think that it is one and systematic, and others, that it is manifold and composite. But what is significant is that both views grant the unity of being.

It is ignorance of the unity of being that is responsible not only for alienating us from the final ideal, but also for leading us to moral evil. We ordinarily feel our otherness from other selves forgetting that we are at the same time one with the rest. The remedy to ignorance (*avidyā*) is knowledge (*vidyā*). But a mere theoretic knowledge of the unity by itself will not improve conduct. The knowledge of unity must become a matter of direct experience if it is to influence life. Our belief in the reality of diversity is immediate. So an equally immediate apprehension of unity becomes necessary to remove it. Seeing is believing. To convert theoretic knowledge into experience, meditation on the ultimate truth of unity is required. The meditation has to continue until the impression of that unity on our mind becomes as deep and indelible as the impression of the difference of one person from others.

Besides ignorance of the unity of being, there are also in ourselves other obstacles to the final ideal. These are narrow selfish impulses (*asaṅga* or *kāma*), which in turn lead to selfish activity (*karma*). Selfish desire is itself a product of ignorance, which requires separate confrontation. To remove selfish desires, moral training in deliberate unselfish activity is required. Institutions such as family, state and so on have the promotion of unselfish activity as their aim. Meditation cannot succeed in effecting direct experience of unity so long as these obstacles are present. Hence meditation, which is the training of the mind, has to be supplemented by moral training, which is training of the heart. Without moral training, "the mind will have neither sustained interest in the Truth, nor sufficient strength of will to concentrate on it."[13] It is also true that in the reverse direction moral training will stand to benefit from meditation. The development of character depends on the deepening of our conviction in the ultimate truth. This combined training will result in the intuition of the final truth.

Thus the aim of philosophy, on the theoretical side, is the removal of ignorance of the final goal; and on the practical side, it is determining the means to overcome narrowness. These two purposes have governed Indian philosophy from the beginning. The life of one who has realized the final freedom even while living exhibits both the features indicated earlier. On the one hand, it is marked by utter freedom from selfishness and, on the other, by love for others. His love for others is not merely a love for them as equals. He loves them as essentially one with himself. As a natural consequence of this love, he works for the same freedom for them as for himself. Work for others earlier involved effort. But now it is quite spontaneous. It is this selfless love issuing in service that is exemplified in the ideal of the *bodhisattva* in Buddhism and in the allied ideal of the *jīvanmukta* in Hinduism.

The Mission of Philosophy

It may be asked whether the final ideal, as represented by the twin features of individual perfection and universal good, is ever attainable. Indian thinkers have uniformly believed in the affirmative. But even supposing that it is never attainable, it will still retain its value; and that is enough to show that philosophy has a high mission to carry out, viz., the promotion of the qualities that indicate the ideal—individual perfection and universal good. What really matters is progress in this direction, i.e., a direction such as *would* culminate in the goal, if it were attainable.

> In other words, the ideals of individual perfection and universal good can serve as regulative principles in the conduct of life; and that is, after all, what all ideals are expected to do.[14]

The very pursuit of the ideal produces some positive results. (i) It frees man from the tyranny of the egoistic self, which works havoc on others and ourselves. (ii) It engenders genuine love for others, which necessarily issues in work for their good. (iii) It incidentally opens the scope for the pursuit of the other higher values of life, like truth and beauty, since freedom from egoism means both the time and the inclination for such pursuits.

4. THE MESSAGE OF INDIAN PHILOSOPHY

The message of Indian philosophy is selfless service to all beings. The highest expression of such service is the result of realizing the final ideal of life. But even the pursuit of that ideal lies in, and through the effort for, selfless service. This is the common lesson of Indian philosophy in spite of its diversity on other matters. Therefore, the ideal of life as conceived in Indian philosophy is not world-negating as critics sometimes make out.

The Common Indian Ideal of Life

On the theoretical side, Indian philosophy presents a rich variety of thought. It includes all types of solutions to the chief problems of philosophy, giving rise to a variety of schools. The diversity of views on theoretical questions appears not only among the schools, but even within many a school, so that we often find schools within schools as in Buddhism and Vedānta. This does not mean that Indian philosophy, even on the theoretical side, is altogether heterogeneous. The differences admit of being reconciled in more than one way. But be that as it may, when we take up the practical side of the teaching of all the schools, there is a remarkable unanimity among them on the question of the value of theoretical teaching. No school of thought indulged in speculation for its own sake. Philosophic truth came to be sought by everyone of them for the light it might throw on the ultimate significance of life. Thus there is a common aim in Indian philosophy, which is to determine the ideal of practical life. And even as regards the nature of this ideal, so far as it is realizable in the present life, it is essentially the same according to the several schools. Thus there is a close linking of theory and practice in Indian philosophy. The common features of the ideal of life as envisaged by the Indian systems generally may now be identified. In full measure they are to be found only in the ideal as realized. But even the pursuit of the ideal involves these features in the making.

Unselfishness

The first and foremost of these features is unselfishness. It characterizes the ideal of practical life not only of the Vedic schools, but also of the non-Vedic schools. In fact, to emphasize its importance, Buddhism goes to the extent of even denying the existence of a permanent self. The doctrine of *nairātmya-vāda* is thus of ethical value, whatever may be its other defects. By unselfishness in the context of the final ideal is to be understood the entire abnegation of self-interest. "An ancient law-giver...defines a cultured person (*śiṣṭa*) as one whose heart is free from all personal desires." (*śiṣṭaḥ punarakāmātmā*).[15] It is for the importance of unselfishness in regard to the final ideal that *saṁnyāsa* is given an exalted place in both orthodox and heterodox schools.

Service

If self-interest is to be totally excluded, it may suggest that the pursuit of the final ideal requires a voluntary forsaking of the world, or asceticism in the negative sense. But it is not so. The Indian view of the ideal is ascetic in a positive sense, which means that it goes hand in hand with altruistic activity. It does not require one to run away from society and seek passive isolation. What diverts man from the ideal is not the world, but his selfish propensities. So what is commended here is not world-renunciation, but self-renunciation. The *Bhagavad-gītā* teaches a life of incessant activity without desire to attain anything for oneself.

The service that is thus recommended is not a separate aim to be pursued merely as a concomitant of renunciation. It is intimately connected with renunciation, being the very means of cultivating it. "Consequently the aim is not renunciation and service, but renunciation *through* service."[16] True detachment cannot be achieved except through active service in the midst of others, but such service should be without any thought of advantage to oneself. Thus the two opposites are harmonized by ridding renunciation of inaction and service of egoism.

If service is to be a means to renunciation, the mode of service cannot be left to the arbitrary choice of the individual. It should be in accordance with one's station in society (and stage in life), in other words, the doing of *sva-dharma*. The doing of service outside the scope of *sva-dharma* is not precluded, but that should not be at the cost of *sva-dharma*. It should be noted that the concept of *sva-dharma* implies the abolition of the distinctions of high and low, for when duty is taken as a means of renunciation, it is the spirit in which it is done that matters and not its content. Whoever discharges the duties of his station and stage in life without any thought of personal gain is virtually a *saṁnyāsin*.

Love and Enlightenment

By renunciation and service self-interest disappears, but the sense of agency remains. The person who has undergone this discipline frees himself from the notion that he is an enjoyer (*bhoktṛ*), but he remains conscious that he is a doer (*kartṛ*). Such self-consciousness is of course necessary for the deliberate conquest of self-interest. But it necessarily involves internal constraint, or strife within oneself. The need for effort is an indication that the final ideal has not been reached, because the final ideal, according to all Indian thinkers, is a state of permanent repose. Hence even the notion of agency, which gives rise to a sense of duty, must be completely transcended. One must forswear selfishness by self-conscious effort and then forswear even this self-consciousness. "...unselfishness which is conscious of itself is not the perfect form of it."[17] We have a sample of such a totally impersonal state, though temporarily, in art contemplation. There are examples even in moral life to show that it is possible. A mother devotes herself to the care of her child. Here the sense of duty merges in love, whereby she becomes completely unself-conscious. Love is stronger than duty. Hence a mother's response to her child is on a higher plane than that of a nurse. The attainment of a similar level of action is the Indian ideal of life. "The agent passes in it from a state of striving morality to that of spontaneous service where he acts as he does, because he cannot but do so."[18] Strife being absent, the activity of one who has reached this level is characterized by supreme joy. He who has reached this culmination of the discipline is no longer a *sādhaka*, but a *siddha*.

How is moral activity involving strife transformed into spontaneous and loving service? Love will not suffice to explain this. In the mother's case the service is restricted to her child. It is an expression of blind narrow love. Her solicitude for her child does not necessarily imply equal solicitude for the children of others. But the service of one who has completely achieved the goal of life knows neither preferences nor exclusions. The love which impels it is universal. Such love is mediated only by comprehensive knowledge. To know all is to love all. The gulf between the common morality of strife and the ideal morality of universal love is bridged only by philosophical knowledge. To acquire such knowledge, a further course of discipline, which is predominantly intellectual, becomes necessary. We shall not go into the details of this discipline. But the need for it shows how philosophic theory in India is related to the ideal of practical life.

As regards the nature of the philosophical knowledge, it varies in the different doctrines. But, for the purpose of fulfilling the final ideal, any doctrine which commends unselfish service and at the same time offers a self-consistent view of the universe will suffice. What is important for us to note is that all the systems aver that, if philosophical knowledge is to influence conduct, it must be properly assimilated. That is to say, all of them insist on the transformation of mediate knowledge into immediate experience, or enlightenment, though one may begin with the former. It is only such a living awareness, and not a mere conceptual knowledge of reality, that can inspire the love which transmutes conduct. A mother's response to her child is also inspired by love. But it is instinctive love, which is a form of attachment (*mamatā*) as shown by its exclusiveness. The love resulting from enlightenment is different. It signifies complete detachment and is, therefore, equal love for all. There is a higher form of love born of faith in God preached by theistic creeds. But the love that we speak of now is different even from this—it is born of insight into the ultimate nature of the universe. This love arising from abiding enlightenment is the third and last feature of the common Indian ideal of life.

The Life of the Enlightened One

In the life of the aspirant (*sādhaka*) renunciation and service are products of effort. But in the case of the enlightened one (*siddha*) both these features become the natural expression of an inner conviction. "...the constraint of obligation is replaced by the spontaneity of love."[19] It is worthwhile dilating on the nature of the service that issues from the enlightened. Earlier we have drawn attention to the importance of *svadharma* in the case of one who strives for the final ideal. But to the one who has reached the goal, the duties of his station as such lose their special significance. Being totally unself-conscious, he reacts to presented situations without relating them to himself. Hence he rises above the moods of self-approbation and self-condemnation. Though still an actor on the stage, he is an impartial spectator. His service will be not only for all, but also will be the best of its kind. It will not merely aim at their material welfare, but will also tend to their spiritual uplift. The enlightened one is, therefore, the true benefactor of all. Even more important than what he does, is the influence which he silently exerts on them by the life he leads. Such is the ideal of *jīvanmukti* which the Indian doctrines hold before us. Even those who accept this ideal only virtually agree with this feature of enlightened and self-forgetting service which characterizes the *jīvanmukta*.

We have many an example of such a sage in the Indian tradition, mentioned not only in scripture, but also in literature, who led a life of disinterested and loving service, of "morality touched with vision."[20] This, then, is the message of Indian philosophy—that man should seek for the fulfilment of his true nature in such service, a service which is the outcome of complete enlightenment and which is expressed in all-comprehensive love and absolute disinterestedness. Owing to the rise of materialistic values over the spiritual, the impact of this message has tended to fade in our own country. The idea of altruistic service has not become absent, but it has lost the scope and quality of the original ideal. Fortunately, the old ideal, though much obscured, has not died out.

> ...our own generation furnishes an outstanding example of it in one whose unselfish labours in the case of not merely his countrymen but of all humanity is shedding fresh light upon our land. The great need of the hour is to revivify our faith in this ideal.[21]

5. THE AIM OF INDIAN PHILOSOPHY

There is a close relation between thought and will, which act and react upon each other. Hence all philosophy has necessarily both a practical and a theoretical side to its teaching. It is not right to assume that any system can entirely dispense with either. But a system may place greater emphasis on either theory or practice. A special feature of Indian philosophy is the care it takes to lay equal emphasis on both. Individual thinkers as well as whole periods in the history of Indian thought stressed the one more than the other. But speaking as a whole, the aim of the teaching is to correlate the two. We may, therefore, describe Indian philosophy to be as much a criticism of life as a criticism of the categories of reality. The reason for this is the fact that philosophy in

India did not take its rise primarily in wonder, as it seems to have done in the West. It originated out of the practical need to overcome the presence of moral and physical evil in life. The consideration of the metaphysical evil of ignorance came in only in connection with this aim. Puzzles of knowledge had to be solved chiefly to find out a remedy, if possible, for the ills of life. From the beginning, Indian philosophy insisted on practical utility (*prayojana*) in addition to intellectual doubt (*saṁśaya*) as the justification for philosophy.

In the Indian view the study of philosophy is to be carried on, not in a merely academic sense, but as a discipline, in the closest possible touch with the student's life. The same process of correlating theory and practice is to be continued till the disciple becomes fitted for *mokṣa*, or deliverance. *Mokṣa*, thus, is the aim of all Indian philosophy. The nature of this aim is now to be delineated.

Jīvanmukti and its Significance

In early Vedic teaching the ideal of *mokṣa* was conceived as eschatological. If this were the final Indian view, then it may be thought that the ideal of *mokṣa* rests on mere speculation or dogma. Such an ideal may be regarded as the goal of religion, but not of philosophy. But the *mokṣa* ideal was soon brought within the sphere of experience and verification, "thanks to the constant presence in the Indian intellectual atmosphere of positivistic thought."[22] This is *jīvanmukti*, or deliverance during life. It was part and parcel of the very influential doctrine of Brahman-Ātman in the Upaniṣads and has since been "woven into the tissue of more than one classical system of thought."[23] Even in doctrines like Nyāya-Vaiśeṣika and Viśiṣṭādvaita, which do not formally accept *jīvanmukti*, there is clearly recognized a stage between enlightenment and actual liberation (*videhamukti*) which admits of being so described, because it marks the culmination of human effort for *mokṣa*, and the disciple has only to bide his time for attaining it. The enunciation of the concept of *jīvanmukti* marks "the acme of Indian thought."[24] And it furnishes the true basis for philosophy and religion having been but one in India. In seeking the experience of *jīvanmukti*, philosophy goes beyond mere intellectual conviction, and religion, beyond mere faith. It may, therefore, be regarded as the point of union of philosophy and religion.

Knowledge (*jñāna*) and self-discipline (*vairāgya*) are both necessary to attain *jīvanmukti*. But the value of *jīvanmukti* itself does not lie in the knowledge acquired or in the self-discipline achieved alone. Primarily, *jīvanmukti* signifies an experience. As a result of the experience, the attitude of mind towards life and the world undergoes a sea-change. So, when it is said that *mokṣa* is the common end of all Indian philosophy, it is this experience and the resulting attitude that is meant. If philosophy is to be a true guide to life, it should emanate from a teacher who has had such an experience, and in turn it should produce a similar experience in the disciple. "The *upadeśa* or precept of the one, as it is said, should evoke a corresponding *anubhava* or experience in the other."[25] A mere academic exercise will be like the blind leading the blind. The experience will certainly transform the pupil's attitude and conduct. But, as already pointed out, the emphasis is on the experience giving rise to this transformation, and not on the outward behaviour which is its expression and, therefore, more or less secondary. Thus the value of *jīvanmukti* lies not in the new conduct and knowledge that are associated with it, but in the inner transformation which gives rise to both.

> Its value lies as little in inducing a person to do what otherwise he would not have done, as in informing him of what he would otherwise have not known; it consists essentially in making him what he was not before.[26]

We have noted that the essence of *jīvanmukti* lies in the transformation of the individual. From this it should not be understood that the ideal is individualistic, or self-involving. Such a narrowing influence is impossible because of the nature of the attitude of a *jīvanmukta*. This attitude is marked by the complete annihilation of desire (*tṛṣṇā*), or egoism (*ahaṁkāra*). Such an attitude is bound to arise by the very nature of the discipline involved in securing the experience. Only the manner in which the attitude is brought about is explained differently according to different philosophic standpoints. According to monistic views the individual is merged in the whole. So the result is the complete effacement of separate individuality. According to dualistic views the individuality of the self is retained, but the individual realizes his exact place in the universe. The result is a willing surrender on the part of the disciple. In such doctrines, whether monistic or dualistic, as are also pessimistic there is the further reason which helps the end of self-effacement or self-surrender, namely "a feeling of the vanity and nothingness of life and a conviction that the best that one can do is to bow to the inevitable."[27] Thus, from whichever point of view we look upon the ideal, it is marked by the total absence of egoism. An ideal thus rooted in self-denial can in no sense be regarded as narrow individualism.

The attitude of a *jīvanmukta* does not exclude activity. But the activity, according to both monism and dualism, is not merely moral, but even goes beyond morality. That it transcends morality is explained in two different ways from the two standpoints. According to monism the very idea of obligation disappears owing to the negation of all contrasts including that between the individual and society. But the enlightened one does not, indeed cannot, cease to act. Only the scope of his activity becomes considerably enlarged beyond the sphere of human society, with which conventional morality is associated. Since he now comes to "think cosmically"[28] by his identification with the rest of being, he will feel equally attached to all that exists, and whatever he does will be inspired by universal love, which knows neither preferences nor exclusions. Such an expansion does not mean that he has less regard for human society now, but only that he has greater concern for the whole of being. Social morality, though it widens the outlook of man, really keeps him isolated from the rest of being, "and all isolation is bondage in this view."[29] To be truly free, man must get rid of not only personal egotism, but also the egotism of the species, and look upon everything as equally holy.

According to dualism, which recognizes the ultimacy of the individual, the consciousness of obligation continues in *jīvanmukti*. But owing to the total transformation of the conception of his own self, he surrenders all his rights. Though the contrast between the individual and the rest of being continues to be felt, that between rights and duties disappears at this stage through the renunciation of the former. To that extent the motive is lifted above that of common morality. Here also the scope of the activity is greatly extended, "since the obligation felt is towards all that is and not merely towards fellowman."[30] Only, the attitude is one of universal sympathy here instead of universal love as in monism.

A study of the nature of *jīvanmukti* shows that the aim of Indian philosophy goes beyond both morality and logical knowledge. This is so according to both the monistic and the dualistic views. In *jīvanmukti* conduct becomes spiritualized, and theoretical knowledge becomes experience. But it must not be forgotten that, though neither morality nor intellectual conviction constitutes the goal, they are the sole way of approach to it. The goal that is reached with their help is characterized by illumination (*jñāna*), which is intellectual conviction ripened into experience, and by self-renunciation (*vairāgya*), which is secure by the revelation of the ontological ground for it. The attainment of such an attitude is the common aim of Indian philosophy. Its pre-eminent characteristic is the peace that comes by the absence of intellectual doubt and moral strife.

6. HISTORY AND BASIC PRINCIPLES OF INDIAN PHILOSOPHY

A General Survey of the History of Indian Philosophy

During its long period extending over several centuries, Indian thought developed practically unaffected by outside influence. The extent and importance of its achievements is evident from the fact that it has evolved several systems of philosophy, besides creating a great national religion, Hinduism, and a great world religion, Buddhism. The history of so unique a development would be of immense value if it could be written in full. But our knowledge of early India is too meagre and imperfect for a detailed account in spite of the remarkable results of modern research. It is difficult not only to trace the growth of single philosophic ideas step by step, but also to determine the relation between one system and another. Significant details are not known, and there is an almost total lack of exact chronology in early Indian history. It may be possible to treat these early developments under different periods, but the limits of these periods are to be regarded as tentative. Another drawback with regard to the history of Indian philosophy is that very little is known of the lives or character of the great thinkers. It has been suggested that this indifference of ancient Indians to the personal histories of their great men was due to the realization that individuals are but the product of their times. It could also be the result of the humble sense which those great men had of themselves.

Buddha is believed to have died in 487 BC. If we take this date as a landmark, we may divide the history of Indian thought into two stages. It marks the close of the Vedic period and the beginning of what is known as the Sanskrit or classic period. To the former belong the revealed texts of the Hindus. Held sacred, they were preserved with remarkable accuracy and therefore regarded as authentic. There is a more extensive literature in the second period. But it contains many additions and amendments. This post-Vedic period itself may be conceived in two stages—the early post-Vedic period and the later post-Vedic period, or the period of the systems. Thus we may treat of Indian philosophy under three periods in all—the Vedic, the early post-Vedic and the later post-Vedic.

A general survey of Indian thought reveals that its striking characteristic is richness and variety. Practically no shade of speculation is excluded. It is partial knowledge of Indian philosophy until recent times that provoked epithets from modern critics like "pessimistic" and "negative." The fact is that excepting a few doctrines, there is no lack of emphasis on the reality of the world or on the optimistic view of life.

Fortunately, such misconceptions are a thing of the past thanks to the publication of comprehensive works on Indian philosophy. It is now recognized that even single schools were not uniform doctrines throughout their history. "The fact is that Indian thought exhibits such a diversity of development that it does not admit of a rough-and-ready characterization."[31]

Underlying the varied development, two divergent currents are clearly discernible—one having its source in the Veda and the other developing independently of it. The second of these currents is later, for it commences as a reaction against the first. But it must have begun quite early, for there are references to it even in Vedic hymns. Originally critical and negative, it develops a constructive side also. Broadly speaking, it is pessimistic and realistic. The other current is very complex and therefore cannot be uniformly described as optimistic. It is important to note that the characteristic marks of the two currents are no longer incompatible, because over a long course of time the doctrines of each happened to be assimilated and appropriated by the other. But the distinction itself has not disappeared, as for instance between Vedānta and Jainism. The two types of thought, though distinct in origin and spirit, exhibit certain common features, and these form the basic principles of Indian philosophy considered as a whole. We shall proceed to consider them.

Recognition of Liberation as the Goal

In India philosophy has never been separate from religion. They begin as one everywhere, for their purpose is ultimately the same, viz., to seek the meaning of existence. Elsewhere they separate and develop on different lines. But in India they are differentiated, but not divorced. This is a striking excellence of Indian thought. Religion in the accepted sense is a yearning of the human spirit for union with God. It is not just in this sense alone of religion that we can speak of the alliance of philosophy with it. We find them allied even in forms of religion which do not recognize any permanent spirit. Therefore, to know the significance of this relationship, it is necessary to know the true meaning of religion. "...it is essentially a reaching forward to an ideal, without resting in mere belief or outward observances. Its distinctive mark is that it serves to further right living."[32] It is only in this broad sense of the word "religion" that we can speak of philosophy as one with it in India as a common characteristic of all doctrines.

The reason for this alliance lies in the fact that philosophy in India goes beyond mere intellectual conviction, which is often mistaken for the goal of philosophy. The ancient Indian philosopher did not stop with the discovery of truth, but strove to realize it in his own experience. He followed up *tattva-jñāna* by a strenuous effort to attain *mokṣa*, or liberation. The conception of *mokṣa* varies from system to system, but it marks for all the doctrines the culmination of philosophic culture. Such a view-point is to be ascribed to the fact that philosophy in India did not take its rise in wonder or curiosity as it seems to have done in the West; it originated under the pressure of a practical need to overcome the moral and physical evil present in life.

> It is the problem of how to remove this evil that troubled the ancient Indian most, and *mokṣa* in all the systems represents a state in which it is, in one sense or another, taken to have been overcome. Philosophic endeavour was directed primarily to find a remedy for the ills of life and the consideration of metaphysical questions came in as a matter of course.[33]

The idea of *mokṣa* is usually taken to be eschatological. It may be objected that such a view of *mokṣa* is purely a matter of religious faith and cannot be the goal of philosophy also. Really, there is no ground for thinking so, for the idea of *jīvanmukti* is prevalent in many schools, if not actually, at least virtually. Liberation is possible in this very life according to some. To others, even if it is to be achieved beyond death, a stage of perfection could be reached in life which almost amounts to release. Hence man's aim is not something to be achieved in a hypothetical hereafter, but one to be continually approximated within the limits of the present life. Such an aim does justice to philosophy as well as to religion. The recognition of it is due to the constant presence in the Indian mind of a positivistic standard right from the stage of the Upaniṣads.

> It points beyond intellectual satisfaction, which is often mistaken to be the aim of philosophy, and yet by keeping within the bounds of possible human experience avoids the dogma of *mokṣa* in the eschatological sense.[34]

The concept of *videhamukti* has also survived as a relic from earlier times, but the retention of it by any school does not really affect its philosophic standpoint of achievement here and now.

Prescription of a Means to the Goal

As a necessary corollary to the recognition of *mokṣa* as the goal, philosophy in India lays down a suitable course of practical discipline for its attainment. Here again philosophy meets religion. It thereby becomes "a way of life, not merely a way of thought."[35] It does not stop with being merely an interpretation of reality, but becomes a guide to life. The discipline differs in the two traditions, orthodox and heterodox. But an ascetic spirit underlies all Indian doctrines as their common feature. All of them agree on the need for renunciation, though for different reasons. The heterodox schools call for renunciation because they believe in the vanity and nothingness of life. Even the orthodox schools, some of which grant the reality of the world and life, recommend renunciation because physical life is not ultimate. Both the traditions differ also on the stage for renunciation. The heterodox schools hold that man should once for all turn away from the world whatever his circumstances may be. Detachment can be achieved at once—any moment of disillusionment about the world sufficing for it. But to the orthodox the renunciation is to be progressively realized in terms of one's *āśrama*, one becoming a hermit at the end of the *āśrama* discipline. They hold that detachment cannot be acquired without a suitable preliminary training undergone in the midst of society. In other words, social training, which involves the cultivation of sympathy and kindness to fellowmen, is indispensable for the perfection of character. But the heterodox tradition looks upon life in society more as a hindrance than as a help to renunciation. This does not, however, mean that it has no regard for society, for according to it also kindness and sympathy to fellowmen are needed, but not as a means to self-culture.

Further, to the heterodox tradition ascetic morality is the sole mode of practical discipline. To the orthodox it is only a preparation for a fresh course of training (which may vary from school to school). But whatever be the differences in matters of detail, asceticism as such serves as a bond of union between the two traditions. Even the ritualism of the Veda involved it, because to gain the fruits in a different world one had to deny oneself the fruits of this world. The principle of detachment implied in ritualism was rendered explicit, and the ulterior motive of self-love was replaced by disinterestedness by the *Bhagavad-gītā*.

Owing to the spirit of renunciation that runs through all of them, it may be said that the way of life which the Indian doctrines prescribe aims at transcending morality as commonly understood. "In other words, the goal of Indian philosophy lies as much beyond Ethics as it does beyond Logic."[36] But the supra-moral attitude aimed at bears a somewhat different significance in the several schools—and this depends on their conceptions of the self. In this respect the distinction does not, as in the previous one, correspond to the two traditions, orthodox and heterodox. Some schools admit the ultimacy of the individual self, while others deny it in one sense or another. Buddhism and Advaita represent the latter standpoint. Buddhism altogether repudiates the individual self as a permanent entity, while Advaita takes it eventually as one with the universal self. But since both ultimately deny the individual self, the contrast between the individual and society gets negated. And since the notion of obligation rests on that contrast, it ceases to be significant finally for both the schools. On the other hand, theism, like that of Rāmānuja, and pluralism, like Nyāya-Vaiśeṣika and Jainism, recognize the individual self to be ultimate. But they teach that, to attain deliverance, absolute self-suppression, or annihilation of egoism (*ahaṁkāra*), is necessary. To them the consciousness of obligation continues, but the disciple devotes himself to its fulfilment with no thought whatsoever of his rights. So far, the motive is lifted above that of common morality. Thus according to both the views, there is in the end total renunciation of personal interest, and thereby the essential duality of the moral world between the individual and the social environment is transcended.

Even in the preliminary stages of discipline, where the distinction between the individual and the environment persists, there is a sense in which the training may be said to transcend morality. Morality as commonly conceived is concerned with the individual's duties to human society. But according to the Indian view the individual's obligations are not confined to human society, but extend virtually to the whole of sentient creation. "Such an extension of the world of moral action accords well with the spirit of Indian ethics whose watchword is devotion to duties rather than assertion of rights."[37] Beings that are not characterized by moral consciousness may have no duties to fulfil, but it does not mean that human beings have no duties towards them to be fulfilled. Indian ethics is rooted in the fellowship of all living beings, and this is best illustrated by the principle of *ahiṁsā*, which is common to all Indian faiths. Such a stand does not ignore the importance of human society. It only shows that human well-being alone should not be the end. Corresponding to its privileged position, mankind has duties to all living creatures. Social morality, though it widens the individual's outlook, really keeps him isolated from the rest of creation. The egoism of the species is as bad as personal egoism, because it leads to the notion that the sub-human world is for man's exploitation. That also must be got rid of to win real freedom. This is possible only when everything is looked upon as equally sacred.

Summary of the Basic Principles of Indian Philosophy

The two elements common to all Indian thought are (i) the pursuit of *mokṣa* as the final ideal and (ii) the ascetic spirit of the discipline recommended for its attainment. They show that Indian philosophy goes beyond intellectual conviction and ordinary morality. "...philosophy as understood in India is neither mere intellectualism nor mere moralism, but includes and transcends them both."[38] That is to say, it aims at achieving more than what logic and ethics can. However, the intellectual and moral efforts are the sole means of approach to the goal of philosophy. Consequently, the goal, when achieved, is characterized by both *jñāna* and *vairāgya*. *Jñāna*, or illumination, is intellectual conviction ripened into immediate experience. And *vairāgya*, or self-renunciation, is at this stage secure by the discovery of its true basis.

The goal thus achieved is an attitude of peace. It is not a passive state, as it involves loving service to others. But this activity is secondary, as it is only the expression of the inner experience, which is primary and but for which such loving service would not have followed. Thus the whole emphasis of Indian philosophy falls on the inner transformation that occurs in *mokṣa*—not either on the new behaviour or the new knowledge that goes with it.

> The value of philosophic training lies as little in inducing a person to do what otherwise he would not have done, as in instructing him in what otherwise he would not have known; it consists essentially in making him what he was not before.[39]

Interaction between the Two Traditions and the Triumph of Vedānta

The two traditions, orthodox and heterodox, though exhibiting the common features outlined above, are fundamentally different. Hence, in the history of Indian philosophy, they have acted and reacted upon each other, giving rise to divergent schools of thought. Their mutual influence has led to a broadening of the basis of thought. At the same time, it has led to considerable overlapping of the two sets of doctrines, with the result that it has become difficult to discover what elements each has incorporated from the other. For instance, it is impossible to say for certain to which of the two traditions we owe the ideal of *jīvanmukti*.

At different times in the course of this progressive movement one school or another was ascendant. At one stage it was conspicuously the case for Buddhism. But finally Vedānta triumphed over all the rest. In the process of interaction it has naturally been transformed much, but its inner character remains the same as it was taught in the Upaniṣads. In fact, even the several phases of growth in the heretical tradition may be looked upon as steps leading to the ascendancy of Vedānta. The Vedānta may accordingly be regarded as the consummation of Indian thought representing the highest type of the Indian ideal.

There are of course different schools of Vedānta, but on the theoretical side, they may be classified under two heads—absolutism and theism. The former is explicitly monistic, and the latter, though avowedly pluralistic, is also governed by the spirit of monism, as it teaches the dependence of everything on God. On the practical side, it was the positive ideal of life that triumphed with the triumph of Vedānta. This shows itself in two ways. First, the ethical discipline acquires a social basis, which Vedānta as an orthodox doctrine commends. Secondly, the conception of the highest ideal comes to mean, not the isolation of the self from the environment (as it does in the negative conception of the heterodox schools), but the conquest of the opposition between the two, because the interests of the self come to be identified with those of the whole of reality. Both the ideals, positive and negative, involve the cultivation of complete detachment. But the detachment in the case of the positive ideal of Vedānta is of a "higher and finer type."[40] Kālidāsa gives the truest expression to such an ideal when he describes it as "owning the whole world while disowning oneself."[41] The Vedānta conception of the highest ideal also implies "the recognition of a cosmic purpose...towards whose fulfilment everything consciously or unconsciously moves."[42] The heretical schools do not generally see any such purpose in the world as a whole, though they speak of individual freedom.

7. THE STUDY OF INDIAN PHILOSOPHY

In the early part of this century very few people thought Indian philosophy as worthy of any attention. Its knowledge was confined to a handful of pandits who had inherited it from old thinkers, and to a few oriental scholars who took what, from the philosophical standpoint, could be described as only "an external interest in it."[43] Things changed rapidly since then. Many universities found a place for study and research in Indian philosophy. Books and articles began to appear. And young people began to evince keen interest in the subject. But a great deal more remained to be done. The subject had to secure a wider recognition in the universities. But more important, investigation had to be carried on into the various branches of the subject and the results made easily accessible to the modern reader. This was Hiriyanna's assessment in 1935.[44] It was an assessment which is relevant even to the present times.

To make Indian philosophy accessible to the modern reader, "it is necessary not only to resuscitate the old thought but also to interpret it."[45] There are some scholars who look upon all attempts at interpretation with suspicion. They might like to confine the work to resuscitation on the ground that interpretation might distort the spirit of Indian philosophy. But Hiriyanna thinks that this literalist position, as he calls it, is neither possible nor desirable. The revival of ancient thought requires its expression in modern terms. But the very process of expressing it in modern terms involves interpretation, "for the concepts out of which that thought is built do not always have equivalents in the speeches of today."[46] For example, how can the idea underlying the word *manas* be conveyed without resorting to interpretation? The Sanskrit word will serve no practical purpose, and the English translation "mind" will only mislead. This shows that the implication of the word *manas* has to be explained in so many words. The object of the interpretation is to make the results of investigation, not attractive or agreeable, but only quite intelligible to those who have no direct access to the old Indian thought. The essential spirit of Indian philosophy is not altered thereby. "It is modernism in expression, not modernism in spirit which would be not merely unhistorical but also unphilosophical."[47] Such a rendering of old thought in modern terminology is no doubt difficult, but it is not impossible for one who approaches the task with knowledge and care. "If we remain content with saying merely what the old works *say* and not what they *mean*, the revival however faithful to the original will be barren of result...."[48] In working towards this aim of interpretation, it is necessary to keep in view certain general principles.

The first is the extension of the bounds of inquiry so that nothing of value may be lost. Some branches of Indian philosophy remain practically unexplored, for example epistemology, aesthetics, and formal logic. Epistemology occupies a very prominent place in Sanskrit philosophical works. At least three different types of theory with many variations are found discussed in them. Aesthetics stands somewhat on a different footing, for philosophical works do not contain much explicit reference to it. But the whole of Alaṅkāraśāstra, which, though not classed under philosophy, is yet closely allied to it, deals with it. "It was not with religion alone that philosophy blends in Indian thought but also with art."[49] Alaṅkāraśāstra comprises a large number of works and yields to no other branch of learning in variety or interest. The attention of the

Sanskritist to it is of recent origin, and if the student of philosophy turns to it, there is a rich harvest to gather. In formal logic the later developments abound in scholastic subtleties. Whatever their use is as means of mental discipline, they are philosophically sterile. But there is enough of valuable information in the earlier works on topics like "the meaning of terms," "the import of propositions," "the theory of the syllogism," "fallacies," and so forth.

Secondly, individual workers should more and more concentrate their attention upon particular problems or upon particular aspects of general ones. What is wanted is an intensive study of special topics, not a general treatment merely. Such a study alone "will make our knowledge of the past fuller and bring us closer into touch with its thought."[50] It may be described as "conquest by division."[51] In addition to enriching our knowledge of the past, such a study may also throw new light on present-day problems in philosophy. The scope for such a selective study in Indian philosophy is ample, for its tradition goes far back and expresses itself in diverse systems of thought, some of which like Buddhism and Vedānta branch out into subordinate schools. Take for instance the conceptions of time and space. It is not only an old problem, but also illustrates the variety of solutions which one and the same problem gets in Indian philosophy. Buddhism makes both of them mental constructions. Nyāya-Vaiśeṣika regards them as objective entities. Midway between these two extremes are the views of Sāṅkhya and Advaita. Sāṅkhya explains them as aspects of *prakṛti*—matter is *behind* both and is not *in* them. To Advaita they are only epistemologically real (*anirvacanīya*) and as such neither strictly objective nor subjective.

Thirdly, the inquiry should follow the historical method. "We should determine the various stages in the development of a doctrine or the growth of a conception for pronouncing judgment finally upon its philosophic worth."[52] In the present state of our knowledge of ancient Indian history, this may not always be possible. But we should have that as our ideal. We should not rest satisfied with a commendation from the merely logical standpoint. The logical development may often coincide with the historical, but there is no guarantee that it will. The possibility of a divergence between the two only shows that conclusions reached without an adequate support for them in history may not be certain. The risk of error in basing our interpretation upon the particulars that happen to be commonly known, without due regard to their historical antecedents, may be illustrated by the so-called Cārvāka doctrine. Our present knowledge of it is meagre. At the same time it is difficult to believe that this school of thought is entirely fictitious and that it was invented by rival schools only for the purpose of demolishing it. There are many indications in the old literature to support the view that it existed at one time or another as a serious system of philosophy. We may cite two.

(i) Our belief that for Cārvāka perception is the only *pramāṇa* seems to be a caricature. On historical grounds we find that the actual intention of the school was not that inference should be done away with, but that it must not be utilized for postulating the supra-natural, as for instance Nyāya-Vaiśeṣika does with the help of *sāmānyato-dṛṣṭānumāna*, which is a variety of *anumāna*. This stand is an excellence and even Mīmāṁsā and Vedānta in a way concede this point—as they set up a distinct *pramāṇa* for the supernatural, viz., *Āgama*. (ii) Not all Cārvākas denied the self by identifying it with the body. There is evidence to show the existence of some Lokāyatas who did recognize the self and denied only its survival after death—a view which cannot be summarily dismissed as unphilosophical. Jayanta contrasts the Suśikṣita Cārvāka with the Cārvāka-dhūrta. The distinction has long been forgotten.

These instances go to show that originally Cārvāka must have represented a serious attempt at philosophy. It stands for "a school of Indian free-thinkers."[53] And free-thinking is traceable to *Ṛgveda*. Cārvāka in all probability goes back to Svabhāva-vāda. Its influence is felt on systems like Sāṅkhya. Its main feature on the theoretical side is its positivistic outlook, and on the practical side its central teaching is that, since there is no surviving self, man should strive for *mokṣa* in this life without postponing it to a hypothetical state beyond death.

On the need for a historical approach it is worth citing the following opinion from Hiriyanna's *Reviews*. He reminds us that the chief systems of Indian thought are all very old and embody the results of a long process of growth. To forget this fact and ascribe a static sameness to any school for its whole history results in a lack of perspective in our view of various doctrines, taken singly or in relation to one another. If a particular view is maintained, for example, in a late Nyāya work, we cannot assume that this view has been present in just that form from the very beginning of the school. In modern studies of Indian philosophy the fact of history has to be constantly kept in view, and efforts should be made to recover as far as possible the details of its development that could have been lost.

> It should not be thought that such efforts will serve only antiquarian interests, for they are sure to unravel many doctrinal intricacies and thus help us to appreciate better the philosophical heritage of India.[54]

The fourth general principle of interpretation is in regard to the results obtained. Here it is necessary to lay special emphasis on what is distinctive of Indian philosophy. Every tradition in philosophy has its own genius, and Indian philosophy is no exception. In our anxiety to find similarities between Indian philosophy and Western or modern thought, we must not overlook differences between them. A superficial examination may show only similarities, but a deeper analysis is sure to reveal differences. Often an apparent similarity may conceal an important difference, which a student of philosophy cannot afford to ignore. Some examples may be cited.

The design argument in Indian systems, for instance in Nyāya-Vaiśeṣika, is usually understood much in the same manner as the argument in the West. This may be all right so far as theistic systems, which use it to prove the existence of God, are concerned. But in India it occurs not only in theistic systems, but also inatheistic ones like Sāṅkhya (unlike in the West). So, as used in Sāṅkhya, it necessarily has a new significance, which is this. In the West the argument was used to prove the *goodness* and *greatness* of God. But one of the weaknesses of the argument as utilized in the West is that the devices in nature—as pointed out by Sāṅkhya—are designed as much to thwart and embitter life as to promote it. Now, the former alternative is wholly incompatible with the goodness of God. (Even in Nyāya-Vaiśeṣika the argument is not taken to point to the goodness of God, but only to his greatness.) But in the Sāṅkhya version of the argument this incompatibility is absent. This is because Sāṅkhya argues from the design of the world, not to its author, but to one who is served by it, viz., the *puruṣa*. So far as the individual is concerned, his lot in life, as is too well known, includes pain and pleasure.

Here is another example of a feature which is peculiar to Indian thought. To the twofold logical division "is" and "is not" the Indian intellect reckoned in two more alternatives, viz., "both is and is not" and "neither is nor is not." These are the conceptions of *sadasat* and *sadasad-vilakṣaṇa*. These additions are not "super-subtleties,"[55] but form the very foundation of the three great systems—Advaita, Jaina and the Mādhyamika. The discussion whether verbal testimony can ever give rise to immediate knowledge, which we find in Vedānta works, is also unique to Indian philosophy. It is full of interest to students of logic and psychology. These examples are sufficient to show how contrast may become more instructive than mere comparison.

In such a study as ours it is differences that are of particular value, for in them we get at the special constructive contributions which a nation has made towards the solution of common philosophical problems. And it is only when we do not neglect such individual features that our study can be described as really fruitful.[56]

REFERENCES

1. Vide *MP*, pp. 1-7.
2. Ibid., p. 46.
3. Ibid., p. 47.
4. Ibid., p. 55.
5. Ibid.
6. Ibid., p. 56.
7. Ibid.
8. Ibid.
9. Ibid., p. 57.
10. Ibid., p. 8.
11. Ibid., p. 9.
12. Ibid., p. 12.
13. Ibid., p. 20.
14. Ibid., pp. 22-23.
15. *QAP*, p. 38, n.1.
16. Ibid., p. 39.
17. Ibid., p. 41.
18. Ibid., p. 42.
19. Ibid., p. 44.
20. Ibid., p. 45.
21. Ibid., p. 46. Expressed in 1939, the implied reference of this view to Mahatma Gandhi is very clear.
22. *PEIP*, p. 20.
23. Ibid.
24. Ibid.
25. Ibid., p. 21.
26. Ibid.
27. Ibid., p. 22.
28. Ibid.
29. Ibid., p. 23.
30. Ibid.
31. *OIP*, p. 16.
32. Ibid., p. 18.
33. Ibid., pp. 18-19.
34. Ibid., pp. 19-20.
35. Ibid., p. 20.
36. Ibid., p. 22.
37. Ibid., p. 23.
38. Ibid., p. 24.
39. Ibid., p. 25.
40. Ibid., p. 26.
41. Ibid., p. 26, n.1.
42. Ibid., p. 26.
43. *IPS—II*, p. 112.
44. Ibid., pp.112-13.
45. Ibid., p. 113.
46. Ibid.
47. Ibid.
48. Ibid.
49. Ibid., p. 114.
50. Ibid., p. 115.
51. Ibid.
52. Ibid.
53. Ibid., p. 116.
54. *R*, p. 142.
55. *IPS—II*, p. 117.
56. Ibid., p. 118.

3

Early Indian Philosophy

1. THE GROWTH OF INDIAN PHILOSOPHY

For the purpose of indicating the general nature of Indian philosophy, Hiriyanna divides its development into three periods: the Vedic, the early post-Vedic and the later post-Vedic. The Vedic period is marked by a growing search for unity. The early post-Vedic period is characterized by the emergence of other currents of thought. Out of the discord among the various currents of thought, Vedic and non-Vedic, a process of systematisation follows in the third period.

Vedic Period

It is in the Veda that we have to seek for the beginnings of Indian philosophy and religion. The Veda is usually stated to consist of two parts, Mantras and Brāhmaṇas. The Mantras themselves may be divided into the early and the later ones. The later Mantras, by their nature, may be considered along with the Brāhmaṇas.

In the early Mantras we find the various powers of nature personified and worshipped for favours. Although their trend is polytheistic, they are not without a suggestion of an underlying unity in the essential oneness of the gods (*devas*). In the later Mantras and Brāhmaṇas the tendency to see unity is fully developed. Some common feature of the gods is raised to the rank of a supreme God. What is achieved is an impersonal monotheism. The idea of a single God behind all the gods also takes various shapes "as if the ancient Indians were mentally experimenting and discovering one concept after another which more nearly approximated to their ideal of the divine."[1] A further tendency is to transform this concept of divinity so as to represent the source not merely of the gods, but even of *all* being. It is a movement towards monism. It takes two directions. In one it analyses the objective universe and arrives at the concept of Brahman. In the other, it searches for the essence of man and culminates in the concept of *ātman*. The movement occurs in the Upaniṣads. Though traditionally classed with the Brāhmaṇas, they really form a separate stratum of thought. The Upaniṣads finally identify the two principles of Brahman and *ātman* in the *mahāvākyas*, which are the crown of Vedic teaching.

Early post-Vedic Period

In the centuries immediately succeeding the Vedic period there arise currents of thought other than Upaniṣadic monism. One current has its source mainly in the Veda and the others are either independent of or opposed to the Veda. (i) The former is monotheism of a personal type. God is regarded as the creator and moral governor of the whole universe. He is either Śiva or Viṣṇu, who are mentioned in the Veda, to whom devotion and rites like temple worship are offered—features which are freely borrowed from a non-Vedic tradition called Āgama. Thus arise two creeds, Śaivism and Vaiṣṇavism, both of which are based on the Veda and the Āgama. (ii) The other currents of thought are diverse. One is Svabhāvavāda, or naturalism, which repudiates belief in the supersensuous and the supernatural. Doctrines like Jainism which are dualistic and pluralistic also arisc. A common feature of Svabhāvavāda and doctrines like Jainism is their antagonism to the Veda. Special mention should also be made of Buddhism, which, in its early form, was not altogether opposed to Vedic teaching.

Later post-Vedic Period or Age of the Systems

In course of time the disaccord among various elements of thought, both Vedic and non-Vedic, necessitate a critical scrutiny of them. As the result of this scrutiny, what are known as the systems of Indian philosophy arise. They are called Darśanas, as each of them represents a particular "point of view" in philosophy. Six of them are orthodox, since they do not question the authority of the Veda. Three are non-Vedic, or heterodox, in origin. The orthodox systems include all varieties of philosophic thought—pluralism, dualism and monism.

Nyāya, Vaiśeṣika and Mīmāṁsā are pluralistic. The ultimate entities are many. Matter consists of atoms. The soul is infinite and eternal but manifold. In its empirical state it is in actual relation with matter, but in its intrinsic nature it is detached from matter. Sāṅkhya and Yoga are dualistic. There are only two ultimates, *prakṛti* and *puruṣa*. The entire physical world is brought under the head *prakṛti*, which is complex in nature. The *puruṣas* are many, but as a category *puruṣa* is opposed to *prakṛti*. Just as in pluralism, the soul is essentially detached from matter, though in the empirical state it is in real association with it. The Vedānta is monistic. The world and the self are eventually traced to Brahman. Vedāntins differ among themselves on two questions. On the relation which the world and souls bear to Brahman, one view is that they are real but dependent on Brahman, and the other is that both are appearances of Brahman. Again, on the nature of Brahman, one view is that it is all-comprehensive (*saguṇa*), and the other is that it is transcendental (*nirguṇa*).

Mokṣa: the Distinctive Feature of Indian Philosophy

The growth of Indian philosophy has been briefly surveyed so far with reference to the problem of reality. A convincing solution to this problem is expected to bring satisfaction to the speculative side of man. Many modern thinkers in the West would say that with this the purpose of philosophy is fulfilled. But Indian philosophers down the ages have held that philosophy must not stop at speculative satisfaction, "but should aim at satisfying the whole nature of man by meeting the practical demands of his moral life also."[2] Why did the Indians take such a view? All the systems inquire into the nature of the self and the physical world, but all of them lay greater emphasis on the self than on the physical world. Hence philosophy in India is known as *adhyātma-śāstra*, or the science of the self. It is more a study of man than of physical nature.

If practical application is the goal of philosophy as a whole, it is particularly so in regard to its highest truth. Each Indian doctrine makes its own distinction between the empirical and the true selves, the true being shown as essentially free from the limitations of the empirical self. The purpose of knowing this truth is not just to gratify theoretic curiosity, but to act upon that truth and realize the higher self, repudiating the lower. All the systems prescribe also a course of practical discipline for achieving it. The discipline has two sides. One consists in the overcoming of narrowness and the cultivation of detachment (*vairāgya*) through the practice of disinterested action (*niṣkāmà-karma*). The other consists in meditation (*dhyāna*) on the true self, about which one has mediately known from philosophy, so that this mediate knowledge may become a direct experience.

As for the question whether *mokṣa* can ever be realized, Indian philosophers have never doubted its possibility. In fact, after originally conceiving it as an eschatological event, they boldly asserted its possibility even within the span of life. The possibility of *jīvanmukti* is literally accepted in systems like Sāṅkhya-Yoga and Advaita. But even the other systems virtually admit it, for they hold that release follows necessarily at the end of life in the case of an enlightened person. The distinction between the two views is only in regard to the question whether discipline is to continue or not during the interval between direct knowledge and death. According to the former view, it need not, but according to the latter, it should.

The life led by a *jīvanmukta* is characterized by two features corresponding to the twofold discipline outlined above. On the one hand it is marked by absolute freedom from selfishness, and on the other, it is signified by spontaneous service to all others so that they too may become free. According to monism, such service is the expression of universal love resulting from the knower's experience of the essential unity of being; according to pluralistic systems, which believe in many selves, it is the outcome of his pity, or compassion, for others.

> Thus, according to all the schools, the knower, after gaining enlightenment and freedom for himself, will spread that enlightenment among others and secure for them the same freedom, so far as it lies in his power.[3]

2. VEDIC THOUGHT PRIOR TO THE UPANIṢADS

The Early Mantras

Vedic thought is represented by the Mantras and Brāhmaṇas. Mantras are metrical hymns. A collection of Mantras is a *saṁhita*. We may distinguish between the early Mantras and the later ones. The later Mantras are akin to the Brāhmaṇas and could be taken along with them.

The early Mantras are religious songs in praise of one or more deities, which are personifications of the powers of nature. They are worshipped either for favours from them or as thanksgiving for favours received. The significance of the worship is a conviction that the visible world is not in itself final and that there is a reality lying hidden in it. It also implies a belief in the uniformity of nature. Thirty-three gods are sometimes reckoned, and they are classified into three groups of eleven each: gods of the sky, gods of mid-air, and gods of the earth. They are regarded as inter-related though none as supreme. It must be noted that, though the Vedic gods are close to nature, they are not complete personifications of its powers. This is a highly favourable frame of mind for philosophic speculation. "...the Vedic Indian did not allow his conceptions to crystallize too quickly."[4] He kept up his sense of mystery about nature until he could arrive at a satisfying solution.

> This characteristic signifies a passion for truth and accounts not only for the profundity of Indian philosophic investigation, but also for the great variety of the solutions it offers of philosophical problems.[5]

An important idea which we find in the early Mantras is that of *ṛta*. The word originally meant the uniformity found in nature, or cosmic order. It later came to include moral order as well. There is physical and moral order in the universe, because its control is in righteous hands. The gods are guardians of *ṛta*. The word almost has ceased to be used in Sanskrit, but under the name of *dharma* the same idea occupies a very important place in the later Indian views of life. According to these early Mantras, the world owes not only its order, but also its existence, to the gods, who have created it. The relation of man to the gods is one of complete dependence; but it is also of an intimate kind marked by love. The chief aim of prayers is worldly prosperity.

The Later Mantras and the Brāhmaṇas

The word Brāhmaṇa "signifies an authoritative utterance of a priest, relating particularly to sacrifice; and the Brāhmaṇas are so-called because they are the repositories of such utterances."[6] The simple worship of gods in the early Mantras is gradually replaced by elaborate sacrifices in the Brāhmaṇas together with the later Mantras. The motive also undergoes a change. The purpose of the early Mantras was to prevail upon the gods to bestow some favour or to ward off some danger. But the aim of the later Mantras and Brāhmaṇas is to persuade and even compel the gods to grant the wishes of the sacrificer. It indicates faith in the efficacy of the Vedic sacrifice as such, which is exalted above the gods. The power of conferring good is thus transferred from the gods to the Veda itself—a logical consequence of which is the denial of gods later by Pūrva Mīmāṁsā. Emphasis thus comes to be placed on the scrupulous performance of the sacrifice in every detail. And the old word *ṛta* is used in this context to mean the correctness of sacrifice, which is the third meaning of the term.

The old idea that man owes his prosperity as a debt (*ṛṇa*) to the gods is still retained, for we find that sacrifice is sometimes regarded in the Brāhmaṇas as a *ṛṇa* due to the gods. It is the first of three obligations (*ṛṇa-traya*). The second is indebtedness to the sages of old for the heritage of culture which they have left behind. It is to be discharged by receiving and transmitting it. The third is due to the race, which is to be met by becoming a householder and begetting sons. The ideal of *ṛṇa* also includes the practice of virtues like truth, self-restraint and kindness.

Thus the idea of morality did not disappear on account of the emphasis on sacrifice.

Neither in the early Mantras nor in the later Mantras and Brāhmaṇas is there any allusion to the transmigration of the soul. But in both phases the idea of the survival of the soul is recognized. The soul is said to be born in another world for the sake of further rewards and punishments. Death does not mean destruction, but only continuance of existence elsewhere, where happiness or misery results according to one's deserts. All this points to the immortality of the soul.

Ritualism marks only one characteristic of the Vedic religion represented by the Brāhmaṇas and later Mantras. Other developments are also found. Though occurring faintly, they are of great importance to philosophy, for they contain the germs of later thought. We shall pass on to them.

Monotheism

In the earlier stage the Vedic Indian sought the causes of natural phenomena, and this led him to recognize the several deities who form the objects of prayer in the Mantras. A longing for simplicity in explanation impels him now to seek their ultimate cause. It is a striving for the one God that controls and rules over all those phenomena—a common power that works behind the several gods. An earlier overlapping of divinities by the mutual resemblance of one natural phenomenon with another (e.g., the Sun, Fire and Dawn) prepares the ground for the unity of Godhead. This is a philosophic rather than a religious conception. But in the initial stage the nature of this unified Godhead is not clearly defined. Various solutions are tried, as represented by names such as Viśvedevas, Viśvakarman, Prajāpati, Prāṇa, and so on. What is noteworthy is that this attempt is to derive a general and virtually impersonal conception of the supreme God. Though the conception is abstract, it does not lack moral exaltation.

Monism

Monotheism is bound to involve dualism. The unity of Godhead is set over against nature, which he makes and guides. This is not an entirely satisfactory conception. So there is a further movement to trace the whole of existence to a single source. Monism is a higher conception of unity than monotheism. It is a definitely philosophical development. It is fully worked out in the Upaniṣads, but it is foreshadowed in pre-Upaniṣadic literature. At this stage the monistic current is often mixed with monotheism—God being regarded as both immanent in and transcendent of nature. Still, the former is clearly discernible. There are at least two shades of monistic thought. To begin with, there is a pantheistic view which identifies nature with God. God is conceived here not as transcending nature (as earlier), but as immanent in it. Although the object of this view is to find unity, it inconsistently retains both the notions of God and nature and hence is not found fully satisfactory. It leads to another conception of unity—an impersonal conception of Godhead which reconciles all opposites within itself. This is regarded as the First Cause which spontaneously unfolds itself as the entire universe, requiring no outside Power to guide and shape it. The best example of this is the "Song of Creation" in the *Ṛgveda.* It brings us to the threshold of Upaniṣadic monism. Thus the idea of unity comes to be emphasized during this period. But, though nature and man are subjected to speculation, the reality of the external world is not yet questioned.

Free-thinking

This is yet another tendency to be noted in this period. Though it does not form part of the teaching of the Veda, there are allusions to it there. This tendency manifests itself sometimes as doubt and sometimes as disbelief. But whatever be the form, it sets itself against the orthodox teaching of the Veda. It is this tendency that later gives rise to the heretical schools.

3. THE UPANIṢADS

The Nature and Importance of the Upaniṣads

Traditionally, the Brāhmaṇas include several of the early Upaniṣads, but in view of their importance, a separate treatment of the Upaniṣads is necessary. They deserve to be reckoned as a separate portion of the Veda. In fact, the three parts, Mantras, Brāhmaṇas and Upaniṣads, stand for teachings that are more or less distinct. "...the Upaniṣads are the very foundation of all Indian thought, and a knowledge of them is essential to a correct understanding of the Indian view of life."[7] If the *Rāmāyaṇa,* the *Mahābhārata,* and the *Bhāgavata* give us an insight into the ideal of practical life, the Upaniṣads reveal to us its philosophical basis. Even apart from their place in the development of Indian thought, their intrinsic value is very great.

Broadly speaking, the teaching of the Upaniṣads marks a reaction against that of the Brāhmaṇas. In more than one place they decry the value of sacrifices, which bring no lasting result as devotion to philosophic truth does. Often the opposition appears indirectly—an allegorical interpretation is substituted for a literal one. For example, the *aśvamedha* sacrifice is transformed into a meditative act in which the contemplative is to offer up the whole universe in the place of a horse and thereby attain true freedom. But the opposition to ritual gradually disappears, and the old teaching is reconciled with the new. Ceremonial life comes to be recognized as necessary, either directly or indirectly, for attaining the final goal of life. Thus the Upaniṣads come finally to represent the teaching of the Veda in its entirety, and not its final portion only.

> Here we see illustrated a characteristic feature of all advance in Indian culture, viz. that when a new stage of progress is reached, the old is not discarded but is, sooner or later, incorporated in it.[8]

The number of the Upaniṣads is very large, about two hundred. But only a dozen of them are genuine portions of the Veda. The rest are all of later origin and are of less value. But they are also called Upaniṣads, because they bear a family likeness in thought and language to the classical Upaniṣads. The term *upaniṣad* signifies "secret teaching." Etymologically, it is equivalent to "sitting" (*sad*) "nearby" (*upa*) "devotedly" (*ni*). It shows that the teaching was a mystery and that care was bestowed on keeping it from the unworthy lest it should be misunderstood or misapplied. Hindu tradition regards the Upaniṣads, like the other parts of the Veda, as *śruti*, or revelation. They contain certain set formulas (*mahāvākyas*) like *tat tvam asi*, and these are preceded and succeeded by expository discourses. They contain the thoughts of many a teacher and so are heterogeneous in nature. Both logically and chronologically, the Upaniṣads form the end of the Vedic teaching, and so in both senses they are called "Vedānta." They are also the basis of all the Vedānta schools. As regards the manner of these works, they are generally in the form of dialogues. Their method is more poetic than philosophical. They indicate truths generally through metaphor and allegory. Sometimes the language is symbolic. The style is elliptical and intended to be orally explained. These peculiarities render their interpretation difficult, with the result that there have been different explanations of them. But the indefiniteness is only in regard to details. The general tenor of the teaching is unmistakable.

The Nature of Reality (Brahman-Ātman)

The Upaniṣads embody several doctrines, some of which are even discordant. But not all these ideas are prominent. The most important teaching in it, namely on the nature of reality, admits of varied interpretation. But it is clear that it is monistic and idealistic. It is monistic as it conveys that the ultimate reality is one and only one. It is also idealistic in the sense that this single reality is conceived of as spiritual in nature. Pluralism and realism are not absent in the Upaniṣads, but they are not conspicuous, being only distant echoes of the earlier portions of the Veda.

The conception of the ultimate reality is arrived at by two currents of thought which eventually merge. One traces the visible universe to a single source named Brahman. This trend is found in the later Mantras in an attempt to account for the whole universe—nature, man and gods—regarded objectively. Several conceptions are tried, which culminate in the conception of Brahman, which is prominent in the Upaniṣads. Brahman is the power, or primary principle, which spontaneously manifests itself as the universe. The term comes from *bṛh*, which means "to burst forth."

A second current of thought, which is just complementary to the above, is also found in earlier literature. It is to discover by introspection the psychic principle, the inner essence of man. The culmination of this inquiry in the Upaniṣads is represented by the concept of *ātman*. The term *ātman* signifies the essential part of anything, more particularly of man, i.e. his self, or soul. But the conception of this essence is not confined to the individual. It is universalized into a world principle, the world itself being looked upon as a cosmic individual. Such a consummation secures the unity of individual selves in the idea of the cosmic self, just as the conception of Brahman secures the unity of the entire outer physical universe.

The two conceptions of Brahman and *ātman*, viewed independently, represent a dichotomy between the self and the not-self, between the inner and the outer worlds. Hence the Upaniṣads do not stop at this stage. The two conceptions are finally identified. "...it is this happy identification of them that constitutes the essential teaching of the Upaniṣads."[9] The fusion of these two conceptions is expressed in the *mahāvākyas* like *tat tvam asi* and *aham brahma asmi*. They mean that the principle underlying the physical universe and that which forms the essence of man are ultimately the same. In other words, the individual and the world are the manifestations of the same reality, and both are, therefore, at bottom one.

It is necessary to see the implication of this identification. The conception of the ultimate reality as mere Brahman carries with it two defects. No doubt, as the source of the whole universe, it is all-comprehensive. But such a cosmic principle need not be spiritual in nature; it may well be a material, or physical, entity. Again, the conception of Brahman is objective; we look upon the ultimate as something not ourselves. Such a conception carries no necessary certainty with it. It could at best be an assumption and a dogma—a mere hypothesis to account for the origin of the universe. There being no compulsion to regard it as actually existing, it would not be illogical even to deny it. The conception of the ultimate as *ātman* has neither of these defects. Our own self is known to us to be spiritual, and we are under an intuitive obligation to admit the reality of our own existence, although we may not know its precise nature. But the conception has another difficulty. In the sense in which we commonly understand it, the self, or *ātman*, is limited in nature. It is determined on the one side by the physical world, and on the other by the other selves. Such a finite entity cannot represent the whole of reality. Even when viewed as the cosmic self, it is set over against nature and is thus limited by it.

Thus, reality cannot be represented as Brahman alone or *ātman* alone. But when the two conceptions are combined, a third is reached which is without the flaws of either taken by itself. The possibility of Brahman being non-spiritual and uncertain is removed by its equation with *ātman*. And the deficiency of finiteness is made good by the *ātman*'s identification with Brahman, the all-comprehensive cosmic principle. This final conception of reality is "neither Brahman nor *ātman* in one sense, but both in another."[10] It may indifferently be termed either Brahman or *ātman*, but it is spiritual and accounts for not only all the selves, but also for the whole of the physical universe. It is this higher reality that is described as *satyam jñānam anantam*, "where *satyam* points to its immediate certainty, *jñānam* to its spiritual nature and *anantam* to its all-inclusive or infinite character."[11] It manifests itself, though not fully, better in the human self than in the outer world, because it appears in the latter as mere insentient matter. "The enunciation of this doctrine marked the most important advance in the whole history of India's thought."[12] The whole process of it is well brought out in the Uddālaka—Śvetaketu dialogue occurring in the sixth chapter of the *Chāndogya Upaniṣad*.

The Relation of the World and Souls to Brahman

The relation in which the world and souls stand to Brahman is presented in two forms in the Upaniṣads. There are passages which teach that Brahman, and nothing but Brahman, is truly real. The physical world is but an appearance, and it has no actual place in the ultimate reality. The individual self is Brahman itself appearing as finite because of its adjuncts like the body, which, being parts of the physical world, are not real in the true sense of the term. Thus Brahman stands above all relations to the perceived universe. And, though beyond comprehension, Brahman is the basis of the universe. It is acosmic (*niṣprapañca*). The Gārgī-Yājñavalkya dialogue in the third chapter of the *Bṛhadāraṇyaka Upaniṣad* represents the teaching.

There are other passages in the Upaniṣads which grant reality to the physical world. But they also maintain that it never exists apart from Brahman. There is also the implication that the individual self is as such real, though it is never apart from Brahman. Brahman is thus immanent in and comprehends the entire universe (*saprapañca*). The teaching is represented, for example, by the Śāṇḍilya-vidyā which we find in the third chapter of the *Chāndogya Upaniṣad*. Brahman is described here as that which gives rise to the world and reabsorbs it and which also supports it (so long as it lasts).

The relative position and importance of these two conceptions is one of the most difficult problems connected with the Upaniṣads. Broadly, there have been two ways of solving this difficulty from which there later evolve two forms of Vedānta. Bhartṛprapañca maintains that the *saprapañca* view is the real teaching of the Upaniṣads. The individual self and the physical universe, though finite and imperfect, are real; but they are not altogether different from Brahman. The three constitute a unity in diversity. Brahman, though one, is complex, as it includes the souls and the world. The complexity is sometimes manifest and at other times latent. That is to say, the world alternately emerges from Brahman, embodying the souls, and merges back into it. This is "the doctrine of self-evolving Brahman" (*Brahma-pariṇāmavāda*). This interpretation retains the monistic idealism of the Upaniṣads. It is monistic in the sense that, according to it, there is no reality outside Brahman. And it is also idealistic, since matter, according to it, has no meaning apart from Brahman.

Śaṅkara, on the other hand, concludes that the *niṣprapañca* view of Brahman is the true teaching of the Upaniṣads. Brahman is the reality. The world is an appearance thereof. And since the physical adjuncts of the soul are part of this appearance, the self is in reality non-different from Brahman. Brahman does not change into the world, but merely appears as it and, consequently, as delimited souls. This is *Brahma-vivartavāda*. But Śaṅkara does not reject the *saprapañca* view outright. According to him, it is a concession for adjusting the final teaching of the Upaniṣads to common, or empirical, ways of thinking, which assume diversity to be real. It represents only the "lower" truth (*aparā vidyā*), which serves as a stepping-stone to the comprehension of the "higher" truth (*parā vidyā*), for which the *niṣprapañca* view stands. This distinction between two levels of knowledge has its basis in the Upaniṣads.[13] The line of interpretation followed by Śaṅkara necessarily involves the notion of *māyā* as the principle which shows the *niṣprapañca* Brahman as the *saprapañca*. But it is not right to maintain that the doctrine of *māyā* is unknown to the Upaniṣads. It is already there, though not with all the features later associated with it in Śaṅkara's Advaita.[14]

In whichever of these two forms (*saprapañca* or *niṣprapañca*) the Upaniṣads present Brahman, they distinguish from Brahman the common things constituting the universe by pointing out that they are merely *nāma* and *rūpa*. *Rūpa* is the specific nature of the thing, and *nāma* is the name, or word, that serves as its sign. In the case of any object, the two terms together signify its particularity, or determinate character. The emergence of the world from Brahman is thus differentiation of names and forms. What is important to note is that, whether we regard these particular things as actual modes or as only appearances of Brahman, they are not real apart from it. Thus, in either case, Brahman is the sole reality according to the Upaniṣads.

On the above consideration, the Upaniṣadic distinction between *parā* and *aparā vidyās* holds good for both the *saprapañca* and the *niṣprapañca* views of Brahman. According to both the views, empirical knowledge is necessarily of the finite (*nāma-rūpa*). Whatever is thought of or spoken about is the particular. The mind and the organs of sense function only within the realm of names and forms. Empirical knowledge is described as lower knowledge (*aparā vidyā*) to distinguish it from knowledge relating to Brahman, which is called higher knowledge (*parā vidyā*).[15] Upto this point the cosmic and the acosmic views agree. It is only as regards the exact sense of the description *parā vidyā* that they differ.

To the cosmic view, Brahman is knowable. And knowledge of Brahman is *parā vidyā*. The knowledge of Brahman gives us insight into the principle of the being of particular things, even as the knowledge of the lump of clay, for example, may be said to do in regard to everything made of clay. In this sense it may be described as complete knowledge, whereas the lower knowledge is fragmentary. There is thus no conflict between *aparā* and *parā vidyās*.

According to the acosmic view, empirical knowledge (*aparā vidyā*) is only knowledge so-called. The world of names and forms is only appearance, and so, from the point of view of Brahman, which is the reality, empirical knowledge is no knowledge at all, but only a sort of *avidyā*. As regards *parā vidyā*, though it has reference to Brahman, it is strictly not *about* Brahman. Brahman transcends the very conditions of knowledge, and so cannot be known in the ordinary sense of the term "knowledge." This is brought out by the Upaniṣads in various ways. Silence is the only way to teach it says one Upaniṣad, which is no longer extant.[16] But to deny the possibility of knowing Brahman does not amount to agnosticism, for the Upaniṣads assert that, though we cannot *know* Brahman, we can *be* it. And being Brahman is what is by courtesy described as knowing Brahman. In the literal sense the term *parā vidyā* applies only to the means leading to such a consummation, viz., *śravaṇa, manana* and *nididhyāsana.*

The details of the things derived from Brahman, the order in which they are derived, and the order in which they are finally retracted, are also discussed in the Upaniṣads. Organic bodies form the abode of the transmigrating souls. Inorganic objects serve as the field in which the souls play their part. As in the earlier literature, the theory of *kalpa*, or the eternal recurrence of creation and dissolution, is not explicit in the Upaniṣads. But the *Śvetāśvatara Upaniṣad*, which is among the latest of the Upaniṣads, points to it in more than one place. The theory is closely connected with the doctrine of *karma.*

The Nature of the Soul

When we speak of psychology in Indian philosophy, it is to be understood in the original sense of the science, or doctrine, of the soul. Such a doctrine is based upon the supposition that the soul exists. For this reason, Indian psychology never branched off from philosophy. Every system of philosophy has its own psychology with its own special features in regard to the exact nature of the soul. To the Upaniṣads, the existence of the soul is a necessary presupposition of all experience. It is the basis of all proof and, therefore, itself needs none. The body would be meaningless without the soul whose end it serves. In the narrow span of a single life we cannot reap all the fruits of our *karma*. Nor can we account for all the good and evil that come to us in the present life by reference to this single life alone. Our belief in moral requital, therefore, demands that we admit a soul that transmigrates. Similarly, the belief in future births gives us hope of redress. There are various suggestions which we find in the Upaniṣads about the existence of the soul.

As regards the relation of the soul (*jīva*) to Brahman, it is conceived differently according to the two views of Brahman. According to the cosmic view, the soul is an actual, though provisional, transformation of Brahman. As such, it is both identical with and different from Brahman. According to the acosmic view, it is Brahman itself appearing as *jīva* and, therefore, not at all different from Brahman. In either case, its state of being a *jīva*, a finite self, consists in its forgetting its essential identity with Brahman. But this forgetting is not without its redeeming features. Occasionally, whenever desire is absent, the soul rises above its belief in finiteness and ceases to be conscious of its individuality. This is an indication that the soul is not in reality a limited entity. In the *Taittirīya Upaniṣad* this self-transcendence is explained as higher than the experience of the conscious (*manomaya*) and the self-conscious (*vijñānamaya*) levels of life. Its essential mark being peace, this higher level is described as *ānandamaya*. Being a passing phase, it is not identifiable with *mokṣa*, but it is a direct indication that the soul is essentially one with Brahman. The best illustration of this state is the contemplation of art, which may be described as midway between common experience and *mokṣa*.

The word *jīva* comes from the root *jīv*, which means to continue breathing. The name gives prominence to the biological, or unconscious, aspect of life, which goes on even during sleep. Two other terms used in the Upaniṣads, *bhoktā*, or experient, and *kartā*, or agent, emphasize the psychological, or conscious, side of life. The principle of unconscious activity is called *prāṇa*, and that of conscious activity, *manas*. Both of them operate throughout the empirical existence of the soul. Only the material body is replaced at every birth. In each life the body, *prāṇa* and *manas* form a sort of empirical home for the soul. The conscious side of the soul's activity is carried on by *manas* with the aid of the five organs of knowledge (*jñānendriya*) and the five organs of action (*karmendriya*). The *manas* is one, though it has many faculties like *vijñāna* and *ahaṁkāra*.

The conscious activity of the *jīva* happens in its waking state, which is evident. But the Upaniṣads take a wider view of life and study the self under three other states—dream, dreamless sleep, and a fourth (*turīya*) state. Of these, dreaming, like waking, falls under psychology proper, for in it the mind functions. But the other two are supra-mental, and are considered with a view to discover the real nature of the soul.

> It is noteworthy that at so early a period Indian thinkers should have thought of studying phenomena under varying conditions, which by eliminating or introducing one or more factors aid the discovery of their true character.[17]

We shall briefly characterize these three states. Dream (*svapna*) is intermediate between waking and deep sleep. In it the organs of sense are wholly quiescent, and the senses are then stated to unite with the *manas*. In waking the *manas* receives impressions from outside, which it builds up into ideas. In dream it fashions a world of forms unaided and by itself. For this purpose, it uses the material of waking hours, generally visual and auditory. Although the content of dream is thus revived impressions of waking, the experience of dream is quite unlike reminiscence. The content of dream is felt as real for the time being, even like in perceptual experience, and is apprehended as present, not as belonging to the past.

Beyond dream is the state of deep, or dreamless, sleep (*suṣupti*). In the waking state both *manas* and senses are active. In dream the senses are quiescent, but *manas* is active. In the dreamless sleep state even the *manas* is inactive. Consequently, normal empirical consciousness is absent. There is no longer any contrasting of one object with another or even of the subject with the object. But it is not a state of blank, or absolute unconsciousness. This is evident from the fact that there is a sense of personal identity connecting the states before and after sleep —the person who slept testifies to his sound sleep. Hence some sort of awareness is associated with sleep. The peculiarity of this awareness is that the consciousness of individuality is absent during sleep, though the individual himself continues to be. It is not an "objectless knowing subject,"[18] for along with the object the sense of being a subject also disappears. It is rather a state of non-reflective awareness. The embodied self during sleep is said to attain a temporary union with Brahman. The state is not identified with release. And so the statement is to be understood only negatively as signifying the absence of individuality. Individuality being absent, the state is above all desire and is, therefore, described as one of unalloyed bliss. The dream state is not disinterested, though the interests of waking are absent. That is why it has its own pains and pleasures. But the perfect peace of sleep we even recollect after waking.

The *turīya* is a state beyond the three states experienced by the ordinary man, viz., waking, dream and deep sleep. Hence it is given the improvised name, *turīya*, which means "the fourth." It is brought about voluntarily by the elimination of discursive thought. It resembles sleep in all respects but one. Like sleep, here also there is withdrawal of normal consciousness, absence of desires, and the consequent manifestation of bliss. But, while the experience of sleep is extremely dim, in the *turīya* the self fully reveals itself. It is a mystic state for which the only testimony comes from the person that is gifted with yogic power. But it is not wholly beyond our understanding. We can get a "conjectural insight" into the nature of the knower's experience from the negative evidence of *suṣupti* on the one hand and from the positive evidence of the "*ānandamaya* phase of experience"[19] on the other. (The latter is a glimpse of the bliss nature of the self in moments when the mind is fully aware, as, for example, in the experience of art.) The attainment of the *turīya* state is the culmination of spiritual training.

Practical Teaching

The basis of the practical teaching of the Upaniṣads is to be found in their conception of evil in life. In pre-Upaniṣadic literature evil is looked upon as having a physical source—it is either offence against the will of the gods or swerving from sacrificial rectitude. The Upaniṣads look upon evil as the result of a metaphysical error, which sees variety alone where there is also the unity of Brahman. It is overcome by the knowledge that unity underlies variety, whatever explanation may be given of that unity-in-diversity. According to the cosmic view, both variety and unity are real, but variety is rooted in unity, and to forget that unity leads to evil. According to the acosmic view, both variety and unity are equally unreal. Reality in itself is beyond both the conceptions. But even in this view, evil disappears the moment unity is realized. Thus there is no difference between the two teachings so far as the problem of ethics is concerned. Evil originates, according to both alike, in the consciousness that diversity alone is true.

Failing to grasp the ultimate reality, empirical thought cuts it up into parts and presents these parts as distinct from one another. It is this mistaken view of reality that gives rise to evil on the practical side, even as it gives rise to finiteness on the theoretical side. Further, this misleading presentation of reality is seen not only in the case of the objective world, but also in the case of the self. Each of us regards himself as distinct from others and thereby strives to guard or aggrandise himself. The *Īśa Upaniṣad* declares that when unity is realized and every being becomes our very self, there can be no delusion or sorrow.[20]

> In other words, all evil is traceable to *ahaṁkāra*, the affirmation of the finite self, and the consequent tendency to live not in harmony with the rest of the world, but in opposition or at best in indifference to it.[21]

The impulse behind this *ahaṁkāra* is not in itself bad. *Ahaṁkāra* signifies the instinct to live and is thus only a manifestation of the desire for self-realization. So it will remain unsatisfied until the knowledge of the ultimate truth avers the wider self in the place of the narrow one. That is the meaning of *ahaṁ brahma asmi*.

The Nature of Mokṣa

The goal of life as conceived in the Upaniṣads is to overcome our congenital ignorance of Brahman by attaining full enlightenment, or *jñāna*. This enlightened state is release, or *mokṣa*. "It is attaining one's true selfhood in Brahman."[22] By *jñāna* is not meant a mere intellectual apprehension of the ultimate truth, but an actual realization of it, an immediate experience of Brahman. On the negative side, *mokṣa* is described as free from all sorrow and pain. On the positive side, it is sometimes characterized as one of joy and at other times as transcending it. What is meant by transcending joy is that it is different from ordinary joy, which is always a complement to sorrow. It is the joy that results when both ordinary joy and sorrow become absent.

> It means that the joy of deliverance is not of the precarious kind with which we are familiar, but is transcendental, such as is meant by the saying of a much later age: *sukhaṁ duḥkha-sukhātyayaḥ*. Rather it is not joy at all but abiding peace, or repose that ever is the same.[23]

The ideal of *mokṣa* is presented in two forms in the Upaniṣads corresponding to the cosmic and acosmic views. In terms of the cosmic view, *mokṣa* is said to be a condition in which the self becomes Brahman, that is to say, attains essential oneness with the all-comprehensive Brahman. Thereby the notion that diversity is ultimate, which is the source of all strife, disappears and the self enjoys eternal bliss (*ānanda*). In terms of the acosmic view, *mokṣa* does not consist in *becoming* something. It is a discovery of what has always been a fact, like the discovery of a hidden treasure. In *mokṣa* the self remains by itself, partless and peaceful, awakening to its true nature as nothing but Brahman. The implication of this view is that the universe is phenomenal. In either case, *mokṣa* is a state of perfection transcending the distinctions which we commonly make between the self and the not-self, and between good and evil.

As regards the stage at which the goal is reached, there is a difference. According to the cosmic view, the attainment of Brahman takes place after the dissolution of the physical body. This ideal of reaching life's goal after death is a relic of pre-Upaniṣadic literature, though the nature of the goal was not clearly defined as *mokṣa* earlier. But what is special to the Upaniṣads is that it introduces the view that Brahman-realization is possible here and now, if one so wills. Such a conception is in accordance with the acosmic view of Brahman. The conception of *jīvanmukti*, as this is called, marks a great advance on the eschatological view of *mokṣa*. It signifies that the present life is adequate to perfect oneself.

> Perfection does not mean...a change of time, place and circumstance. It is rather rising above them all, or overcoming every form of narrowness through knowledge and self-discipline.[24]

A person who has realized his true nature as Brahman even while the body lives may continue to see variety, but he is not deluded by it. The reason is that the spiritual unity of all that exists is now a matter of personal experience to him. Consequent on this experience, his devotion to the good of others also undergoes a sea-change. Every desire vanishes of itself, and his natural unselfishness spontaneously expresses itself in loving service to all.

> *Jīvanmukti*, if we rightly understand the spirit of Indian philosophy, is indeed the highest and the most truly philosophical of all conceptions of deliverance, and may be said to represent a landmark in the history of philosophic thought in India. It is one of the points where Indian philosophy emerges clearly from Indian religion and what was once a mere speculation is thought within the range of practical life.[25]

The dissociation of the body from the *jīvanmukta* is regarded as final release (*videhamukti*).

Those who are fit for *jīvanmukti* are so few, for one has to succeed in killing every passion and acquiring complete enlightenment in this life. Of the rest, who are the majority, the Upaniṣads make two broad divisions—those who pursue the right path of life though they are not capable of enlightenment in this life, and those who yield to natural impulses lacking self-control. The former progresses from one state of existence to a higher until at last they find release. This is progressive realization (*krama mukti*). Some Vedāntins consider this to be the sole form of release taught in the Upaniṣads. The latter class of people, i.e., those who lack self-control, are born again and again according to their *karma*. Incidentally, it shows that the *karma* doctrine is a characteristic feature of the Upaniṣads.

The Means to Mokṣa

The most important means taught by the Upaniṣads for the attainment of *mokṣa* are *jñāna*, or knowledge of the ultimate reality, and *vairāgya*, or complete detachment. Of these, *jñāna* is the direct means to release. Evil is due to a misconception of the nature of reality. Hence its removal can only be through right knowledge. The cultivation of detachment is laid down as necessary only to render the acquisition of such knowledge possible. By *jñāna* what is meant is not a mere intellectual apprehension of the view that reality is one, but an actual realization of it in one's own experience.

> ...the aim of studying philosophy is not merely to gratify theoretical curiosity, however disinterested that curiosity may be; it is also to live the right kind of life, consciously adjusting one's conduct to one's intellectual convictions. It is in this sense of devotion to worthier living and not in the sense of dogma or superstition, that religion is blended with philosophy in India.[26]

Acquiring such enlightenment means a long course of training involving three steps: *śravaṇa*, *manana*, and *nididhyāsana*. *Śravaṇa* is the formal study of the Upaniṣads. The truth taught in the Upaniṣads has to be learnt with faith from a proper preceptor (*guru*). The insistence on the need for a teacher defines the place of precept and tradition in the training. "It also means that the influence of an ideal is never so great on us as when we are brought into personal contact with one who is a living embodiment of that ideal."[27]

Manana is continued reflection upon what has been learnt with a view to get an intellectual conviction regarding it. Merely to accept the teaching, though true, would be blind faith; it becomes philosophy only when its rational support is sought out. Facts relating to the ultimate reality are beyond the reach of reason and, therefore, cannot be absolutely demonstrated. But philosophy should at least point to the *likelihood* of their being true. This is the significance of *manana*. "It means that philosophy, though it may begin as faith, does not end there."[28]

Nididhyāsana, or *dhyāna*, is constant meditation on the truth about which one has become intellectually convinced until that conviction becomes a matter of direct experience. Meditation assists directly in the realization within oneself of the unity underlying the multiplicity of the universe. The need for this part of the training is as follows. Our belief in the reality of diversity is the result of perception and is, therefore, immediate. So nothing but an equally immediate apprehension of unity can effectively remove it. Seeing is believing.

> That is why the Upaniṣads speak of *darśana* or 'spiritual perception' in respect of the *ātman* or Brahman. A mere reasoned conviction is not enough, though it is necessary to give us the mark, as it were, at which to shoot.[29]

The direct knowledge resulting from the pursuit of *nididhyāsana* will lead to *mokṣa*—later according to the cosmic view, and at once according to the acosmic view.

Nididhyāsana is the highest form of meditation. It consists in contemplating Brahman as identical with the contemplative's own self. This is possible only after considerable practice in concentration of thought. Hence the Upaniṣads prescribe several meditative exercises of a preliminary character. They are usually called *upāsana*, and the Upaniṣads give them the same prominence which the Brāhmaṇas give to rites. The *upāsanas* are mainly of two forms. (i) The thought may be directed wholly outwards, and two selected objects, both external, may be mentally identified as in the meditation of the universe as a horse. (ii) Only one external object may be chosen, and it may be thought of as identical with the contemplative's own self. While the former affords exercise only in concentration, the latter, in addition, gives scope to the cultivation of sympathetic insight—the power to place oneself in the position of another. Hence the second serves as a more direct aid to Brahman-realization. Another important point about *upāsana* is that the object of contemplation may be either a real object or only a symbol. In either case, it is to be thought of as one with Brahman. Among the real objects mentioned, we often find conceptions which were once taken for the ultimate reality itself, for example *prāṇa*. Among the symbols for Brahman, the most famous is the mystic syllable *Om*. Whatever form the meditations take, they prepare the disciple for the final mode of contemplation as *ahaṁ brahma asmi*. This is *nididhyāsana* proper. When *nididhyāsana* transforms mediate knowledge of Brahman into an immediate certainty, the spiritual goal is attained.

The Upaniṣads state that only a few can achieve the goal of release. The majority, as already noted, are born again after death. *Saṁsāra* is the constant stream of births and deaths. Not only the non-virtuous, but even the virtuous who lack right knowledge, undergo it. All are born according to their *karma*. Each life with its pains and pleasures is the result of the past and becomes, through its own activities, the cause of future births. Thus all suffering is due to ourselves, and there is no cause for bitterness against God. Since the future lies in our own hands, the belief in *karma* is a perpetual incentive to right conduct. This principle is essentially different from the earlier notion of good as a gift of the gods. The doctrine of *karma*, which we find for the first time in the Upaniṣads, does not embody a demonstrable truth. Nevertheless, its value as a hypothesis for rationally explaining the observed inequities of life cannot be denied.

The origin of this doctrine is not clear. It was not present before the Upaniṣads, though the idea of repeated birth and death in another world occurs in connection with sacrifices. The idea of rebirth in this world is purely Upaniṣadic. In its initial form, as enunciated by Yājñavalkya, the doctrine does not imply any interval between the end of one life and the beginning of the next. But in a later modified form it teaches a twofold reward or punishment, first in the world beyond and then in a life here.

Vairâgya is the pre-condition for acquiring knowledge about Brahman. The main obstacle to Brahman-knowledge is *ahaṁkāra*, which stands for narrow selfish impulses. And *vairāgya* is that attitude towards the world which results from the successful eradication of narrow selfish impulses. Even the first stage in the path of knowledge, *śravaṇa*, where one betakes oneself to a proper *guru*, requires this moral qualification.

> The necessary pre-condition for starting on the course of Vedāntic life is detachment. In other words, no one that has not undergone a course of ethical training calculated to kill all egoistic impulses is qualified for a serious study of the Upaniṣads.[30]

This was the idea underlying the practice of keeping the Upaniṣadic teaching a secret and imparting it only to true and tested pupils. It was feared that an indiscriminate broadcasting of the truth that all is one might lead to its distortion and bring it into discredit.

The accomplishment of *vairāgya* requires a long course of training through three *āśramas,* or disciplinary stages—those of the religious student (*brahmacarya*), of the householder (*gārhastya*), and of the anchorite (*vānaprastha*). *Āśrama* means "toil." So, they are stages of strife where selfishness is slowly but steadily rooted out. The training leads to *saṁnyāsa*, but in the Upaniṣads this word does not bear its later significance of a formal stage of spiritual ascent. It there means only "the transcending of the triple mode of *āśrama* life, and is regarded as a consequence of Brahman-knowledge rather than a means of attaining it."[31] The conception of *saṁnyāsa* as a means to knowledge appears later.

It should not be thought that the cultivation of detachment means the neglect of social duties. In fact, detachment cannot be cultivated in the abstract. *Saṁnyāsa*, which symbolises it, is only the fourth *āśrama*, and fitness for it is to be secured through the three earlier stages, particularly that of the householder with its multifarious social duties. The *āśramas* are grades in the moral discipline according to the capacity and temperament of the persons in question. The Upaniṣads clearly teach "that man ought not to break away from society until he has discharged his duty towards it and gained its goodwill, so to speak."[32] *Vairāgya*, being the final outcome of such training, cannot be characterized as unsocial, or purely negative. A doubt may occur at this stage. It may be conceded that the steps leading to *saṁnyāsa* involve social activity. But is not *saṁnyāsa* in itself negative? The answer of the Upaniṣads is "no". The one who has achieved self-denial does not necessarily withdraw from society. He continues to discharge his obligations to his fellow-beings, but (unlike as in previous stages) he does not think of reaping any personal benefit from such service. Hence *saṁnyāsa* signifies self-renunciation and not world-renunciation.

The Upaniṣads primarily address their practical teaching to the *saṁnyāsin,* the one who has successfully undergone the training of the previous stages and has acquired *vairāgya*. They do not go into the details of the three earlier stages. This does not mean that the value of the preliminary ethical training is ignored. It is fully recognized, but taken for granted. But where they refer to it, the Upaniṣads definitely bring out its importance. For example, in the *Kaṭha Upaniṣad* Yama does not teach Naciketas the truth about the self without testing his spirit of renunciation. In the *Bṛhadāraṇyaka Upaniṣad* Prajāpati's in-struction to gods, men, and demons indicate the necessity for grades in moral discipline. The failure to recognize this fact has led critics to imagine that common morality with its social implications is ignored in the Upaniṣads.

The Place of Theism in the Upaniṣads

Theism in the ordinary sense is belief in a personal God who is objective, i.e., apart from the soul, worship of which is necessary for salvation. We cannot properly look for such a view in the Upaniṣads, as their main concern is with the philosophic Absolute. However, a theistic rendering of the Absolute is sometimes found, the Absolute being personified and spoken of as God. It is the cosmic view of Brahman that lends itself easily to such transformation. But the true self of man (*ātman*) being identical with Brahman, the idea of God so derived can only be an inner principle and not an object of adoration distinct from the self that adores. "The Upaniṣads explicitly repudiate an objective conception of God."[33] Thus the idea of God in the Upaniṣads differs fundamentally from the old Vedic idea of *deva* and even from the idea of Prajāpati occurring in the Brāhmaṇas, both of which are presented as external to us. It can be described as theistic only by courtesy. The God of the Upaniṣads is described as the "inner ruler immortal" (*antaryāmyamṛtaḥ*) and as the thread (*sūtra*) that runs through all things and holds them together. As the central truth of both animate and inanimate existence, he is not merely a transcendent, but also an immanent principle. He creates the universe out of himself like a spider and retracts it again into himself. For this reason, in later Vedānta he is described as at once the efficient and the material cause of the universe (*abhinna-nimittopādāna-kāraṇa*).

4. EARLY POST-VEDIC PERIOD

The Nature of the Period

There is a long interval between the end of the Vedic period and the emergence of the systems of philosophy. It is a period of great intellectual stir involving many streams of thought, some a continuation of old trends and some which arise newly. It is a period when diversity of thought becomes pronounced not only within the Vedic tradition, but also in opposition to it. Heterodox thought emerges clearly in Early Buddhism and Jainism. Another variety of heterodox thought is naturalism for which there are only stray references in the works of other currents, especially the *Mahābhārata*.

A common feature of all these various strands of thought is that they are intended, broadly speaking, to all without distinction. Orthodox thought does this through the later Upaniṣads, the Epics, especially the *Mahābhārata*, and the Kalpasūtras, the last being more religious than philosophical in character. The *Mahābhārata* is designed chiefly for those who have no direct access to the sacred scriptures, viz., women, Śūdras and degenerate Brahmins. But all these are in Sanskrit. Buddhist and Jaina thought seek to reach out to the common people through a popular medium, mostly of Prākṛta languages.

The thought of this period is predominantly realistic, i.e., world-affirming. Buddhism and Jainism are avowedly so. Hinduism retains its old idealistic background, but it also manifests a certain concern to emphasize the reality of the external world. As such, it prefers to dwell on the idea of the cosmic Absolute rather than on that of the acosmic. The result is that a well-defined theism emerges.

Sources for the Period

For Jainism and Buddhism among the heterodox schools, besides Sanskrit works, there is a vast literature in one or other of the Prākṛta languages. As regards orthodox thought, our sources of information are some of the later Upaniṣads, the Kalpasūtras and the epics, especially the

Mahābhārata. The later, or minor, Upaniṣads develop on theistic and realistic lines. Unlike the classical Upaniṣads, their teaching is not uniform. They fall into groups, each dealing predominantly with a special topic. For example, there are Upaniṣads treating of contemplation (*yoga*) or of renunciation (*saṁnyāsa*). There are others glorifying Śiva or Viṣṇu conceived as God supreme. Not all of them are definite sources, as there is doubt as regards the date of many of them. The Kalpasūtras consist of concise aphorisms. They fall into three divisions, the Śrauta, Gṛhya and Dharma Sūtras. The Śrautasūtras systematize the sacrificial lore of the Brāhmaṇas. The Gṛhyasūtras portray the ideal of life from the point of view of the family and describe the ceremonies connected with it. The Dharmasūtras deal with customary law and morals and thus set forth the norm of life from the standpoint of society. But all of them, like the Mantras and the Brāhmaṇas, are concerned chiefly with priestly life. So their interest for philosophy is only indirect. A more valuable source of information on this period is represented by "the older sections" of the epics, especially of the *Mahābhārata*, which is regarded as a great storehouse of post-Vedic mythology and teaching. Within its vast and heterogeneous content, the biggest philosophical section is the Mokṣadharma of the Śāntiparva. The *Bhagavad-gītā*, although part of the epic, deserves separate treatment by virtue of its importance. Although the early teachings of Buddhism and Jainism belong to this period, it would be convenient for us to include them under a chapter on Metaphysics. In the present chapter we shall confine ourselves to the other trends of thought during the early post-Vedic period. All the four currents of thought found in the earlier periods are found herewith important modifications, viz., ritualism, absolutism, theism, and heretical thought.

Ritualism

Of the three sources which we are considering, it is the Kalpasūtras that are chiefly concerned with ritual. In fact, the aim of the Kalpasūtras is to elaborate and systematize the ritualistic teaching of the Veda. For this purpose, they consolidate the Veda by defining the limits of the Veda and laying down strict rules for its study and preservation. They lay particular stress on the *āśrama* of the religious student, by whom the Veda is to be studied, and of the householder, to whom most of the Vedic behests are addressed. The Kalpasūtras regard tradition as an inviolable authority. Respect for tradition is implicit in the Brāhmaṇas, but it is formally recognized here. The tradition itself is twofold: it is either that of the Veda or of *samaya*, which means the habitual observances of the cultured Āryans (*śiṣṭa*). But the Kalpasūtras point out that such observances are themselves based upon the authority of the Veda in one form or another.

Of the three kinds of Kalpasūtras, the Śrauta and Gṛhya Sūtras avowedly deal with ritual. The Śrauta describe the elaborate rites of the Brāhmaṇas. The Gṛhya deal with the simpler domestic rites of the family, such as marriage. The Dharmasūtras speak from the standpoint of society, but they also have a significance for ritual. They regulate the conduct of the individual by requiring him to perform certain duties. They thus fit him for ritualistic life, according to a principle recognized for long, viz. that rituals will become fruitful only in the case of those who are morally pure. They are called Dharmasūtras, because they lay down the standard of *dharma*. In this connection it is worthwhile to consider the meaning of *dharma*.

Literally, the term *dharma* means "what holds together" (*dhāraṇāt dharmam ityāhuḥ*).[34] *Dharma* is thus the basis of all order, whether social or moral. The term is thus allied, in its ethical aspect, to the earlier concept of *ṛta*. In fact, the term virtually replaces the other during this period. It is sometimes used as a purely moral concept, meaning virtuous conduct. But its more usual meaning now is religious merit, which in some unseen way (*adṛṣṭa*), is supposed to secure good for the doer in this life or after it. Even in this predominantly ritualistic meaning, it has an ethical significance, viz., the attainment of moral purity, without which rituals would not fructify. That the idea of moral purity, though only as a means to success in ritualistic life, emerges at all in this period is important for us.

The ethical significance of the Dharmasūtras will be evident from their attitude to the obligatory duties prescribed by them. These are of two classes: *sādhāraṇa-dharma* and *varṇāśrama-dharma*. (There are two other kinds of *karma*, which we need not consider here, viz. *kāmya*, or optional deeds, and *pratiṣiddha*, or prohibited actions.) The general significance of the obligatory duties is that they conduce to the cultivation of personal virtues in the doer as well as to the promotion of social welfare.

Sādhāraṇa-dharma comprises duties that are obligatory on all irrespective of their special position, like self-control, kindness and truth-speaking. Those duties among them that have a bearing on others cover not only human beings, but also sub-human beings, which are regarded as having rights, though they have no duties. *Varṇāśrama-dharma* comprises duties that are special to each class in society and each stage in the life of an individual. Āryan society was divided into four classes (*varṇa*), and the life of an individual belonging to the higher three among them was divided into four stages (*āśrama*). Each class and each stage has its own specific duties to perform. So it is wrong to think that the *saṁnyāsin* has no obligation to discharge. One who enters into this order gives up only the ritualistic life of the householder. He does not become indifferent to the welfare of others. Like *sādhāraṇa-dharma*, *varṇāśrama-dharma* also cultivates private virtues on the one hand and contributes to common good on the other.

The usual view of the Dharmasūtras is that the discipline of the four stages is to be gone through in order. This is the same as in the Upaniṣads. Thus the assumption of *saṁnyāsa*, which is the last stage, presupposes the training of the other stages of life, particularly that of the householder. There are in the Dharmasūtras references to a view which denounces *saṁnyāsa*. This accords with the ritualistic outlook of the early portions of the Veda, which hold out heavenly happiness as the goal of life. But on the whole, the Dharmasūtras synthesize ritualism with the Upaniṣadic view of liberation. The ultimate goal to be reached is described as the "world of Brahma" (Brahma-*loka*)[35]—a goal which resembles the ideal of progressive realization of liberation (*krama mukti*) set forth in the Upaniṣads.

We have so far described the view of the Kalpasūtras on ritualism. In the later Upaniṣads there is, as in the Kalpasūtras, a tendency to revert to sacrificial worship as taught in the Brāhmaṇas. The *Maitrī Upaniṣad* regards adherence to the Veda as indispensable to a knowledge of the self. But at the same time, unlike in the Kalpasūtras, these Upaniṣads contemplate a stage when obligation to perform Vedic rituals is transcended. The *Maitrī Upaniṣad* denies the need for ritual in the case of one that has passed the stage of preliminary discipline. Here we find a new conception of ritual which becomes quite prominent later. Ritual is not a means for seeking material favours from the gods, but a "cure for sin" (*durita-kṣaya*)—a means of purifying the heart and thereby making oneself qualified for the pursuit of the knowledge that brings liberation. As for the attitude of the *Mahābhārata* to ritual, it is indefinite. Some passages glorify sacrifice, but some others are unfavourable or even antagonistic to ritualism.

Absolutism

As in the case of the earlier Upaniṣads, the prevailing teaching of the later Upaniṣads is monism, but, as in the earlier ones, there is sometimes ambiguity as to its particular form. But the general tendency is to lay stress on the cosmic standpoint, looking upon the physical world as an actual emanation from Brahman, and to dwell upon the distinction between soul and Brahman as well as between one soul and another. The distinction of soul from Brahman is not intrinsic; it is due to the association of the *jīva* with the physical body. It is overcome and oneness (*sāyujya*) with Brahman is attained when the soul realizes the truth. Yet the recognition of its provisional separateness from Brahman implies the admission that the physical world is real.

Under the influence of the Upaniṣads, monism appears as a prominent feature of the *Mahābhārata*. As regards the particular form of monism, both the cosmic and the acosmic forms often appear even in the same section. But considering the popular character of the text, the cosmic conception is set forth with added detail. The creation of the universe is by transformation in Brahman. But Brahman himself is uncreated. There is no place for *māyā* in the scheme of creation. The Creator is said to have his own "day" and "night", each of infinite duration. Creation takes place each day of the Creator at dawn, and at the close of the day what is created is withdrawn into Brahman. This process is cyclical, involving the idea of *kalpa*. The order of dissolution is the reverse of the order of creation.

Monotheism

The theism found in Vedic literature is of an impersonal kind. It acquires a personal form during the present period. The first deity to be raised to the status of the supreme God is Brahmā. The concept is derived from that of Prajāpati of the earlier literature. His supremacy gradually wanes, and his place is, in course of time, taken by two other deities, viz., Śiva and Viṣṇu. Their conception is personal, and this personal character becomes more and more pronounced as they gain in importance. Their complete personification must have been influenced by the belief of common people. The personality of both Śiva and Viṣṇu are so clearly outlined that it is impossible to identify either with the other. This distinctness explains, at least partly, the sectarian character of theism in the present period.

Śaivism

Śiva is conceived as the supreme God. The concept of Śiva can be traced to the concept of Rudra in the early hymns of the Veda. Rudra is the personification of the destructive powers of nature. In the later portions of the Veda Śiva becomes his distinctive name, and he is also called Mahādeva. In course of time, Śiva becomes benignant also, an object of love and fear. In the *Śvetāśvatara Upaniṣad* he comes to be blended with the Absolute. He is knowable through devotion (*bhakti*), and his grace (*prasāda*) is necessary for salvation. The Upaniṣad thus introduces a characteristic feature of all personal theism, viz. that the grace of God is a necessary counterpart of man's devotion to him. These features become more prominent in the sections of the *Mahābhārata* glorifying Śiva. Images and emblems of Śiva are found among the relics of Mohenjo-Daro, but their exact relation to the Vedic faith in Rudra-Śiva is not known. The Śiva creed is probably of a mixed origin from Āryan and pre-Āryan conceptions. One indication of this is that Śiva worship is largely based upon Āgamas (literally "tradition"), "which are not, according to some thinkers like Śaṅkara, entirely in agreement with the teaching of revelation or the Vedas."[36]

Vaiṣṇavism

This also has a Vedic origin. In the Mantras Viṣṇu is represented as one of the solar deities and is thus associated with light and life. By the time of the Brāhmaṇas, this worship of the sun gradually transformed itself into the worship of Viṣṇu, "the pervading,"[37] regarded as the supreme God. The *Aitareya Upaniṣad* speaks of reaching the abode of Viṣṇu as the goal of life. Viṣṇu is also conceived as Nārāyaṇa, "the abode or resting place of men."[38] The conception of Nārāyaṇa, which originates in the *Ṛgveda*, is developed in the Brāhmaṇas. In the *Mahānārāyaṇa Upaniṣad* his cosmic character is described. In the *Mahābhārata* he is called "the son of *dharma*,"[39] thereby highlighting his ethical character. A third element that goes to form Vaiṣṇavism is the concept of Śrī Kṛṣṇa, or Vāsudeva, which has a non-Vedic origin, viz., the Bhāgavata cult. In the *Mahābhārata* Viṣṇu-Nārāyaṇa comes to be blended with this concept. This combination contributed to make the God of Vaiṣṇavism even more personal than that of Śaivism, which sometimes shows an impersonal phase. The form of worshipping the supreme which Vaiṣṇavism commends is mostly based on the Āgamas. Vaiṣṇavism, like Śaivism, lays great emphasis on loving devotion (*bhakti*) as a means of redemption. It also discards the animal sacrifice of Vedic religion.

A distinguishing feature of Vaiṣṇavism is that Viṣṇu assumes different incarnations called *avatāra*. The word *avatāra* signifies that "God brings himself down in order to present to us a higher ideal of life, and thereby to exalt us to him."[40] It is a general Hindu belief that progress in the world is not continuous. At times things grow worse and worse when God descends to inaugurate a reign of justice and happiness.

> This theory of *avatāras* helps what has all along been a noteworthy feature of Hinduism, viz., its absorption of other creeds into itself by explaining the gods worshipped in them as but manifestations of the one supreme Being.[41]

The Lord says in the *Bhagavad-gītā* that those who worship other gods also worship him, though but imperfectly.[42] Such absorption "does not extirpate those creeds, but re-interprets them and utilizes whatever elements of truth they may contain."[43] In fact, it was through such re-interpretation that Śrī Kṛṣṇa himself was assimilated into Vaiṣṇavism. Later on a place was found for Buddha among the *avatāras* of Viṣṇu.

Monotheism, whether Śaivism or Vaiṣṇavism, makes a distinction between God, the soul, and the world. The soul is conceived as eternal, but as entirely dependent on God. As such, it is the duty of man to make himself a willing instrument of God's purpose. Though the conception of the goal is presented in diverse forms in early Indian theism, generally speaking, it is "reaching the presence of God or becoming godlike."[44] *Prasāda*, or grace, is necessary for redemption. *Bhakti* is the chief means to secure it besides *caryā*, or good conduct.

Heretical Views

By this term is meant views antagonistic to the Vedas, particularly to their sacrificial teaching and the customs and institutions directly connected with it. Opposition to Vedic religion is very old, but it gets strengthened during this period. Heretical views appear in diverse forms. But there is no detailed exposition of heretical doctrine in early Sanskrit literature. It appears now and then in the *Mahābhārata*, but this account is the only considerable one from which we can draw our information. The *Śvetāśvatara Upaniṣad* also mentions diverse heretical views. The part played by heretical views in the development of Indian philosophy is not insignificant.

> It has greatly helped the progress of Indian thought as a whole, opposition instilling strength into the exponents of both sets of doctrines.[45]

Three main heretical tendencies, mentioned in the *Mahābhārata*, are of philosophical importance. One of them called Yadṛcchāvāda, or Animittavāda, can be described as "accidentalism." It maintains that the world is a chaos and ascribes whatever order is seen in it to mere chance instead of to any definite cause. In contrast to this, there is another called Svabhāvavāda or "naturalism." It recognizes that "things are as their nature makes them." While the former denies causation altogether, the latter acknowledges its universality, but only traces all changes to the thing itself to which the change belongs. Every object is unique, and its entire history is predetermined by that uniqueness. So it is not a lawless world in which we live; only the law governing it is within the world and not external to it. It is self-determined and not either undetermined or externally determined. There is a necessity governing all phenomena, but the necessity is inherent in the very nature of a thing. It is by our ignorance of this fact that we either imagine that everything is left to chance or that we can alter them as we like. Both Yadṛcchāvāda and Svabhāvavāda agree on one point, viz. that nature does not reveal the existence of any supernatural, or divine, agency working behind it. It is in Yadṛcchāvāda that we have to look for the source of the later "sensualist doctrine of the Cārvāka,"[46] which also attributes the events of life to mere accident. But it is Svabhāvavāda that is of real philosophical importance.

Svabhāvavāda is positivistic in character. It was because of its "mundane metaphysics" probably that the doctrine was described in later literature as *lokāyata*, which means that it was "restricted to the experienced world."[47] Svabhāvavāda denies a transmigrating soul, "although it might have admitted a self lasting as long as life does."[48] In fact, the very aim of this doctrine is to repudiate such transcendental entities. Since it rejects a permanent soul, Svabhāvavāda does not believe in the law of *karma* either. In so far as we rely on the *Mahābhārata*, we have no clear indication of its answer to the problem relating to the source of the material world.

The third tendency mentioned in the *Mahābhārata* is not entirely opposed to the Veda. It seems to be a modification of the Absolutism of the Upaniṣads under the influence of Svabhāvavāda. According to the cosmic view, Brahman undergoes modification to bring forth the world of diversity (*Brahma-pariṇāmavāda*). Especially this aspect of the doctrine seems to be modified here. The notion of the Absolute is retained. *Puruṣa* and *prakṛti* are regarded as distinct from, but subordinate to, the Absolute. Instead of the Absolute, *prakṛti* is taken to be the source from which the whole physical universe emerges. *Puruṣa* and *prakṛti* are sharply distinguished. *Puruṣa* is regarded as many and permanent. It is the subject of experience. And the products of *prakṛti* are its object. Man is usually ignorant of the distinction between *puruṣa* and *prakṛti*. And knowledge of the distinction qualifies him for release. The important point here is that the Absolute comes to be conceived as passive, creative activity being transferred entirely to *prakṛti*. The recognition of permanent souls distinguishes this doctrine from Svabhāvavāda. But in endowing matter with the exclusive power to unfold the universe out of itself, it resembles Svabhāvavāda. It differs from Absolutism by admitting matter as virtually a second entity by the side of spirit. It is thus dualistic. These characteristics anticipate the Sāṅkhya doctrine. It may, therefore, be described as "proto-Sāṅkhya or Sāṅkhya in the making."[49] Its importance in the history of Indian thought is great. It inaugurates a new stream of tradition in ancient India, which can be described neither as quite orthodox nor as quite heterodox, a middling doctrine, which, however, leans more towards orthodoxy than towards heterodoxy. Accordingly, orthodox belief itself henceforward may be said to run in two channels—one a continuation of the old orthodoxy and the other a somewhat heterodox modification of it. The distinction between them often leads to important controversies (such as the question whether the Veda is *pauruṣeya* or not).

Practical Teaching

We find that three modes of discipline are commended during this period for reaching the goal of life, viz., *karma, yoga,* and *bhakti.* They are respectively associated in a predominant way with ritualism, absolutism, and theism.

Karma

As used in this period, the term stands for the sacrificial rites and the acts allied to them as taught in the Brāhmaṇas as well as for certain duties and practices which had become sanctified by tradition. But this does not mean that ordinary virtues, whether social or self-regarding, were ignored, for ethical purity was regarded as the necessary condition for entering upon the path of *karma. Karma* in the above sense is of three kinds. (i) Some are "permitted, or optional" (*kāmya*), and they aim at specific results such as the attainment of heaven. (ii) Some are "prohibited" (*pratiṣiddha*), and indulgence in them will lead to sin and suffering. (iii) Some, again, are "obligatory, or unconditional" (*nitya*), and they comprehend the duties appropriate to the four classes, or *varṇas,* and the four stages in life, or *āśramas.* A few principles underlying this view of discipline may be mentioned.

(i) The whole code of conduct presupposes that there is a self which survives death and that the present life is a preparation for the coming one. Whatever may be the metaphysical basis of such a view, the value of this belief for discipline is clear. It discountenances present indulgence in all its forms and cultivates self-restraint. The discipline does not abolish desire altogether, for it promises the agent's welfare in a future life as its reward. What it denounces is pursuing the goods of this world for their own sake.

(ii) The discipline prescribed is not arbitrary, but oriented to what is regarded as the true ideal of life. This is well indicated by the formulation during this period in a definite way of what are called the *puruṣārthas,* or human values. They are said to be three (*trivarga*)—*dharma, artha,* and *kāma*. *Mokṣa* is not excluded from the Kalpasūtras, but it does not find a prominent place there. The pursuit of *artha* and *kāma*, or wealth and pleasure, are accepted as legitimate. But *dharma*, or religious merit, is to be preferred in all circumstances. *Dharma* brings in its train worldly benefits, but even if it does not, it matters little. Thus *dharma* assumes great importance here. The word literally means "what supports or upholds."[50] It represents the governing principle of the universe and is thus comparable to the earlier word *ṛta*. But in the present period it stands for all the established ways of living—secular, moral and religious. This comprehensive meaning introduces some vagueness in its use. But what is clear in this period is that *dharma* is believed to bear fruit in a future life and implies moral purity as a necessary condition for earning it. The authority for deciding what is *dharma* or *adharma* is the Veda and the tradition traceable to it. Thus *dharma* is extra-empirical. This is the significance of the term *vidhi*, which stands for a behest from above.

Yoga

The term literally means "harnessing."[51] Yoga is essentially a process of self-conquest. It was often resorted to in ancient India for the acquisition of supernatural, or occult, powers. But such an application of the technique was denounced as "malevolent" (*abhicāra-para*). Its true purpose is to serve as a means to securing release. Such a use is described as "benevolent" (*dharma-para*). The practice of *yoga* used for release is the same as *upāsana* taught in the Upaniṣads. It is predominantly associated with Absolutism, where it is prescribed for converting mediate knowledge of reality into an immediate experience. It should, therefore, follow the intellectual conviction resulting from *śravaṇa*. It is, thus, a joint aid with *jñāna*, or right knowledge. In the Upaniṣads it is prescribed under the name *nididhyāsana* for securing unity with the Absolute. It undergoes systematization during this period. It must be observed that *yoga* as practised in this sense, i.e. for release, presupposes moral purity. Thus, like *karma,* or the practice of rituals, it should be based on common morality.

Bhakti

This is "loving devotion" and is appropriate to theism, which believes in a single personal God. Speaking generally, *bhakti* is a social attitude, while *yoga* is an individual one. *Bhaktas* find spiritual exaltation in the company of other *bhaktas* and, therefore, congregate for worship. *Yogins*, on the other hand, are apt to seek God or the Absolute in the silence of solitude. *Bhakti*, again, is predominantly emotional, while *yoga* is predominantly intellectual. As regards the origin of the Bhakti cult in India, it has been suggested by some that it came from Christian sources. But there is no warrant for this assumption. There is sufficient evidence both in the Mantras and in the Upaniṣads to show that the attitude of loving devotion towards the Godhead was familiar to the Vedic Indian.

> Thus the ideas of devotion to God and of his grace (*prasāda*), the reward for it, were well known to the Indians long before the Christian era; and there is no need to seek for their source outside India.[52]

Of the three Gods who are regarded as supreme during this transitional period, Brahmā, Viṣṇu and Śiva, Viṣṇu-Kṛṣṇa is most prominently connected with the idea of *bhakti*, though it is found in connection with the others also.

Discipline in the Heretical Schools

Of the three modes of discipline described above, only *yoga* can be associated with the heretical views. But here it can be only a way of withdrawal from the world, and not a means of attaining union with the ultimate. The ideal man for heterodox thought is the "world-renouncing *yogin*," not "the half-divine *ṛṣi*" of the orthodox. As in the case of other doctrines, the need for moral purity as a condition for *yoga* is recognized. But in this process of cleansing, only common morality is called for. The cleansing effect of Vedic *karma* is not recognized. Moreover, the moral training prescribed is noted for its stoic severity. It is a discipline of denial and is intended to free man from all personal desires, which are regarded as the source of all evil in life.

The Concept of Saṁnyāsa

Over and above these modes of discipline, *saṁnyāsa*, or formal renunciation of the world, is recognized in this period, particularly in the heretical schools. But among the orthodox, it is not universally so. Some of them refuse to include *saṁnyāsa* and *vānaprastha* in the normal scheme of life. Next to studentship, the only legitimate *āśrama*, according to them, is that of the householder. The other two are explained as intended only for those who, for some reason or other, are disqualified for performing the *karmas* of a householder. This is probably the oldest view of *saṁnyāsa* put forward by those who are wedded to ritualism. Other orthodox schools of this period accept *saṁnyāsa* as a normal stage of life, but it is to be assumed only last. It is only in later times that this restriction comes to be relaxed and it comes to be admitted that whoever has acquired detachment could assume *saṁnyāsa*, no matter when. From the standpoint of *saṁnyāsa*, the modes of discipline could be said to fall into two types, one positive and the other negative. The first is the path of *pravṛtti*, or active life, insisting on Vedic ritual and the duties taught in the Kalpasūtras. The second is the path of *nivṛtti*, or quietism, and demands an escape from social and sacrificial life for complete devotion to a life of contemplation.

The Goal of Life

What is the aim of the whole discipline? To those who subscribe only to the first three values (*trivarga*) the goal of life is the attainment of heaven by means of earning religious merit (*dharma*) in this life. There are others who recognize *mokṣa* as the highest ideal to be realized. But *mokṣa* itself is conceived in more than one way. It is union with the Absolute according to Absolutism. It is reaching the presence of God according to theism. To some of the heretical schools *mokṣa* is a negative state, where one escapes from the trammels of *saṁsāra*. In fact, the name *nirvāṇa* (literally "blowing out")[53] often given to it brings out its negative character. But in whatever way *mokṣa* is conceived, the idea that it can be attained in this very life (*jīvanmukti*) continues and receives greater emphasis in this period. Though many orthodox schools believe in it, the ideal of *jīvanmukti* specially fits in with the world-view of heretical schools. For example, the conception of liberation after death is incompatible with Svabhāvavāda, which does not believe in a future life.

5. THE BHAGAVAD-GĪTĀ

The Nature and Importance of the Gītā

The importance of the *Bhagavad-gītā* in the religious and philosophical literature of India is next only to that of the Upaniṣads. It is also a highly popular work. "It has always commanded great admiration and "its popularity now, if anything, is on the increase."[54] It is part of a great popular epic and is written in a simple and charming style. But it owes its attractiveness chiefly to the specific message it gives. And in conveying this message, it breathes throughout a spirit of toleration, which is an outstanding characteristic of Hindu thought. It teaches that "it is not so much the nature of the object worshipped as the spirit in which the worshipper turns to it that counts."[55] Another reason for its popularity is that it does not discuss the subtle and recondite details of ethics or metaphysics. It deals only with the broad principles underlying them and relates these principles to the basic aspirations of man. Further, it undertakes this task not in an abstract manner, but in the context of a specific situation involving a moral dilemma and points out how it is overcome. "The concrete mode of treatment, with the suggestiveness natural to it, very much widens the scope of the teaching and makes its appeal almost universal."[56]

The popularity of the *Gītā* should not lull us into thinking that the work is easy of understanding. It is one of the hardest works to interpret and has invited numerous commentaries, each differing from the rest in some essential point or other. This diversity of interpretation is partly due to the assumption that the *Gītā* not only concerns itself with the problem of conduct, but is also a treatise on metaphysics. But it must be realized that metaphysical questions form only the background to its ethical teaching. The focus of the work is distinctly practical. Another cause of difference among the interpreters of the work is their expectation that it provides a complete theory of morals. It must be noted that the occasion for the *Gītā* is a particular one, and in enunciating a course of conduct suited to it, the work draws attention to *some* of the principles of right living while omitting others, though they may be important in their own way.

As regards the sources of the *Bhagavad-gītā*, the poem, which appears as an inset of the *Mahābhārata*, shares the heterogeneous character of that work. While in some places it is based on the Upaniṣads, in others it presupposes the theistic view of the Bhāgavata religion. Hence in the matter of details the work offers some perplexity. But there is no doubt as regards the central point of its practical teaching. The present treatment is to explain that teaching and identify the principles that underlie it.

The Teaching of the Gītā in Conspectus

The teaching of the *Bhagavad-gītā* comes in response to Arjuna's mood of despair on the battlefield. To understand the exact bearing of the teaching, we have to note two aspects of his mood. First, he forgets his station in life as a warrior, whose duty is to fight when occasion demands it. He wants to renounce the world when he is not yet spiritually fit for it. Secondly, he wrongly feels that the fight, which he wants to avoid, is for the good of himself and his clan. In other words, his standpoint is really one of selfishness. In fact, it is under this wrong notion that he desires to renounce the world. It is in answer to these misconceptions that the *Gītā* stresses the importance of social duties. But in emphasizing it, the *Gītā* makes an innovation, which marks its whole significance. Social duties were originally (i.e. in the Dharmasūtras) conceived as advancing the common good, i.e. of society and of the individual agent. But the *Gītā* says that such duties should be done with no thought *whatsoever* of the good that may follow, whether to society or to the agent himself. That is to say, the notion of duty becomes entirely separated from the idea of its consequences, whatever they may be. This innovation has a psychological justification. Social and individual good cannot really be correlated, except when the same line of conduct serves to promote the interests of both. But the two interests often collide, when it becomes impossible to reconcile their rival claims. It is to avoid this conflict that the *Gītā* commends that duty should be performed in a totally disinterested way (*niṣkāma-karma*). It may be said that the conflict could be avoided if the agent abandoned all selfish interests and pursued only the good of the society of which he is a member. "But such conscious assumption by anyone of the role of a social benefactor is likely to result in a sense of self-importance which is ruinous to all spiritual growth."[57] Hence the *Gītā* teaches that both aims are to be discarded.

A doubt may arise at this stage. If the idea of duty is thus separated from that of its consequences, there will be no means of determining the content of duty in any particular context in life. The *Gītā* may tell us *how* to act, but not what deeds we should do. But really there is no such lack of guidance in the teaching. The *Gītā* points out that the duties which a person has to undertake are determined by the place he occupies in society. It says that one's own duty (*sva-dharma*), be it ever so low, is superior to another's.[58] Here is another important principle enunciated in the *Gītā*. It is a principle whose knowledge has filtered down to the lowest ranks of our society, as illustrated by the words of the fisherman in Kālidāsa's *Śākuntalam*.

> The significance of this principle is to elevate the moral quality of actions above their content. What really matters is the motive inspiring their doing—how actions are done and not what they are.[59]

The actions of an ordinary man bear no comparison with the historically important work of Arjuna. Yet, in point of their moral worth, which, according to the *Gītā*, consists in detachment from results, the two do not differ in the least. Such a detached performance of one's duties, whatever they may be, is called *karma-yoga.*

Another clarification is also necessary. The *niṣkāma-karma* taught by the *Gītā* does not mean the total exclusion of consequences from the motive of the action. "Disinterested activity, in the literal sense of the expression, is a psychological impossibility."[60] So what is meant is only a reorientation of interest. There are two sets of consequences for any good action—those that accrue to society in the form of its welfare and those that bear upon the agent in the form of worldly benefits. Both these get transmuted in *niṣkāma-karma.* The consequences to society become "implicit" and those to the agent become "spiritualised."[61] The *Gītā*'s insistence that one should perform the duty of one's own station in life spontaneously paves the way for the maintenance of social order. Thus, instead of social welfare being the motive to the action, it becomes the consequence that necessarily follows from the action. Similarly, in the case of the agent also there is a transformation of motive. The agent is expected to cease thinking of the *diverse* external purposes that will fall to his lot in life as a result of his action. Instead, he should be inspired by *one and the same* spiritual end of his moral improvement, the cleansing of his heart (*sattva-śuddhi*), in other words, the building up of his own character. Thus, as in all volitional activity, there is here a personal end; "only it is of a higher type, because it shuts out altogether the desire for inferior or utilitarian values, and aims solely at subjective purification."[62] It should further be noted that this subjective purification is only the proximate end of duty; it is meant to subserve the ultimate aim of liberation (*mokṣa*). However, the utility of *karma-yoga* to *mokṣa* is not direct. *Karma-yoga* prepares the mind for the acquisition of right knowledge (*jñāna-yoga*), and it is *jñāna-yoga* that directly leads to liberation.

What we have explained above is only one of the ways in which *karma-yoga*, as taught in the *Gītā*, is to be practised. It is based on the absolutistic view of Brahman. There is another way according to the standpoint of theism, which is also genuine to the *Gītā*. From this standpoint, the *Gītā* teaches that one should perform one's duties for the fulfilment of God's purpose. Here also the duties that one has to perform are those of his station in life; but he should perform them subordinating his will completely to the divine will. This is dedicating all work to the

Lord and working for him (*Īśvarārtha*). *Karma-yoga* thus becomes *bhakti-yoga*. Here also the general result of *karma-yoga* is the same as in the previous view. By working for the Lord, the agent renounces the fruits commonly associated with duties and thereby purifies his heart. But, unlike as in the previous view, salvation is achieved here through the grace of God rather than through *jñāna*. For this reason we may say that the only difference between the two teachings is that while the former, being somewhat difficult, may suit the few whose minds are well cultivated, the latter has decidedly a stronger appeal to common people who simply trust in God.

Karma-yoga—the Central Message of the Gītā

To understand the meaning of the expression *karma-yoga*, it is necessary to consider separately the two terms constituting it. *Karma* literally means "what is done," "a deed." In this general sense the word does appear sometimes in the *Gītā*. But what the word usually signifies in the work are the duties that were at that time found associated by custom and tradition with particular sections, or classes, of people, i.e. *varṇa-dharma*. (There is not much reference in the work to *āśrama-dharma*, the twin companion of *varṇa-dharma*, which are duties belonging to particular stages in the life of an individual.) The word *karma* is also sometimes used in the sense of divine worship and devotional acts connected with it such as prayer. But when thinking of *karma-yoga* as taught in the *Gītā*, we should ordinarily take the word in its predominant sense stated above: of social obligations. The word *yoga* means "harnessing" or "applying oneself to." So *karma-yoga* may be rendered as "devotion to the discharge of social obligations."[63]

A characteristic of any voluntary deed is that it is preceded by a desire, or motive, for something, which is described as the result, or *phala,* of the deed. In the present case Arjuna is actuated by a desire for sovereignty over his ancestral kingdom, which has passed on to his wily cousins. And he has undertaken to fight for regaining it. The *Gītā* teaches that such an undertaking would not be devotion to *karma*. It is devotion to its *phala*, for which *karma* becomes only a means.

> For *karma-yoga*, the act should be viewed not as a means but as an end in itself. That is, the idea of result, which is to ensue from the action, must be dismissed altogether from the mind before as well as during the act.[64]

There is no doubt that a result follows from the deed done, but the *karma-yogin* pays no thought to reaping it. "Your concern is with action—never with its fruit."[65]

An important advantage of following this principle of action is that one acts with complete equanimity. Desire, or self-interest, may blind us to what is right. Even when we choose the right, eagerness to secure its fruit may deflect us from the path of rectitude. In one place the *Gītā* explains the term *yoga* as signifying just this equanimity (*samatvam*).[66]

> This teaching that we ought to engage ourselves in our work as members of a social order in the usual way and yet banish from our mind all thought of deriving any personal benefit therefrom is the meaning of *karma-yoga* and constitutes the specific message of the *Gītā*.[67]

Karma-yoga—a Combination of Renunciation and Action

The importance of the above teaching will become clear if we remember that two ideals of conduct were prevalent at the time of the *Gītā*. One was the negative ideal of renunciation (*nivṛtti*), and the other was the positive one of active life (*pravṛtti*). The first consisted in giving up all *karma* and withdrawing from society; the second was living in society and undertaking all social obligations. The second did not exclude selfishness. Ritualistic activities, for example, were meant for one's own good in another life, though not in this. They were thus at bottom selfish. And as regards activities which were not other-worldly, social obligations, for example, the agents were as much conscious of rights as of duties and expected others to requite their actions. To that extent they were selfish. The *Gītā* propounds the golden mean between *pravṛtti* and *nivṛtti*, or action and contemplation, pre-serving the excellence of both. This is *karma-yoga*.

> While it does not abandon activity, it preserves the spirit of renunciation. It commends a strenuous life, and yet gives no room for the play of selfish impulses. Thus it discards neither ideal, but by combining them refines and ennobles both.[68]

The attitude which renunciation signifies remains without looking askance at action. "In other words, the *Gītā* teaching stands not for renunciation *of* action, but for renunciation *in* action."[69]

Arjuna at the outset undertakes to fight under the influence of the ideal of *pravṛtti*. But when despondency overcomes him, he soon falls under the influence of the other ideal of *nivṛtti*. In resolving to renounce the world and withdraw from the contest, he forgets that *nivṛtti* requires as a condition real detachment, which he hardly has. His dispassion (*vairāgya*) is not genuine as it springs not from true enlightenment, but only from narrow-mindedness, viz., love of kith and kin.[70] The undercurrent of this narrow love is the distinction he makes between them and his subjects, whose interest becomes for him secondary.[71] His detachment, or rather his disinclination to fight, is the result of weakness—surrendering to the power of the moment. It is also the result of the subtle diffidence and fear that he might not after all win the battle. So at bottom it is faint-heartedness (*hṛdaya-daurbalyam*). It is "eventually *rāga*, not *virāga*."[72] His inaction is based "on empirical, not on ultimate, grounds."[73] That his detachment is not genuine is finally proved by his despondency (*viṣāda*) and doubt. "Neither doubt nor sadness is a sign of true spirituality which would result in a feeling of triumphant freedom."[74] The narrow selfish impulses of which sadness and doubt are the sign should first be overcome; and the way to do it is to live in the midst of the storm and stress of social life, doing one's duty without any thought of recompense. This is Śrī Kṛṣṇa's teaching.

The teaching has been traced by some to earlier sources. It is mentioned, for example, in the *Īśa Upaniṣad*, but without any elaboration. But even granting that the ideal of *karma-yoga* is not entirely new, its impressive enunciation in the *Gītā* is responsible for its acceptance by all the subsequent creeds and schools of thought in the orthodox tradition. To all of them detached action becomes the starting point of life's discipline. The earlier view of the ideal of *pravṛtti* as activity pursued for its fruit becomes completely transformed as a result of the *Gītā*. This is "one of the chief contributions of the *Gītā* to Hindu thought."[75] It is to be added that, through this transformation of the ideal of *pravṛtti*, the *Gītā* teaching becomes particularly relevant to modern times. The danger to spiritual life is no longer from the extreme view of *nivṛtti* as of old. The one-sided ideal of a monastic withdrawal from social obligations holds no appeal to the modern man. "Ours is an age of self-assertion, not of self-suppression."[76] The danger, therefore, comes from the other side—of looking upon a life of action (*pravṛtti*) as a means of self-gratification. Such a view of action is likely to erode all sense of duty. "In our eagerness to claim our rights and exercise them, we may ignore our duties."[77] The life of action requires as much to be corrected now as the life of renunciation did in an earlier age. "Hence the need for the teaching of the *Gītā* now is as great as ever. Its value has not lessened through lapse of time; and that is a mark of its greatness."[78]

The Occasion for the Teaching

It has already been said that the *Gītā* teaching arose in a particular context. But this does not mean that it is confined to that context. Its message is universal. The occasion which it chooses is not isolated but typical. The appeal of the *Gītā* is to all men who find themselves placed in a dilemma in life similar to that in which Arjuna found himself. It also requires to be noted that the particular situation that gave rise to the *Gītā* is the most appropriate to it. The teaching was imparted on the battlefield. "...nowhere else is the subordination of individual aim to the general good so complete."[79] The soldier may know the cause for which he is fighting, but he hardly knows the outcome. Even if he knew that it would be favourable to the cause, he may not live to share its joy. This uncertainty does not reduce his responsibility and value as an agent. But he must forget that he is to participate in the good that may result from his duty. In other words, while he should realize to the full that he is a *kartā*, he should altogether forget that he is a *bhoktā*. What he serves is the cause of a wider entity than himself. His thought should not go beyond realizing his individual responsibility as an actor in the cause.

> That represents the highest form of self-sacrifice—to work for no profit to oneself, but yet to exert oneself to the utmost; and the finest exhibition of this spirit in the world is to be seen on a battlefield.[80]

Thus the *Gītā* addresses itself to all men through the telling case of Arjuna. In making this wider appeal, it recognizes that activity is natural to man and that no view of life that ignores or minimizes its importance can be right. No one can abjure activity altogether.[81] What the *Gītā* teaches is that this natural activity, instead of being utilized for selfish, or material, ends, should be properly directed towards the higher end for which one lives.

Karma-yoga in Svadharma

As already remarked, the *Gītā* does not purport to be an exhaustive treatise on conduct. It does not attempt to teach what types of duty are incumbent on man. There is no allusion, for example, to the general obligations of all men, except incidentally, as in distinguishing the worthy from the wicked in chapter Eighteen. The main concern of the *Gītā* is *how* duties are to be discharged. *Karma-yoga* is the principle along which duty is to be directed. And in explaining this principle, it practically confines itself to what is called *svadharma*. It comprises the special duties that pertain to various classes in society (*varṇa*) and the different stages in the life of the individual (*āśrama*). Of these, the *Gītā* is almost silent on *āśrama-dharma* and devotes itself mainly to *varṇa-dharma*. This is as required by the context in which the *Gītā* is delivered.

That is to say, it is to *svadharma* in this restricted sense that the *Gītā* applies the principle of *karma-yoga*. It enjoins on all the performance of the duties that devolve on them by virtue of their station in society.[82] They are obligations which everyone owes to society according to his station, and are calculated to secure and preserve the solidarity of society. The *Gītā* is least concerned with the intrinsic nature of the deed so long as it is one's own *dharma* performed with detachment. What these duties are, the book does not elaborate, but leaves their determination to the good sense or immediate judgement of the individual. This proves "the severely practical character of the teaching."[83] This does not leave the matter vague, for at the time of the *Gītā* social organization was simple. There is no doubt as to the *svadharma* of Arjuna. The *Gītā* emphasizes the social character of man and, generally speaking, does not look upon him apart from the community.

The Motive of Karma-yoga—Two Conceptions

Karma-yoga is not motiveless action. There is no voluntary activity without some motive or other. The motive behind *karma-yoga* is conceived of in two ways in the *Gītā*. One is *ātma-śuddhi*, or cleansing of the heart,[84] and the other is subserving the purposes of God (*Īśvara*).[85] The spirit in which one engages oneself in activity is also said to be different according to the two aims. In the former case what is done, is done for the sake of the social whole of which the doer is a member. In the latter it is done for the sake of God, surrendering the fruit of action to him. Action in the one case is regarded as duty to others; in the other it becomes service to God. In the former case the agent is directly conscious of his relation to his environment, which demands his fealty. In the latter case he is conscious only of God, conceived as a personality in constant touch with the world, and regards whatever he does as God's work, which has to be done. But whether the work done is looked upon as duty or as divine service, it is not "disinterested" in the literal sense of the term. The motive of the former is subjective purification; of the latter it is the security that God guarantees to those who serve him.[86]

Though the immediate and direct motive of *karma-yoga* is thus either self-purification or divine service, the ultimate and indirect aim is one and the same, viz., the higher end of life, or liberation. The doctrine of *karma-yoga* teaches that "an active life led without any thought of securing the worldly results it may yield, sets free the springs of that inner life whose development is the one aim of man."[87] *Karma-yoga* does not do away with motives altogether. It is disinterested only in so far as it turns our mind from worldly results and directs it towards the true end of life. It thus "furnishes *one and the same* motive for whatever we may do, viz. the betterment of our spiritual nature."[88] By insisting on social obligations at all costs, the doctrine may appear to ignore the individual. But it does not really do so, since thereby it provides for his advancement on a higher plane of life.

The Nature of the Final Goal

Corresponding to the two ways in which the motive of the *karma-yogin* is presented, the final goal to be reached is also conceived in two ways. Where the motive is "cleansing the heart", the goal is self-realization. It is to be understood much as in the Upaniṣads. It is becoming Brahman (*brahma-bhūyam*).[89] If the motive is "subserving the purposes of God," the end is God-realization, or reaching the presence of God.[90] It is sometimes also described as merging in God.[91]

An important question in this context is whether individuality persists in the final stage. The absolutistic view of release denies the persistence. The purely theistic view admits it, but it says that the individual's will merges in the divine will. But in whichever of these two ways the goal is conceived, it is clear that *saṁsāra*, which is the realm of good and evil, is transcended.

Another question is whether the goal is reached within the limits of this life or after death. There are statements in the work which indicate that the goal—particularly of the theistic conception—is reached after death.[92] But the prevalent idea in the work is that the goal can be realized within the limits of this life.[93] Of the person who has perfected himself thus there is more than one beautiful description.[94] And in the eleventh chapter there is a thrilling account of a direct perception of God by the devotee.

The perfected state, in so far as it is granted to be attainable in this life, is variously described as "the life absolute" and "dwelling in God."[95] The distinctive feature of this state is peace. Only the attitude is predominantly one of *jñāna* in the case of self-realization and one of *bhakti* in the case of God-realization. The former is a state of enlightenment, which enables the perfected one "to see oneself in all beings and all beings in oneself."[96] The latter is a state of loving communion with God, and through him, with all his creatures. "But whether we look upon the *Gītā* as the gospel of enlightenment or of love, it is equally the gospel of action."[97]

The Activity of the Perfected One

In connection with the nature of the goal there is a point to which special attention needs to be drawn. It is that the perfected one, according to the *Gītā*, does not and cannot remain passive. He continues to work even in this perfected state, and there is nothing incompatible between outer activity and inner peace. Thus the *Gītā* assigns an exalted position to work. There is no period when activity may be wholly renounced. Passivity is as reprehensible as wrong activity. The examples cited are King Janaka and Śrī Kṛṣṇa. The former has attained perfection, and the latter has always been perfect, and both alike are active.[98]

> Such a view totally transforms the notion of *saṁnyāsa* by dissociating it from all inaction; and in this transformation of the ideal of *nivṛtti* consists another important contribution of the *Gītā* to Hindu thought.[99]

Karma-yoga accordingly falls under two stages. The earlier stage is a stage of strife when the disciple is continually weaning himself from selfish activity. The later stage comes at the dawn of truth when the strife is over and right conduct becomes quite spontaneous. *Karma-yoga* in the first sense is ancillary,[100] and this forms the essential theme of the *Gītā*. The second is a characteristic of the goal to be kept in view by the aspirant, and this appears in the work now and then.

The Nature of the Struggle Involved in Karma-yoga

Karma-yoga, as we have seen, involves the deliberate abjurement of selfish desires and the performance of duty with the sole motive of spiritual betterment. This implies that our life occupies two levels, which the *Gītā* represents as two selves. And it calls for the conquest of the lower self by the higher.[101] The lower may be styled the sensuous self. It is to this that evil dispositions appeal. The senses and mind are its habitation. And through them it deludes us by evoking love or hatred in respect of every sense object. If this were our only nature, there would be no point in persuading man to adopt the right path. The lower self is the source of impulses, and no moral responsibility would attach to man if he was only a slave of impulses as in the case of animals. Moral judgement applies only to actions that are willed by the agent. But the *Gītā* explains that fortunately the lower self is not our true self. We are conscious also of the presence in ourselves of a higher self. So, we have the opportunity to act differently after appropriate reflection. We are not driven to evil against our desire (*anicchan*) as Arjuna wrongly assumes. The higher self may remain half-concealed, but it is still there giving rise to a conflict between wish and will.

It is the consciousness of this conflict that makes right choice possible. This is because the nature of the higher self is such that it will not allow itself to be subordinated to the lower. The *Gītā* beckons us to steady the (lower) self by the (higher) self[102] and "commends activity without any reference to the ends which the lower of the two selves may like to pursue."[103]

It is not practicable to replace the lower aim by the higher one only as and when a selfish motive presents itself. So we are asked to be forearmed by adopting the higher ideal permanently and to see that all our actions become the expression of this single coherent purpose. This is the meaning of telling us that we should uniformly substitute the betterment of our nature for the divergent ends of our numerous actions. Progress in this course is difficult, but the *Gītā* assures us that "nothing of what we do for self-development really runs to waste."[104] It is to encourage us to persevere in this course that the *Gītā* clarifies the notion of the true self.

Freedom of the Will

The *Gītā* discussion of this topic is in the context of *karma-yoga* and is restricted to the question whether man can choose the path to the higher life. The teaching relating to *karma-yoga* presupposes the belief in *karma*. The doctrine of *karma* implies that the agent is bound to reap the fruits of his action, whether they be good or bad. But the principle of *karma-yoga* calls for effort in doing good actions without expecting their rewards. Now, the question arises, how, in view of the necessity involved in *karma*, man is free to engage in *karma-yoga*. In answering this question, it is pointed out that every deed that we do leads to a double result—the direct result of pain or pleasure following from it (*phala*) and the indirect one of a tendency to repeat the same deed in the future (*saṁskāra*). The *phala* is inevitable; even the gods cannot prevent it. But that is all the necessity involved in the *karma* theory. Although the *saṁskāras* are also established as a result of past actions, since they lie latent in the mind, we have within us the full power to regulate them as they tend to express themselves in action. "There is thus nothing in the doctrine which either eliminates responsibility or invalidates self-effort."[105] Even the necessity that governs the *phala* and renders escape from it impossible, instead of unnerving us, should stimulate us to exertion. Thus the *karma* doctrine, paradoxical though it may seem, "inspires us both with hope and resignation at once—hope for the future and resignation towards what may occur in the present."[106]

Theoretical Teaching

The theoretical teaching of the *Gītā*—its metaphysics—occupies only the background, and, as such, its details are not clearly determinable. But it is evident that there is a mixture of doctrines. There is a current of Upaniṣadic thought, stressing the cosmic conception of the Absolute. Throughout the work expressions drawn from the Upaniṣads, and sometimes even quotations from them, are found. Another stream of thought which mingles with the Upaniṣadic teaching is the theism of the Bhāgavata type. Thus the theoretical teaching of the *Gītā*, like its practical one, is a blend of these two distinct creeds. In fact, the two streams on the practical side are the natural counterparts of those on the theoretical.

A third current of thought is also suggested by some scholars, viz., the Sāṅkhya. It is claimed that the Sāṅkhya is as old as the Upaniṣads, and that the Bhāgavata creed made use of it in a modified form to furnish itself with a metaphysical basis and, through this channel, influenced the *Gītā*. But although there are ideas in the *Gītā* which sound like those of Sāṅkhya, this element of the *Gītā* is not fully identifiable with the Sāṅkhya system as known to us, for there are some vital differences. For instance, the super-soul (*uttama-puruṣa*) recognized in the *Gītā*[107] is unknown to Sāṅkhya. Again, in the *Gītā* there is no reference to the negative ideal of *kaivalya*, or spiritual aloofness, found in Sāṅkhya. The goal of life as represented in the *Gītā* is different, being positive—it is either "becoming Brahman" or "reaching the presence of God." The *Gītā* no doubt thereby implicitly teaches the soul's separation from nature (*prakṛti*), but, instead of being the end itself as in Sāṅkhya, it is regarded as the means to the end of realizing the ultimate.

There is no doubt that the Upaniṣadic doctrine as contained in the *Gītā* does not retain all its old features, but shows some advance towards realism and dualism. For example, the *Gītā* exhibits a tendency to separate God, soul, and the world and conceive of them as coeval, though the latter two are held to be dependent on God. Again, the physical world, instead of being traced to Brahman as in the Upaniṣads, is traced to *prakṛti*, which is distinguished from *puruṣa*. But such partial resemblances to Sāṅkhya do not by themselves establish the antiquity of Sāṅkhya and its influence on the *Gītā*. On the contrary, it is preferable to regard the Sāṅkhya element in the *Gītā* as a step in the movement of Upaniṣadic thought towards Sāṅkhya in its classical, or systematic, form.

REFERENCES

1. *PEIP*, p. 109.
2. Ibid., p. 112.
3. Ibid., p. 114.
4. *OIP*, p. 33.
5. Ibid.
6. *EIP*, p. 14.
7. *PEIP*, p. 69.
8. *EIP*, p. 19.
9. Ibid., p. 21.
10. *OIP*, p. 57.
11. Ibid.
12. Ibid., p. 58.
13. Vide *Praśna Upaniṣad*, I.1; V.2.
14. Vide *OIP*, p. 63.
15. Vide *Muṇḍaka Upaniṣad*, I.i.4-5.
16. Vide *OIP*, pp. 69-70.
17. Ibid., p. 70.
18. Ibid., p. 71.
19. Ibid., p. 72.
20. Vide *Īśa Upaniṣad*, 7.
21. *OIP*, p. 73.
22. *EIP*, p. 25.
23. *PEIP*, p. 72.
24. Ibid., p. 73.
25. *R*, p. 7.
26. *EIP*, p. 25.
27. *OIP*, p. 77.
28. *EIP*, p. 26.
29. *OIP*, p. 77.
30. *EIP*, p. 28.
31. *OIP*, p. 75.
32. Ibid., p. 76.
33. Ibid., p. 82.
34. *EIP*, p. 37, n. 11.
35. Ibid., p. 39.
36. Ibid., p. 34.
37. Ibid.
38. Ibid.
39. Ibid., p. 35.
40. Ibid.
41. Ibid., p. 36.
42. Vide *Bhagavad-gītā*, IX.23.
43. *EIP*, p. 36.
44. Ibid.
45. Ibid., p. 40.
46. *OIP*, p. 104.
47. Ibid.
48. Ibid., p. 105.
49. Ibid., p. 106.
50. Ibid., p. 109.
51. Ibid., p. 110.
52. Ibid., p. 112.
53. Ibid., p. 114.
54. Ibid., p. 116.
55. Ibid.
56. Ibid., p. 117.
57. *EIP*, p. 54.
58. Vide *Bhagavad-gītā*, II.31; III.35; XVIII.47-48.
59. *EIP*, p. 55.
60. Ibid.
61. Ibid.
62. Ibid., p. 56.
63. *OIP*, p. 119.
64. Ibid.
65. *Bhagavad-gītā*, II.47.
66. Vide ibid., II.48.
67. *OIP*, p. 120.
68. Ibid., p. 121.
69. Ibid.
70. Vide *Bhagavad-gītā*, I.31; II.6.
71. Vide ibid., I.33.
72. *OIP*, p. 121.
73. Ibid.
74. Ibid., p. 122.
75. Ibid.
76. Ibid.
77. Ibid.
78. Ibid.
79. Ibid., p. 123.
80. Ibid.
81. Vide *Bhagavad-gītā*, III.5; XVIII.11.
82. Vide ibid., XVIII.47-48.
83. *OIP*, p. 124.
84. Vide *Bhagavad-gītā*, V.11.
85. Vide ibid., III.30; IX.27.
86. Vide ibid., IX.31.
87. *OIP*, p. 125.
88. Ibid., p. 126.
89. *Bhagavad-gītā*, XVIII.53.
90. Vide ibid., IV.9; IX.25.
91. Vide ibid., VIII.5.

92. Vide ibid.
93. Vide ibid., V.19 and 26.
94. Vide ibid., II.55-58; XIV.22-25.
95. Ibid., II.72; XII.8.
96. Ibid., VI.29.
97. *OIP*, p. 127.
98. Vide *Bhagavad-gītā*, III.20-28.
99. *OIP*, p. 127.
100. Vide *Bhagavad-gītā*, V.6; VI.3.
101. Vide ibid., III.33-43.
102. Vide ibid., III.43.
103. *OIP*, p. 129.
104. Vide *Bhagavad-gītā*, II.40; VI.40.
105. *OIP*, p. 130.
106. Ibid.
107. *Bhagavad-gītā*, XV.17-18.

4

Metaphysics—Part One

I. INTRODUCTION TO THE SYSTEMS

Emergence of the Systems

By about the third or fourth century BC a great mass of philosophical material had accumulated. The heterogeneity of this material called for systematization. The details relating to the early stages through which the systems of thought arose are lost. The primary sources that can be identified for the Vedic systems are the *sūtra* relating to each school. The non-Vedic systems also have primary authorities of a more or less similar nature. The object of all these treatises is to consolidate the teaching of the respective schools and to criticize others where they differ from them. They are thus critical as well as constructive. The *sūtras*, or aphorisms, are so laconic that they are not intelligible without the aid of commentaries, which, therefore, came to be written. Further commentaries were written on the earlier commentaries themselves. Each school produced also independent treatises (*prakaraṇa*), which treat of either the whole doctrine for beginners or aspects of it for advanced students. Thus the literature of each school developed over a very long period ending only a century or two ago. All these developments comprise what we have earlier described as the later post-Vedic period.

The chief indication of the process of systematization in this period is to be found in the attention that comes to be paid to the nature and function of knowledge. Upto the evolution of the schools Indian philosophy may be described as largely consisting of results. Attention was hitherto centred on the nature of reality. The conclusions reached should of course have been arrived at by definite methods of inquiry. But very little is now known as to what those methods were. The philosophy of the present period gives not only the conclusions of the various schools, but also the methods by which they have been arrived at. In fact, since the nature of the results depends on the process of knowing, several systems set about their subject-matter only after having entered into a critique of knowledge and considered how we come by truth. "In other words, Indian philosophy becomes self-conscious at this stage; and Logic emerges as an explicit branch of it."[1] The exact cause of this shift is not known. But this much is certain that the growth and consolidation of heterodox doctrines must have contributed much to it. The increasing conflict of thought in regard to the metaphysical problem necessitated a critical re-examination of the tools of knowing by different sets of thinkers.

The spirit of this change is well represented by the fact that every school of Indian philosophy contains and most often starts with an investigation into the *pramāṇas*. *Pramāṇa* is defined as the proximate means to valid knowledge, or *pramā*. The object known is called *prameya*, and the knower, *pramātā*. *Pramāṇas* are usually regarded as a help not only in acquiring new knowledge, but also in verifying what is already known. Thus logic as conceived in India is a science of both proof and discovery. There is much divergence of opinion among Indian thinkers in regard to the scope and nature of *pramāṇas*. The number of *pramāṇas* is another topic on which there are wide differences. And one of the commonest, though mechanical, classification of the schools is according to the number of *pramāṇas* they accept, ranging from one to six or even more. Most of the schools, however, agree in accepting three of them—perception (*pratyakṣa*), inference (*anumāna*), and verbal testimony (*śabda*). The inclusion of verbal testimony among the *pramāṇas* is peculiar to the Indian view of philosophy, and it has special significance in determining the nature of metaphysics in the schools. We shall, therefore, devote some attention to it here.

Two aspects of *śabda* have to be distinguished—its sound and sense. When a sentence is uttered, we hear the sounds occurring in a certain order. This is purely a case of perception. *Śabda* as a *pramāṇa* does not mean simply this, for the sounds as such are rather a *prameya*. What has been heard must be interpreted. It is with reference to the meaning of the sentence, its semantic aspect, that *śabda* is regarded as a *pramāṇa*. A further distinction which we have to make is between the utility of *śabda* and its validity. The usefulness of *śabda* as a means of acquiring knowledge cannot be questioned. Only a portion of what we know is known by our own observation or deduction. For the rest, we depend entirely on the testimony of others, which comes to us through spoken or written words. But the mere utility of *śabda* cannot make it an independent *pramāṇa*. To be regarded as a *pramāṇa*, *śabda* must also be valid. Thus the dispute regarding the acceptability of *śabda* as a *pramāṇa* turns solely on its logical status, and not on its usefulness.

What is the scope of *śabda* when accepted as a *pramāṇa*? In the beginning *śabda* stood only for tradition (*aitihya*), which means what is handed down from the past, or ancient belief. (To the orthodox stream of thought tradition is represented by the Veda; to others it is the expression of individual seers.) In course of time the scope of *śabda* was extended so as to include all verbal statements whether they were connected with ancient belief or not. We shall for the time being confine our attention to the original sense of *śabda* as tradition and consider the exact significance of regarding it as a *pramāṇa*. The material of tradition that had accumulated by the time of the systems was very vast. And it was felt that the contributions of history to philosophy should not be ignored. The recognition also indicates the reverence with which the authority of tradition was regarded then. But from this we should not conclude that those systems which took their stand on tradition relinquished all independent judgement. Such a course was impossible as matters stood at that time. On the one hand, the whole teaching of the Veda handed down from the past was itself complex. On the other, a mass of heterodox thought had resulted from free thinking in different circles, exhibiting a good deal of diversity. Philosophy as embodied in tradition was thus riddled with internal conflicts; and the need was felt for testing whether the elements constituting each creed were mutually compatible. Both orthodox and heterodox thinkers accordingly set about examining their traditional beliefs and tried to interpret them consistently. This involved a great deal of independent reasoning. And so, when it is said that *śabda* in the sense of tradition is taken as *pramāṇa,* what is meant is not mere tradition, but tradition as subjected to reasoned inquiry. "The *pramāṇa*, therefore, signifies not tradition in general, but systematized tradition."[2] In the case of the Mīmāṁsā system, for example, the essential aim is the systematic interpretation of the teaching of the Veda.

The acceptance or otherwise of *śabda,* or tradition, as a *pramāṇa* marks a radical difference in the metaphysical outlook of Indian schools. Tradition in both orthodox and heterodox circles stands for truths that lie beyond the range of common experience, or what cannot be known by perception and inference. But according to an old point of view represented by Svabhāvavāda, reality is confined to what is perceivable, and perception and inference are the only means of knowing it. This view may be described as empiricism, or naturalism, and it appears later as different forms of the Cārvāka school. It rejects verbal testimony as a separate *pramāṇa*. Verbal statements, according to it, will be valid only when they are based directly or indirectly on perception and inference. Hence, these two are the only *pramāṇas*. The other schools hold that, so far as the world of sense experience goes, there is no doubt that verbal statements should be based on perception and inference. But they say that to assume that reality is confined to the sensible realm is unwarranted. They argue that, though the human mind may not be definitely aware of what is beyond the reach of perception and inference, it is not altogether unconscious of it. "The very statement that common experience exhausts reality implies, by placing a limit on it, that the mind has travelled beyond that limit. Our reach exceeds our grasp."[3] But there is need for an appropriate *pramāṇa* whereby we may definitely know of it, since perception and inference fail to be of help here. It is on such a consideration that verbal testimony has been accepted in Indian philosophy as a separate *pramāṇa*. According to Jaimini, the chief function of verbal testimony in this transcendental application is the communication to us of a knowledge of the two higher ideals of *dharma* and *mokṣa* and of the proper means to their realization.

Among those who accept verbal testimony embodying tradition as an independent *pramāṇa,* there is an important difference as regards the source of *śabda*. According to the heterodox schools, Jainism and Buddhism, *śabda,* or tradition, at no stage goes beyond human (*pauruṣeya*) experience. Human experience is not confined to perception and reasoning. There is a higher faculty, belonging to gifted individuals, which may be described as intuition, or insight, which can apprehend what is beyond perception and reason. Thus tradition, for these thinkers, stands for truths that lie beyond the reach of common men, but which have been directly apprehended by those who possessed spiritual vision. *Śabda* has its origin in the intuitive insight of a saint (*yogi-pratyakṣa*). Jainism, for example, traces its truths to the insight of great prophets like Mahāvīra. Our knowledge of what transcends common experience depends entirely upon the authority of individual insight. It is described as *pratyakṣa,* because it is taken to give immediate knowledge to the *yogin*. This intuitive power is found in all men, but in a latent form, and a good deal of practice in meditation is needed to develop it, besides a cleansing of the mind. "The association of moral purity with what is essentially a logical means of knowledge indicates, we may observe by the way, the close connection that has always subsisted in India between religion and philosophy."[4] In view of the difficulty in acquiring this intuitive power, its successful cultivation is not possible for ordinary men. They have to depend on others, and the knowledge so gained by them is mediate. The schools that recognize verbal testimony in this sense are generally realistic, and we may take Jainism as a typical example of it.

Other schools see a risk in appealing to individual insight on transcendental matters. In their view, nobody's private insight can carry with it the guarantee of its own validity. The vision of a single saint may after all be an illusion. This is not to question the good faith of the saint. It only means that the excellence of the character of a teacher does not rule out the possibility of his being self-deluded. To avoid this possible defect of subjectivity, the opponents of the previous view postulate verbal testimony in another sense as *pramāṇa*. This is *śruti*, or "revelation," otherwise called Veda. The Veda, it is claimed, will not mislead, as it is supernatural in some sense or other. Since its origin cannot be traced to any mortal being, *śruti* is that tradition which is immemorial (*sanātana*) in character. The belief in such an authority implies that "the realm of transcendental being is not directly accessible to the mind of man, however gifted morally and intellectually he may be."[5]

The significance of this distinction in the source of *śabda* is that it connotes a difference in the conception of reality. From the heterodox point of view, the realm of human experience exhausts reality. Even what lies beyond perception and reason, the transcendental sphere of being, is open to human experience of a special kind. And to place anything beyond the reach of human powers is as good as denying reality to it. From the orthodox point of view, the realm of the transcendental is such that it is not open to human experience, however gifted a person may be. Human experience may be sufficient to understand nature, but not what lies beyond it. *Śruti*, or revelation, is the sole means of acquiring knowledge of it.

> The question what *śabda* or tradition represents in the two schools thus resolves itself eventually into one of general philosophic outlook and connotes a fundamental difference between them in the conception of reality.[6]

The verbal expression of a saint's vision is spoken of in the heterodox schools as *smṛti*, by which term they mean "(mere) tradition," or tradition in the general sense of "what is remembered."[7] The word *smṛti* is used by the orthodox schools also, but for them it stands only for such tradition as has a basis in *śruti*, or revelation, directly or indirectly.[8] In other words, it applies only to such works of a human origin as help to recall the teachings of *śruti*. Thus, for the heterodox, the word *smṛti* signifies verbal testimony of primary importance; for the orthodox, it connotes only verbal testimony of a secondary value. Tradition in the heterodox sense of *smṛti* may be described as *āgama*, and tradition in the orthodox sense of *śruti* as *nigama*.[9]

The acceptance of *śruti* in the sense of revelation has its own risk. Anything could be claimed to have been revealed and come to be believed. Realizing this danger, the ancient Indian hedged in his view of revelation by certain conditions. These conditions show how revelation stands in relation to experience in general and to reason in particular. The first condition is that the revealed truth should be new, or extra-empirical (*alaukika*). It should be something not known by any other means. For example, revelation should not be cited to show that heat destroys cold, as this is a matter of common experience. But revelation should speak to us in terms of our experience, for otherwise it will be unintelligible and will, therefore, fail to fulfil its purpose. "Even the scripture cannot teach the unknown through the unknown, so that the theme of revelation cannot be wholly out of relation to human experience."[10] When the condition of novelty is taken along with this fact, it comes out that the teaching of revelation "cannot be altogether new, but can only be a new *way* of constructing our experiences."[11]

The second condition is that what is revealed should not be contradicted (*abādhita*) by any of the other *pramāṇas*. It may transcend common experience, but it cannot go against it. The condition of non-contradiction implies that the content of revelation must be internally coherent also. It does not stand to reason that one part of revelation should be in conflict with another. Thus, though the content of revelation may be above reason, it should not go against reason. Even the fact that conditions are laid down for determining the validity of revelation shows that it cannot be opposed to reason.

The above condition shows that revelation is negatively related to reason. But this is not the only relation. The third condition expresses a positive relation to reason. It lays down that reason should foreshadow what revelation teaches. Reason should prepare the ground for revelation by showing that the revealed truth appears probable. This does not clash with the first condition of novelty, for it means only "a rough forecast of the truth under consideration by means of analogies drawn from the empirical sphere."[12] The analogies are not proofs of the revealed truth; they serve only to remove in advance any improbability that may be felt about the truth in question. "In this sense they are known as *yukti* or *anukūla-tarka*, not *anumāna* or inference proper."[13] The appeal to reason which we come across often in the Upaniṣads is explained by the orthodox schools as really of this kind. In their views, reason by itself is incapable of discovering transcendental truths. At best it may lead to two or more conclusions equally plausible, ultimately giving room for scepticism. Reason can only be an aid to scripture, which is the only authority in these matters. The survival of the self after death is a good instance of a truth taught in the Veda which also satisfies reason negatively and positively. It is not accessible to reason. At the same time there is nothing in it to contradict reason. Reason could even suggest its probability, as when we cite the demand for moral justice.

A fourth condition is also sometimes laid down to obviate a possible objection. The Veda is said to be supernatural (*apauruṣeya*) on the ground that the realm of the transcendental is not directly accessible to the mind of man. But still it must be admitted that the truths for which the Veda stands should eventually have some human connection. This fact seems to be implied in the description of those truths as having been *seen* by the inspired sages (*ṛṣis*) of old. It may be objected that, if it be so, the Veda also must be reckoned as the result of the yogic perception of individual seers. It thus becomes *pauruṣeya* just as in the heterodox view. But there is an important difference as seen from a fourth condition which is sometimes laid down by the orthodox as being essential to all revealed teaching. It is that the revealed truth "should have proved acceptable to the best minds of the community (*mahājana-parigraha*)."[14] That is to say, "it should be in harmony with what may be described as race-intuition."[15]

This may appear to be only a begging of the question at issue, for the non-Vedic schools also claim that their teaching, which is intuited by seers, is acknowledged by the general mind of the community. But what the Vedic schools mean by this new condition is that if a doubt arises as to the validity of the views handed down from the past, appeal is to be made to a community of minds which they have to satisfy. Such an appeal is not contemplated by the non-Vedic schools. It is this sanction of the community in case of doubt that in the end distinguishes orthodox *śruti* from heterodox *āgama*. Thus the standard here becomes eventually a society of men, and not an individual. The deliverances of *śruti* thus come to acquire an objective value, and by virtue of this status, they possess an authority which cannot belong to those of anybody's private intuition. Herein lies the superiority of *śruti* to yogic perception, to mere *smṛti* in the sense of the non-Vedic schools. Mīmāṁsā and Vedānta are the systems that accept revelation in this sense.

We have so far spoken of *pramāṇas* to which special attention comes to be paid during this period. The results arrived at by means of *pramāṇas*, whichever they may be, is described by the general name *darśana*, which literally means "sight." In this sense the word expresses a distinguishing feature of Indian philosophy in general, namely that it does not rest content with a mere intellectual conviction, but aims at transforming such conviction into direct experience. Sometimes the name *darśana* is substituted by the word *dṛṣṭi*, which is an equivalent for it. Hence it seems more probable that *darśana* means "philosophic opinion and signifies a specific school of thought as distinguished from others."[16]

From the standpoint of verbal testimony Indian schools are, as we have seen, divisible into two groups. One assumes that reality is confined to what is given in common experience and may, therefore, be described as positivistic, or empirical. The other holds that the realm of being is by no means exhausted by sensuous experience and acknowledges the unique *pramāṇa* of *śabda* for knowing what lies beyond. The latter group is again divisible into two classes on the basis of the two interpretations of *śabda* given above. One of them believes that individual insight is a sufficient source of this *pramāṇa*; the other insists that verbal testimony in regard to the transcendental should be of the nature of revelation, or *śruti*. Both, however, may be described as intuitionistic, since both alike mean that ultimate philosophic truths are neither deduced from postulates nor constructed from common experience, but are directly seen. Though six systems are reckoned as orthodox, only two, viz. Mīmāṁsā and Vedānta, are directly based on the Veda. The other four, viz. Nyāya, Vaiśeṣika, Sāṅkhya, and Yoga in their present form declare allegiance to the Veda, though they put their own interpretation on it. But it is doubtful whether they were Vedic from the very beginning of their history.

The six systems of orthodox philosophy fall into three pairs—Nyāya-Vaiśeṣika, Sāṅkhya-Yoga, and the two Mīmāṁsās—as the members falling under each pair agree either in their general metaphysical outlook or in their historical basis or in both. To these orthodox (*āstika*) systems may be added the three heterodox (*nāstika*) ones—Materialism, Jainism, and Buddhism. Later Buddhism has a fourfold division into Vaibhāṣika, Sautrāntika, Yogācāra, and Mādhyamika. Hence the heterodox systems are also sometimes described as six in number.

The germs of practically all these schools are to be found in the literature of the previous periods, but their full development and systematization belong to the present period. When once systematized, the *darśanas* determined the main channels along which Indian philosophic thought ran for ever afterwards. The schools are usually ascribed to individual thinkers who were responsible for their systematization. Thus we speak of the Nyāya of Gautama, the Vaiśeṣika of Kaṇāda, the Sāṅkhya of Kapila, the Yoga of Patañjali, the Pūrva Mīmāṁsā of Jaimini, and the Uttara Mīmāṁsā, or Vedānta, of Bādarāyaṇa. But the *darśanas* in their present form are really the outcome of the thought of a long succession of teachers. It is difficult to assess the exact contribution of each of these thinkers, for even the greatest among them sank their individualities for the sake of the systems for which they worked. Such a phenomenon gives proof of the complete disinterestedness with which they sought the truth.

The *darśanas* are described as "systems," because each is a logical whole of well-coordinated thoughts. They are systems also in the sense that each is regarded as *closed* (*siddhānta*) in essentials, though not in matters of detail. Many of them are more than philosophy as now understood, since they include on the one hand, religion, and on the other, what may be described as science. The value of the science contained in the systems is very little now, and it may be omitted except when it has a clear philosophic bearing. The case of religion in them is different, in view of the close alliance of philosophy with it in India. But when we speak of the religious element in these systems, it is the final goal of life as conceived by a system that really matters and not the details of its belief. And even of that goal, whatever is of purely eschatological reference—the kind of existence that a system promises to an enlightened person after life—is of little interest to philosophy. On the contrary, the value of these philosophical systems is to be estimated by the kind of actual life which it expects a person to lead after enlightenment and before physical death, that is in that condition which is described in some systems as *jīvanmukti*, or being an *arhant*.

The Doctrine of Karma

Notwithstanding their wide differences, the systems of Indian philosophy exhibit remarkable agreement on two basic features. One of them is the belief in *karma*. This ancient belief has had a profound influence on the life of the Indian people. To understand the significance of this belief, it is necessary to distinguish between two aspects of it. The first is the necessity involved in it. It teaches that just as every event in the physical world is determined by its antecedents, everything in the moral realm is pre-ordained. But this does not mean that the doctrine amounts to fatalism, leaving no room for freedom. To realize this, we have only to look into the true meaning of freedom. To be controlled by external factors is certainly no freedom. But freedom is not mere caprice or unrestricted licence. It consists in being determined by one-self. What the belief in *karma* precludes is external determination and not self-determination. The doctrine traces the causes which determine an action to the very individual that acts. Since all the causes cannot be found within the limits of a single life, the doctrine of *karma* postulates the existence of the self in a succession of past lives. Similarly, since all the effects of action done in this life cannot be expected in this life itself, it postulates the possibility of future births as well. Thus the theory of transmigration (*saṁsāra*) is a necessary corollary of the *karma* doctrine.

At this stage a question may be asked as to when the responsibility for one's actions was *first* incurred. Such a question is really inadmissible, for it takes for granted that there was a time when the self was without any disposition at all for action. Such a view of the self is a meaningless abstraction. There can be no self without any disposition whatsoever just as there can be no disposition except as belonging to some self. This is what is meant by all schools when they describe *karma* as beginningless (*anādi*). "It means that no matter how far back we trace the history of an individual, we shall never arrive at a stage when he was devoid of all characters."[17] Thus the self is always with a stock of disposition which determines how it acts. The *karma* doctrine implies self-determination at all stages without any imposition of constraint from outside.

Necessity in the sense of self-determination is only one aspect of the *karma* doctrine. The other aspect is the freedom involved in it. This will be evident if we look into the implications of the nature of moral necessity. It may be objected that, although we are ultimately accountable for whatever happens to us now, we cannot alter the course of our past *karma*, which leads to those happenings. There can, therefore, be no freedom of action. In meeting this objection, it is necessary to point out in the first instance that there is absolute justice in the moral retribution underlying the *karma* doctrine. Whatever we knowingly do will bring the result we merit. What we sow, we must reap. That is to say, the *karma* doctrine signifies not merely that there is no escape from the results of our past actions, but that there is perfect justice in the rewards and punishments that fall to our lot in life. "The law of *karma* accordingly is not a blind mechanical law, but is essentially ethical."[18] This conviction that there are no iniquities in life has sunk so deeply into the minds of even common people in India that they blame neither God nor their neighbours, but only themselves whenever any misfortune befalls them. The absence of any trace of bitterness in the wake of pain and sorrow, which is noticeable among them, is one of the most wholesome consequences of the *karma* doctrine.

The implication of this idea of justice in retribution is that it commits man to the ideal of moral advance. The rewards and punishments that the *karma* doctrine signifies are not ends in themselves, but only the means to bring about moral growth. They serve as incentives for self-reformation. Now, the presence, in the mind of man, of an ideal to be pursued implies also that he is free to pursue it. An "ought" implies a "can." Although there is no helping the past, so far as the present is concerned, man can choose between alternative ways of acting. Hence freedom of action "is not merely compatible with, but is actually demanded by, the law of *karma*."[19]

We have seen that both necessity and freedom are implied in the law of *karma*. Man cannot avoid the consequences of the past, whether they are pleasant or unpleasant. There is strict necessity in that respect. But there is also freedom in present action in respect of ethical advance. There is no contradiction in this, for the necessity and the freedom refer to different aspects of *karma*. The explanation is this. Every deed that we do has a double result. It produces its direct result (*phala*), which is the pain or pleasure following from it according to the nature of the deed done. At the same time, it has an indirect result: it establishes in us a tendency (*saṁskāra*) to repeat the same type of action in the future. The necessity involved in the *karma* doctrine is only in regard to the former of these results. But the latter, the tendencies, are entirely under our control. We can regulate and direct them as they tend to express themselves in action. Again, this double significance of *karma* does not lead to any bifurcation of life's interests, for ethical advance in respect of the tendencies should be the sole purpose of *all* our activities. While enduring the results of the past, man should make effort to improve his character for the future. This is what the *Bhagavad-gītā* teaches. "By thus adopting the betterment of one's moral nature as the goal of all endeavour, one may grow indifferent to what happens in the present as the inevitable result of past *karma*."[20]

The Ideal of Mokṣa

All the schools recognize that liberation from the cycle of births and deaths (*mokṣa*) is the highest of human values. Belief in the ideal of *mokṣa* was not accepted by all in earlier times. For instance, the ritualistic teaching of the Brāhmaṇas seems to recognize only *dharma*. But this view has for long been superseded, and *mokṣa* has come to be acknowledged by all schools (except Cārvāka) as the highest of human values. The ideal of *dharma* is not abandoned, but it becomes subordinated to *mokṣa* on the ground that ethical discipline is necessary for the pursuit of *mokṣa*.

The various systems differ widely in their conception of the nature of *mokṣa*. But generally, it is represented as self-perfection. It may be recalled that, while some Indian thinkers maintained that liberation can be achieved only after the expiry of life (*videhamukti*), others held that it could be achieved in this very life (*jīvanmukti*). This distinction persists in the age of the systems also. But what is important to note is that all the schools assume that *mokṣa* is actually attainable, whether here or hereafter. All the schools, including the heterodox, believe that the evil of *saṁsāra* carries with it the seeds of its destruction, and that it is bound to be superseded by freedom from it. None of the Indian systems, therefore, is finally pessimistic. The faith of the Indians in the ultimate goodness and rationality of the world is undoubted. Corresponding to this belief on the practical side, on the theoretical side there is the belief that ignorance, which leads to error and evil, will be replaced by truth. "If either evil or error were final, the world would be irrational."[21]

In connection with the means to *mokṣa*, an important point may now be mentioned. There are two ways of life—one of action (*pravṛtti*) and the other of renunciation (*nivṛtti*). Though they were originally conceived as exclusive to each other, it soon came to be admitted that *pravṛtti* is to lead to *nivṛtti* after a person reaches a certain stage in self-discipline. This practice continued to prevail in the non-Vedic tradition even in the age of the systems. But a profound change came about among the Vedic schools in regard to the relation between these two ways. Instead of the positive way of life completely yielding place to the negative way, the positive way itself comes to be transformed by the incorporation in it of the essence of the negative one. Even in its earlier conception, the path of action involved numerous checks on natural impulses. But the self-restraint in it was only partial, as there was room for a person to seek private happiness, provided he did so without prejudice to the interests of the community. In contrast to this, the later conception of *pravṛtti* stands for the total exclusion of self-interest from action. It is not just a subordination of self-interest to the interests of society. It is the performance of action without any self-interest whatsoever. The path of action now comes to lay the same emphasis on self-renunciation as *nivṛtti* did in the earlier view. It must be noted that there is no reduction of social activity in this new conception of the relation of *pravṛtti* and *nivṛtti*. Active social life is at no stage to be abandoned, according to this view; it must be pursued in a spirit of absolute detachment. This combination of the two paths elevates both. "Asceticism thereby becomes much more than self-denial, and activity is freed from all egoistic motives."[22] We owe this remarkable change chiefly to the teaching of the *Bhagavadgītā*, which presents this new idea in a splendidly devised setting.

2. MATERIALISM

Svabhāvavāda

The origin of the Cārvāka school is to be found in two heretical tendencies of the early post-Upaniṣadic period, namely Svabhāvavāda and Yadṛcchāvāda, which may be rendered as "naturalism" and "accidentalism," respectively. It is Svabhāvavāda that is of real philosophical importance. The influence of Svabhāvavāda is transparent in more than one sphere of Indian thought. It has also contributed important elements to the growth of systems like Sāṅkhya. It is a distinctive current of thought running parallel to the orthodox tradition over a long period. In spite of its importance, no detailed exposition of Svabhāvavāda is to be found anywhere in Sanskrit literature. The *Mahābhārata* contains references to it. Both Svabhāvavāda and Yadṛcchāvāda are mentioned separately in the *Śvetāśvatara Upaniṣad.*

Yadṛcchāvāda believes that the world is a chaos and whatever order is seen in it is by mere chance (*yadṛcchā*). But Svabhāvavāda holds that things are what they are by virtue of their nature. Hence, according to Svabhāvavāda, the world in which we live is not a lawless, or undetermined, world, but a world which only has no external principle governing it. It is self-determined. The nature of a thing entirely determines its history. As reactions of Vedic religion, both these views are at one in rejecting the idea that nature reveals any divine, or transcendental, agency working behind it. Yet, their distinction is important as they lead to two kinds of the Cārvāka school—the "cultured" (*su-śikṣita*) and the "vulgar" (*dhūrta*).[23] The former owes its origin to Svabhāvavāda and the latter to Yadṛcchāvāda.

Svabhāvavāda is positivistic in character. It believes only in perception and inference, which is based upon perception. It does not accept anything that is the result of mere speculation. *Āgama*, or tradition, is also condemned as decoying the unwary. In its rationalism and empiricism it would appeal to the spirit of modern Western thought. It rejects dogma and mysticism. Its metaphysics is confined to the world of common experience—a "mundane metaphysics." It is by virtue of this character that in later literature it is more generally described as *lokāyata*, which means "restricted to the experienced world."[24]

Svabhāva is the unique nature of an object or a group of objects. This implies that things in the world can be classified according to their resemblance to one another. But the classification will be such as will ultimately leave diversity as the characteristic of the universe. The prefix *sva* means "one's own" and implies contrast with "the other." Thus the conception of reality is pluralistic.

Svabhāvavāda denies the existence of an immortal, transmigrating soul. In fact, the very aim of this doctrine is to deny on the basis of common experience transcendental entities. However, it admits "personality," by which is meant "a certain unity of the differences characterizing a person."[25] And "personality" lasts as long as life does. This is an important admission, as it enables the doctrine to explain satisfactorily psychical phenomena like memory and to find scope for self-discipline in terms of an ideal. This "personality" is not present before birth; nor does it endure after death. It is something that emerges when a stage of complexity is reached in the concatenation of the elements constituting the physical body.

Svabhāvavāda encourages freedom of thought. But this does not mean that it tolerates licence in conduct. It imposes a stoic discipline on life. Evil cannot be eliminated, but can only be endured. Such an attitude may be described as "rational pessimism."[26] It is neither hedonism nor cynicism. The wise man will regard pain and pleasure with equal indifference. Thus the view insists on purity of character. This is to be supplemented by enlightenment (*jñāna*). By *jñāna* is here meant dispelling the delusion (*moha*) that there is a permanent soul for whose sake we can modify the nature of things. It is this *moha* that is the source of selfish desire (*tṛṣṇā*), which leads to pain. By the discipline recommended, man can attain peace, which is here called *jīvanmukti*. But the term is understood here in a peculiar sense unlike in Sāṅkhya or Advaita. It simply means the passionless serenity that results from enlightened resignation to the state of things during the tenure of life.

Since the doctrine does not believe in a permanent self apart from the body, this peace is said to last only so long as the body lasts.

The Cārvāka School

We have already referred to two kinds of Cārvāka, a sensualist one and a refined one. It is the latter, which owes its origin to Svabhāva-vāda, which we have to consider now under the philosophical schools. It is difficult to give any detailed and definite account of this viewpoint in Indian philosophy. There are two reasons for this. One is that later thinkers often confused this school of thought with its crude variety and on that basis condemned Cārvāka wholesale. In fact, the very name "Cārvāka," which is generally applied to both these varieties, more properly belongs to the lower type, as the word probably stands for "sweet-tongued" (*cāru-vāka*) and describes its superficial attractiveness. The Cārvāka school has, therefore, been for long condemned and ridiculed by orthodox thinkers for its ostensibly sensualist appeal on the ethical side, which tended to undermine the foundations of social order and moral responsibility.

The second reason for the indefinite information about the school is that no original treatise relating to it has survived, although it is ascribed to a teacher named Bṛhaspati, who is said to have left behind a *sūtra* on the doctrine. This deficiency makes it difficult to judge how far the teaching could be called a *darśana* and how far it merited condemnation by others. The only account of the doctrine we now have is in the summary given in the works of other schools for the purpose of refuting it. Such accounts are naturally meagre, omitting many details. It is also probable that they exaggerate the weak points of the doctrine and even misrepresent its tenets. Thus, what we generally have is a caricature of Cārvāka. In spite of all these limitations, the system is important in the sense that it affords evidence for the many-sidedness of philosophical activity in ancient India and for the prevalence of a great deal of liberty of thought as well as freedom of expression. In regard to epistemology and metaphysics, there must have been more than one school of thought within Cārvāka as shown by evidence scattered here and there in old works.[27]

Cārvāka admits the validity of only one *pramāṇa*, viz., perception. It rejects not only verbal testimony, but also inference. The reason given for rejecting inference is that there can be no finality in its conclusions. Inference depends on an inductive relation (*vyāpti*), which is ascertained on the basis of observed instances only. The truth of this relation, though it may be highly probable, is never demonstrably certain. There is no guarantee that it will hold good for uninvestigated cases also. Not all types of Cārvāka appear to have repudiated reasoning as a *pramāṇa*. There is reference to one type of Cārvāka[28] which admitted inference in general as a legitimate channel of valid knowledge and rejected only a certain variety of it, viz., inference by analogy. Some schools of Indian philosophy make use of inference by analogy to establish such important points as the existence of God and the survival of the self. But this variety of Cārvāka refuses to admit that on the basis of mere analogy we can jump from a knowledge of the sensuous to that of the supra-sensuous. "Such a discrimination in using reason alters the whole complexion of the Cārvāka view "[29] This position may be called "higher materialism"[30]—a position which would secure the whole-hearted support of many modern rationalists.

As a consequence of rejecting inference, Cārvāka cannot speak of any order, or system, in the world. Perception by itself gives only piece-meal knowledge of things, without connecting them by means of any necessary relation. So far it is realism and pluralism. The Upaniṣads speak of five elements. But Cārvāka admits only the four of them given in perception. It discards ether, which is not so given and is merely inferred by others. But the four elements are recognized only in their gross form as given in perception. Their so-called subtle state, which is merely deduced by others, is not admitted by Cārvāka.

For the same reason that it is not given in perception, Cārvāka denies also the soul, or *ātman*, as a surviving entity apart from the body. It does not deny consciousness, or mind, but explains it as a property of the body. Consciousness comes into being when the elements enter into a peculiar concatenation to form what is called the living body, and disappears with the death of the body. It is simply this conscious principle which is coeval with the body that people really mean when they speak of a soul. As a matter of fact, consciousness is always experienced in association with the body and is never found apart from it. For example, the feelings of pleasure and pain bring about a change in the condition of the body. So they are really attributes of the body and do not belong to a separate entity called the soul. Thus the Cārvāka theory of consciousness is a rough Indian counterpart to the view found in the West that mind is a function of matter.

The concept of the *ātman* occupies an important place in all other Indian systems. Naturally, its denial by Cārvāka provoked a keen controversy. Theoretically speaking, the position of Cārvāka that the *ātman* in a non-physical sense cannot be *demonstrated* is irrefutable. That is why some Indian thinkers seek to meet this argument in an indirect way by pointing out that the identity of the *ātman* with the body cannot equally be demonstrated.

The Cārvāka theory of consciousness as a product of matter carries no conviction with it, since it accounts for the higher principle of mind by the lower one of matter. In starting with the assumption that everything is matter or a function of matter, Cārvāka has already taken for granted that there is no mind, although it is as much given in experience as matter. In fact, we have no conception of matter except as it appears to an observing mind. Hence the assertion of matter implies the admission of a mind that perceives it. The belief in the existence of the one carries with it the belief in the existence of the other.

Consistent with its view of reality, the Cārvāka school does not believe either in a life after death or in liberation of the soul (*mokṣa*). It is content with the pursuit of the worldly values of pleasure (*kāma*) and wealth (*artha*). But it is also represented as discarding morality (*dharma*) and preaching a life of "good digestion and no conscience."[31] Accordingly, the Cārvāka ideal is said to be one of hedonism, pure and simple. Pleasure in this life—and that too of the individual—is the sole aim of man. There is no conception of a general good to which the interests of the individual are to be subordinated. Virtue is either based on convention or the result of worldly prudence. The good is what is useful. Pain is a fact of life, but that is no reason to avoid pleasure. Freedom from pain being impossible, it is wisdom to seek the maximum of pleasure that is possible.

No serious thinker could conceivably have inculcated a teaching such as this. A school of thought may be without the ideal of *mokṣa*. But it is impossible to think of one without that of *dharma* also. One may hold that death is final and nothing remains afterwards; but to think of a life devoid of *dharma* is to reduce man to the level of a brute. Hence it is difficult to believe that there could ever have been such a school of thought. It may well be that Cārvāka was reacting against the free speculation and austere asceticism of its times. But even this purpose could have been served by inculcating less objectionable principles, which, we can surmise, it should have done once. If any proof for this is required, it is that the self-indulgence which it is said to teach is something which need not be taught. We could also suspect that Cārvāka should have been so negative a doctrine as made out—mostly denying what is accepted by the other schools and contributing very little of its own to the sum of Indian thought. "The form in which it is now presented has an air of unreality about it."[32]

3. JAINISM

Jainism is a very old form of non-Vedic religion, much older than Buddhism. It is probable that it arose in the later Vedic period. Though there were earlier teachers, Vardhamāna, its greatest teacher, gave it a fresh impetus by ridding it of corruptions in the sixth century BC. Jainism resembles Buddhism in its rejection of the Veda, its pessimistic outlook on life, and in its refusal to believe in a supreme Being. But it differs from Buddhism in other respects such as in its recognition of permanent entities like self and matter. Unlike Buddhism, its influence is confined to India. Jaina teaching appears in a Prākṛta language (Ardhamāgadhī).

The distinguishing mark of Jaina metaphysics is the belief in the eternal and independent existence of spirit and non-spirit, or the animate and the inanimate, described as *jīva* and *ajīva*, respectively. But spirit represents here only the individual self, and not the supreme Self as in the Upaniṣads. The *jīva* is conceived to be of limited, but variable, magnitude to explain how it adjusts itself to the dimensions of the physical body which it occupies. (Indian thinkers generally believe in the unalterable nature of the *jīva*.) Knowledge is its very essence; and empirical knowledge is a manifestation of it under the limitations of the body occupied. The ultimate aim of life is to cast off these limitations and let the soul reveal its true nature of omniscience. It is then in direct intuition with all things. This full and comprehensive knowledge is called *kevala-jñāna.*

The *jīva* is manifold. It is subject to transmigration according to its *karma*. While Hinduism generally believes that it is God who allots rewards and punishments according to *karma*, Jainism holds that *karma* is self-sufficient to explain the kind of birth one takes. In this respect it strangely resembles the old school of Mīmāṁsā. Again, to Hinduism, *karma* is non-material. But to Jainism, it is subtle particles of matter (a sort of *ajīva*), which soils the nature of the soul. The implication is that the soul consists of parts to provide for such ingression of *karma* particles.

Whatever is devoid of consciousness is *ajīva*. It is regarded as five-fold: matter (*pudgala*), time (*kāla*), space (*ākāśa*), motion (*dharma*), and rest (*adharma*). The first three are more important. Matter consists of atoms, but it is only as aggregates of atoms that matter can be perceived. There is no distinction in atoms as such, but when they combine in different ways, qualitative differences among objects emerge. Time is infinite and all-pervasive. All things are in time and change in time. The universe as a whole has neither an origin nor an end, though things in it undergo change. Space also is infinite and all-pervasive, and extends beyond the world.

The notion of reality here is dynamic as in Buddhism, but it is not the same. Buddhism denies a constant element; and so the change it recognizes is a change of nothing. In Jainism the change occurs to an enduring substance. Consequently, Buddhism accepts the many, but denies the one. Jainism admits both—reality is a one-in-many. To the question how unity and diversity can co-exist in reality, Jainism replies that our sole warrant for speaking about reality thus is experience. When experience vouches for such a character in reality, it must be admitted to be so.

Jainism regards the object known as existing outside and independently of knowledge. There is an object that is known as surely as there is a subject that knows. Experience without something that is experienced is meaningless. For this reason, Jainism is realistic. It is also pluralistic, as it believes in the manifoldness of both spirit and matter.

A special feature of Jaina metaphysics is the *sapta-bhaṅgī*, or the "sevenfold predicable." According to Jainism, reality admits of contradictory features like permanence and change. So reality is indeterminate, i.e., it cannot be defined absolutely in one way or another. It is so complex in its structure that it cannot be adequately expressed in any single step. The universe may be looked at from many points of view, each view yielding a different conclusion (*anekānta*). Altogether seven steps in expressing reality have been worked out (*sapta-bhaṅgī*), each being true so far as it goes, but none completely so.

(i) Maybe, a thing is (say, as A).
(ii) Maybe, it is not (as A when it becomes B).
(iii) Maybe, it is (as A once) and is not (as A later).
(iv) Maybe, it is inexpressible (because it cannot be A and B at the same time). By combining the fourth with each of the first three, three more steps are derived.
(v) Maybe, a thing is and is inexpressible.
(vi) Maybe, a thing is not and is inexpressible.
(vii) Maybe, a thing is, is not, and is inexpressible.

The general significance of these seven steps is that, according to Jainism, whatever view we take about reality is purely relative, no single view being adequate to describe it. Jainism has, therefore, been described as "the doctrine of maybe" (*syādvāda*). "The doctrine indicates extreme caution and signifies an anxiety to avoid all dogma in defining the nature of reality."[33]

It may be readily admitted that our knowledge of reality so far as it goes is relative. But it is impossible for the mind to stop with relativism. Relativism as a final view is self-contradictory. The very notion that a view of reality is relative implies an absolute standard by which we judge that view to be relative. But if we grant such a standard, it means there is a knowledge of reality which completely satisfies that standard and is, therefore, absolute. And in that case the claim that knowledge of reality can only be relative stands self-stultified. Jainism, in fact, grants the possibility of such absolute knowledge in its acceptance of *kevala-jñāna*, or "perfect knowledge." It is said to comprehend all things and all phases of them and is also conceived as supra-sensuous and unique. Hence the characterization of knowledge as relative becomes meaningless. In the alternative, the relativistic view will have to be confined to common experience, but this will render the truth of *sapta-bhaṅgī* a mere truism.

Reality, according to Jainism, is characterized by interdependence and multiplicity. Nothing is wholly independent and can be fully understood by itself. Jainism believes that he alone who knows all things, knows anything completely. It means that if we have to understand one thing, we have to take it in relation to everything else. Since this is impossible in common experience, we have to grant that there is a higher experience in which it should be possible. Interdependence, if pushed to its logical conclusion, leads to monism. But Jainism stops at the first analysis of experience, disregarding its implication. The implication can be demonstrated by taking the case of spirit and matter. Jainism reduces the entire variety of the physical universe to one kind of substance, namely, *pudgala*. It also concludes that all *jīvas* are of one kind. But when it comes to the question of the relation between matter and spirit, it fights shy of tracing them to a common basis, and tries to maintain their contrast. Sāṅkhya also contrasts matter and spirit, *prakṛti* and *puruṣa*. But it is consistent in its dualism. It holds that there is no real relation between *prakṛti* and *puruṣa*; they only appear to be related. Jainism, on the contrary, admits that *jīva* and *ajīva* are in actual relation with each other, *karma*, which is itself a kind of matter, serving as a link. Yet no attempt is made to look for a common principle behind them.

The other feature of reality in the Jaina view is its plurality. Material objects as well as souls are manifold. But if we analyse this view, it inevitably points to monism. Matter is divided into an infinite number of atoms. But since all atoms are said to be of the same kind, it becomes impossible to distinguish one atom from another. The implication is that there is only a single material substance behind atoms. Similarly it is said that there is no intrinsic difference between one soul and another. All distinctions among souls are empirical; and they are adequately explained by their physical adjuncts. Even their moral differences are explained by *karma*, which is a form of matter. Such an admission points to a single spiritual substance encountering a single material substance. This dualism must, in turn, point to monism, since the two substances are said to be interdependent. In other words, there must be an Absolute as the basis of both *jīva* and *ajīva*. This is the inevitable consequence of the Jaina view, which the school is averse to accept.

> The half-hearted character of the Jaina inquiry is reflected in the sevenfold mode of predication (*sapta-bhaṅgī*), which stops at giving us the several partial views together, without attempting to overcome the opposition in them by a proper synthesis.[34]

The goal of life is to restore the soul to its native omniscience (*kevala-jñāna*). It is intuitive knowledge comprehending all things and all aspects of them. With such knowledge comes also infinite peace and infinite power. It is freedom from both good and evil, merit and demerit. The discipline prescribed for attaining it consists of right faith, right knowledge, and right conduct. The first is belief in the scriptures of Jainism; the second is knowledge of its principles; the third is practising what one has learnt. These are to be supplemented by *yoga*, or mental concentration. Of the various virtues to be cultivated, *ahiṁsā* occupies the foremost place. The whole course of discipline is marked by severity. The reason for this is to be found in the Jaina conception that *karma*, which is the link between *jīva* and *ajīva*, is matter in an extremely subtle form. The soul in its mundane condition is permeated by such *karma*-matter, binding the soul to the world. To attain freedom, the soul has to extricate itself from all *karma*.

Liberation is actually attained after death. It is a state of inactivity and bliss. It is described as *nirvāṇa*, as in Buddhism. But enlightenment may be attained even while the body lives. During the period intervening between enlightenment and actual release the *jīva* dwells without any fresh influence of *karma*. During this interval the *jīva*, which is virtually liberated, is described, as in Buddhism, an *arhant* ("the worthy one"). He becomes a *siddha* ("the perfected one") at actual release. The state of being an *arhant* resembles the ideal of *jīvanmukti* in Hinduism.

Jainism rejects the idea of a supreme Being, God, as self-discrepant. If God created the world, he cannot be supreme, for there must have been some want in him that led him to create. So, there is no God, and the world was never created. In this respect Jainism is in agreement with Mīmāṁsā. Theism conceives of the ultimate reality in the image of man. But Jainism looks upon the perfected man with the veneration given by theism to God. With the rejection of the concept of God, Jainism rejects also the idea of grace as a condition for *mokṣa*. *Mokṣa* is attained by one's own effort, keeping before one the example of those who have already attained self-perfection.

4. BUDDHISM

Early Buddhism

It is generally believed that Buddha was born in 563 BC. No direct record of his teachings has come down to us. The earliest literature available to us on Buddhism is the canon written in Pāli a couple of centuries after Buddha. Time was when scholars took for granted that the form of the doctrine as taught in the Pāli scriptures was essentially true to what Buddha taught originally. But this view has considerably changed, and attempts are made to reconstruct the original form of the creed from the Pāli scriptures. The Pāli scriptures themselves, it is said, are not homogeneous, but consist of strata which belong to different periods.[35] Though there is no unanimity among modern scholars in regard to the precise nature of Buddhism as originally taught, all are agreed that it was far more positive than one would gather from a study of the Pāli scriptures. It was also constructive, while Pāli Buddhism was analytic in character.

It is obvious that Buddhism began as a religion and that it was, in course of time, forced to become a philosophy since it had to defend itself against the metaphysical schools of Hindu and Jaina tradition. It is now generally believed that original Buddhism was an expansion within Vedic Hinduism. Its protest against Hinduism was mostly on the ritualistic side, against the over-elaborate ceremonialism of the Brāhmaṇas. As a consequence of this, emphasis was placed on moral practice. Adverse references to the teaching of the Upaniṣads are fewer, which shows that early Buddhism did not diverge from it much.

It is wrong to say, as is often done, that Buddha either denied the self or identified it with the body and the mind. He recognized the self as spirit, or the ideal self, which man ought to realize. He also believed that, as spirit, the self, or *ātman*, persists here as well as hereafter. There is an inner urge in man to realize this true self. And the effort for this end results in the "waning out" of his lower nature, which is all that is meant by liberation, or *nirvāṇa*. "It is not annihilation of the self, but only the extinguishing of selfhood in the ordinary acceptation of the term."[36] Buddha's teaching is thus a gospel of hope, and not a gospel of despair as it is commonly represented to be. As for the means to liberation, while the Upaniṣads laid stress on *yoga* as the immediate means to it, Buddha's emphasis is throughout on *dharma*, or perfect conduct.

We have to note three general features characterizing early Buddhist thought. The burden of its teaching is that all is suffering (*sarvaṁ duḥkhaṁ*). In so far as Buddhism recognizes the fact that life is full of misery, it may be described as pessimistic. But at the same time it admits the possibility of attaining freedom from pain here and now if only man makes an earnest effort. Another important feature is its positivism. The period just preceding Buddha was marked by excessive discussion of the supernatural. Buddha brought thought down to the hard facts of life. His teaching largely excludes whatever is not positively known. The general spirit of his teaching suggests that "Buddha did not recognize anything beyond the sphere of perception and reason."[37] We must also note that Buddhism is thoroughly pragmatic. Buddha generally avoided discussing metaphysical questions. This was not because he was an agnostic or knew nothing of the nature of reality. In fact, he was credited with enlightenment. The reason for his silence was that he saw no immediate use for metaphysics in lifting man from the vale of misery. He was practical and asked his disciples to set about the task of overcoming evil first. But this does not mean that metaphysics is totally absent in Buddha's teaching. There is in it a good deal of metaphysics in an implicit form. "There may be no metaphysical *aim* in what he taught; there certainly is a metaphysical *view* underlying it...."[38]

Buddhism goes along with common sense in recognizing a distinction between the soul and the material environment in which it is placed. The common belief is that sensations like heat or cold and thoughts like love or hatred do not stand by themselves, but belong to an unchanging entity known as the self. Buddhism admits the transient sensations and thoughts, but not the self as the possessor of them. The sensations and thoughts, together with the bodily frame, are themselves what is called the self. The self is an aggregate (*saṅghāta*) of mental and physical states. The Upaniṣads explained these changing states as not ultimate and regarded their substratum to be real. Buddhism does the opposite by denying the substratum and taking the mental and physical states themselves as real.

A similar explanation is given of material things. We have sensations of certain attributes like colour. Common sense believes that these attributes which we sense *belong* to the object. To Buddhism the attributes, or sense-data, are themselves the object. There is no self-sustaining substance apart from them. The reason is that there is no means of knowing it as there are in the case of the attributes. Thus material things, like the self, are also aggregates (*saṅghāta*) having no underlying unity. This doctrine is called *nairātmyavāda*, or "the doctrine of no-self," taking the word *ātman* as meaning just the essence of anything. The term *nairātmya* tells us what objects are not, while *saṅghāta* states what they are. The name given to an object is merely a symbol for an aggregate of components. It is important to note that the doctrine of *nairātmya* applies equally to the soul and material things; it is not confined to the soul alone as it is apt to be taken. It stands for the denial of a self-contained soul-substance and equally so of a self-sufficient material substance.

So far we have looked at reality without reference to time. When we consider reality in time, the aggregates, according to Buddhism, do not remain the same even for two moments. The self and the material world are each a flux (*santāna*), like a stream of water and a flame. Everything is only a series (*vīthī*)—a succession of similar events. The notion of fixity which we have of anything is wholly fictitious. This view denies both the being and the non-being of reality. Since things originate, they are not non-being. And since they perish, they are not being. Hence reality is only a becoming. There is no underlying reality to which change occurs. Change itself is the reality. Thus Buddha did not deny reality, but gave a dynamic explanation of it. Buddha himself seems to have taught only the impermanence of things. But through the force of its inherent logic, the doctrine comes, in course of time, to be transformed into one of the momentary disintegration of all things. This view that everything changes from moment to moment is known as *kṣaṇikavāda*.

The law governing the process is very important to Buddhism. If everything is a series of similar states, what is the relation between two consecutive members of the series? One explanation that was available at the time was that it was accidental. Another was that the relation owed itself to supernatural intervention like that of God. Buddhism rejects both these explanations. The relation is not accidental, because there is uniformity in nature. Buddhism is also averse to bringing in any supernatural element in explaining natural phenomena. Moreover, in neither case could men interfere with the course of things. Buddhism adopts a solution similar to that of Svabhāvavāda but with a difference. According to Svabhāvavāda, there is an inner necessity in the cause to produce the effect. Buddhism accepts the concept of necessity, but not in the same sense as above. The effect is not the mere unfolding of what is inherent in the cause. It is the result of certain external factors cooperating with the cause. "It is necessary succession, but yet the constraint implied by it is of a contingent kind."[39] It is contingent because a series does not begin until certain conditions are fulfilled; it is necessary as the series once begun will continue so long as the conditions persist. The flame-series, for example, is dependent on conditions like wick, oil, etc. This is the law of "dependent origination" (*pratītya-samutpāda*). The implication of this doctrine is that by sundering the conditions sustaining the effect, a series can be arrested. Such an admission has tremendous practical value. Buddha believes that misery can be ended, because we know the conditions that sustain it.

The practical teaching of Buddhism is in accordance with these two doctrines, viz., insubstantiality and impermanence. Since all things in the world are insubstantial and transient, it is futile to desire any of them. And since the self also is so, the craving for the preservation of the self is equally meaningless. It is ignorance of this truth that is the source of all misery. This has been illustrated in the four noble truths that Buddha is said to have preached. The first truth is that life as it is ordinarily lived is evil, i.e., full of pain. The second truth is that the origin of evil is ignorance (*avidyā*), which consists in not knowing the true nature of the self as insubstantial and impermanent. The third truth assures us that evil can be overcome. Evil has a cause, and whatever is caused is removable. There are twelve links in the cause of evil. At the bottom of the chain is ignorance. If ignorance can be ended, the cycle of birth and death can be ended. It is the principle of causation conceived in this context that was later extended to all things. Since ignorance is the cause of evil, right knowledge (*prajñā*) is the means to remove evil. This is the fourth truth. Right knowledge is enlightenment on the true nature of the self. To secure it, one requires moral training (*śīla*) and meditation (*yoga*) on the four noble truths. The discipline includes five more elements, thus making the "eightfold path."

Nirvāṇa, to which the whole discipline leads, has two meanings—"blowing out" and "becoming cool."[40] Taken in the former sense, it is a state to be attained following death. It signifies a state of annihilation. When it is reached, the false self, which is a constant procession of mental and physical states, disappears once for all. Salvation then becomes literally "the unmaking of ourselves."[41] The ideal thus presented is extremely negative in character and may not serve as an incentive to man to pursue it. Hence it is pointed out that it is more important to take the term *nirvāṇa* in the other sense of "becoming cool." So conceived, *nirvāṇa* is a state that can be attained within the span of life. It is the condition that results when perfection, or enlightenment, is reached and while yet the "individual" continues to live. This corresponds to *jīvanmukti* in other schools. It is a state where the passions and narrow desires of common life have disappeared and the person leads a life of perfect peace and equanimity. He that has attained it is known as an *arhant*, or "the worthy one." It is this state that the Buddhist really *aims at* and means by *nirvāṇa*. An *arhant*, after the dissolution of his body and mind, may come to nothing, that is to say attain *nirvāṇa* in the other sense. But this idea need not stultify the teaching, for the goal which Buddhism presents is not annihilation, but the state which precedes it. "Annihilation is only a further consequence, not the motive of the training which Buddhism prescribes."[42] To show this distinction, *nirvāṇa* after death is described as *pari-nirvāṇa*.

Before we conclude, the Buddhist position regarding *karma* and transmigration may be referred to. The Buddhist belief in transmigration seems to be inconsistent with its denial of an enduring self. To this it is replied that there could be transmigration without a transmigrating agent. Though the dead person does not survive, his disposition is transmitted to another body. It is character, not any soul, that transmigrates. *Karma* pursues the character into the next life. In this sense, the good or evil done recoils on the doer. Buddha conceived of *karma* as an impersonal law working by itself. The fruits of action are not allotted to the doer by a divine agent as in Hinduism. Nor is *karma* any subtle matter sticking to the *jīva* as in Jainism.

Later Buddhism

There was some vagueness in Buddhism as originally taught. This gave rise to great divergence of views among its followers in the later period. Moreover, Buddha passed over the theoretical basis of his practical teaching. There now springs up a remarkable interest in the theory as a result of conflict with Hindu thought. Indian thought becomes richer by this conflict.

> All the different shades of philosophic theory—realistic and idealistic—are found within Buddhism itself; and we have, so to speak, philosophy repeated twice over in India—once in the several Hindu systems and again in the different schools of Buddhism.[43]

The period is also marked by the rapid spread of Buddhism outside the country. The influence of Buddhism within the country, however, gradually declines under the stress of strengthening Hindu thought. The literature of this period is vast, and several works are written in Sanskrit.

The various views falling under later Buddhism are classifiable under two heads, Hīnayāna and Mahāyāna, which literally mean the lesser and the greater ways to salvation. From the inferiority accorded to the former it is clear that the names were devised by Mahāyāna. Hīnayāna believes in the reality of the external world, but Mahāyāna does the opposite. Hīnayāna is content to stop with pointing out the way to individual salvation, but Mahāyāna teaches that the enlightened one should work for the spiritual uplift of humanity.

The distinguishing features of early Buddhism were (i) its belief that everything is a flux (*santāna*) and (ii) its belief that everything is an aggregate altogether lacking substance (*saṅghāta*). These features continue to characterize later Buddhism; but they receive greater emphasis and formal elaboration now. A special point with regard to the doctrine of change requires to be mentioned. The idea, which started as one of impermanence in early Buddhism, gradually becomes the idea of total and perpetual change. When a seed, for example, causes the shoot, nothing of the seed survives in the shoot. Moreover, the seed is never inactive, or static. It is itself a series. When the seed is said to cause the shoot, what is meant is that the seed-series is replaced by the shoot-series. Further, no extraneous causes are necessary for destroying a thing. The germs of destruction are inherent in every object. Hence nothing can last beyond a moment.

The four Buddhist schools of this period differ sharply among themselves in respect of perception. In fact, the division of Buddhist thought into the four schools is based chiefly upon this difference. In the first instance they fall into two classes—realistic and idealistic. The former, which belong to Hīnayāna, believe in the existence of objects outside and independently of knowledge. Of course, this position is subject to the Buddhist postulate that everything is momentary. The latter group, which belong to Mahāyāna, deny external objects altogether.

In the Hīnayāna group Vaibhāṣika holds that objects are directly perceived, and Sautrāntika that they are known indirectly. The objection of Sautrāntika to the former view is that, according to the doctrine of momentariness, objects cannot be present at the time they are perceived. If things are really momentary, it is only a past thing that can be perceived. Though what is apprehended in perception does exist, it is not apprehended at the moment when it exists. Thus the so-called perception really refers to the past and resembles an inference. A member of the object-series, before it disappears, leaves its impression on the percipient mind; and it is from this impression, or idea (*ākāra*) that we come to know of the prior existence of the corresponding object. Thus what we directly know is not the object as such, but only its representation. It is through this representation that we indirectly come to know of the object. Though Sautrāntika compares the method of knowing to inference, it does not really mean that it is inference. The statement that the object is indirectly known only means that, consistent with the doctrine of momentariness, the object is postulated as a *hypothesis* to account for the fact of perception.

Vaibhāṣika may be described as pluralistic realism. In accordance with the doctrine of momentariness, it holds that the content of perception is always a bare unrelated particular, a member of a series. It is represented by the term *sva-lakṣaṇa*, which means that everyone under this head is unique. The basis of the external world is an indefinite number of *sva-lakṣaṇas*. They are diverse, having no unity among themselves. Every *sva-lakṣaṇa* is produced by the preceding one in its series and in turn produces the succeeding one.

Sva-lakṣaṇas are apprehended directly by the senses. But the act of perception is accompanied by certain subjective determinations (*kalpanā*), which are of five classes; generality, quality, action, name, and substance. Everything that appears to us appears through their medium. Thus perception includes much more than what is actually presented to the senses. Mental forms are superimposed on the *sva-lakṣaṇas*. These conceptual elements are called *sāmānya-lakṣaṇa*. *Sva-lakṣaṇas* alone are real. The *sāmānya-lakṣaṇas*, which are constitutive of the mind, appear transferred to the object. Therefore, they are illusory and have no ontological status. But, though imaginary, these mental forms are the basis of our practical life as they help us to distinguish and relate objects. In view of these subjective elements, Vaibhāṣika is not naive realism. Sautrāntika agrees with this analysis. The only difference between these two schools is that while Vaibhāṣika admits that *sva-lakṣaṇa* is directly cognized, Sautrāntika regards it as indirectly known.

The complicated explanation of perception given by Sautrāntika may be said to prepare the way for the idealistic school of Yogācāra. If, as Sautrāntika maintains, objects are really known only indirectly, i.e. through the occurrence of images, or ideas, in the mind, there is no need to assume the existence of the object at all. We may account for the occurrence of the idea by saying that it is generated by the mind itself. The so-called objects are not encountered by the mind, but are created by it. Secondly, if relations between objects (*sāmānya-lakṣaṇa*) are subjective, as both Vaibhāṣika and Sautrāntika hold, we may as well regard the objects (*sva-lakṣaṇa*) as subjective. Thus Yogācāra abolishes the logical distinction between *sva-lakṣaṇa* and *sāmānya-lakṣaṇa*, and regards the very concept of externality as subjective. The only reality is *vijñāna*, or knowledge-series; its whole content is false. Knowledge is a succession of ideas. The specific form which an idea assumes is determined, in this view, not by any external object, but by the impression left on the mind by the previous experience. Since Yogācāra believes in nothing except ideas (*vijñāna*), it is called Vijñānavāda.

Yogācāra assumes that the *vijñāna*-series is of unlimited number. The doctrine is thus pluralistic, though idealistic. It is objected that in the absence of externality it is impossible to assert the existence of more than one self. And the logical result would be solipsism. If external objects could be rejected, the existence of all selves besides one's own must also be rejected. Though such a conclusion cannot be proved to be wrong, it stultifies the very basis of practical life. There are indications to show that to overcome this difficulty, some adherents of Yogācāra have postulated a cosmic, or absolute, *vijñāna*-series of which everything is regarded as but an appearance. On this basis, the doctrine is found described as Vijñānādvaita and classed with Ātmādvaita of Śaṅkara.[44] Such a development suggests the influence of the Upaniṣads; but the Buddhist commitment is not abandoned as even the ultimate *vijñāna* is only becoming. On the whole, the Yogācāra reasoning has a negative force, which cannot be easily thrust aside. Its strength lies in pointing to the indemonstrability of the opposite view maintained by realism.

Yogācāra, while denying the reality of external objects, takes for granted that the subject-series at least is real. Mādhyamika denies the reality not only of external objects, but also of the self. Such a position is reached by showing that the scrutiny of the things of common experience leads nowhere. The very notion of things, whether physical or psychical, is riddled with contradictions. This is best illustrated by the interpretation by this school of the old Buddhist idea of causation. The other Buddhist schools believe that there is nothing that is uncaused. But Mādhyamika points out that the very notion of an object originating is inconceivable. If it exists prior to origination, it does not require to be produced. And if it is non-existent then, it is impossible to produce it, for what is nothing cannot become something. Hence the notion of causation is itself a delusion. And if we take this conclusion along with the admission that everything is momentary, we shall see that the whole universe is self-discrepant. The only escape from such difficulties is to regard objects as having no intrinsic character (*nissvabhāva*), in other words as illusory. The same argument is extended to *vijñāna*, or stream of ideas, and it is also dismissed as devoid of self-essence. This line of reasoning leads Mādhyamika to conclude that knowledge as a whole is invalid. It accordingly believes neither in outer reality nor in inner, and is described as Śūnyavāda, or "the doctrine of the void."

However, it is necessary to add that the denial of reality by this school is only from the ultimate standpoint. The system grants a sort of reality (*saṁvṛti-satya*) to the subject as well as to the object in order to explain the activities of everyday life. Thus things are real relative to common life, but their final significance is nothing. For this reason the system may be called "relativism." But it is impossible to speak of a relative reality without recognizing an absolute one. Moreover, it is impossible to deny the self altogether, for to think of the absence of consciousness is itself a state of consciousness.

It may be asked whether the Mādhyamika teaching is entirely devoid of anything positive. Hindu and Jaina works represent it as totally nihilistic. And for this reason they denounce it as self-contradictory. They point out that the negation of everything is inconceivable without implying a positive ground (*avadhi*). "Nothing can be proved false, if nothing is taken as true."[45] But Candrakīrti, a later exponent of this school, points out that the nihilism of Mādhyamika is different from common, or vulgar, nihilism. It is not dogmatic denial, but is the result of a logical scrutiny of experience.

Some modern scholars see a positive implication in Mādhyamika.[46] To them the word *śūnya* does not mean absolute nothingness, but nothingness *as it were*, since reality is altogether incomprehensible. The ground for this view is the Mādhyamika definition of the ultimate reality, according to which, nothing can be predicated of it. "It excludes all conceivable predicates, including that of non-existence; and the ultimate has accordingly to be viewed as beyond all conception, and not as absolute nothing."[47] Such an interpretation is logically involved in the doctrine, since the negation of anything necessarily implies a positive ground (*avadhi*) as demanded by critics. So, the system may be said to accept an Absolute, though ineffable. If the above positive interpretation is accepted, along with the idea of absolute consciousness in Yogācāra, the goal of life in Mahāyāna Buddhism should be merging in the Absolute, not annihilation as in Hīnayāna Buddhism.

In spite of the extreme position maintained by Mādhyamika, we can say that the difference between Mādhyamika and the other three schools of Buddhism is not much. All the four are idealistic in varying degrees, for according to all of them alike, common knowledge contains elements which are superimposed by the mind. All are agreed that what are regarded as the general features of things (*sāmānya-lakṣaṇa*) have no objective reality and are entirely due to the nature of thought. ". . . scholastic Buddhism as a whole regards the greater part of common knowledge as only conventionally true. The Mādhyamika merely extends this principle to all experience."[48]

To all the four Buddhist schools, inference is only of provisional value. Inference is based on a supposed relation between two terms, but according to all the four Buddhist schools, relations are all false, as they are only mental forms read into external objects. Therefore inference can have no final validity, though it serves the purposes of practical life. As regards perception, Mādhyamika regards even this as only of provisional value, as it rejects all reality, external and internal. Yogācāra may be placed on the same footing, since it also refuses to recognize external objects. In the Sautrāntika view also the validity of perception is not absolute, since it postulates the external world as a mere hypothesis to explain perception. It is only in the Vaibhāṣika school that perception can claim any logical value, in so far as it admits that external objects are real and are directly known. But even here perception is not without a subjective element.

We may add a word about the practical teaching of later Buddhism. The Hīnayāna scheme of discipline is virtually the same as in canonical Buddhism. But Mahāyāna modifies it in two important respects. The attainment of liberation by the individual is no longer considered the ultimate aim. The person who succeeds in acquiring enlightenment (*arhant*) has, according to the earlier doctrine, only to wait for his liberation (*nirvāṇa*). But in Mahāyāna he is expected to work for the similar uplift of all his fellow beings. Such a one is called a *bodhisattva*, which literally means "wisdom-being."[49] It is definitely an ideal superior to that of the *arhant*. The *bodhisattva*, it is believed, can even transfer his own good deeds to others, thereby mitigating the rigour of their *karma*. Such a feature naturally evokes devotion (*bhakti*) towards the *bodhisattva*. Buddha himself thus comes to be deified in Mahāyāna, whereas he is essentially a gifted human being to Hīnayāna.

REFERENCES

1. *OIP*, p. 177.
2. Ibid., p. 179.
3. *EIP*, p. 44.
4. *PEIP*, p. 27.
5. *EIP*, p. 45.
6. *OIP*, p. 180.
7. Vide *EIP*, p. 44, n. 19.
8. Vide ibid., p. 204, n. 19.
9. Vide *OIP*, p. 180, n. 1.
10. Ibid., p. 181.
11. Ibid.
12. Ibid.
13. Ibid., p. 182, n. 1.
14. *PEIP*, p. 28.
15. *OIP*, p. 182, n. 4.
16. Ibid., p. 183.
17. *EIP*, p. 48.
18. Ibid.
19. Ibid., p. 49.
20. Ibid., p. 50.
21. Ibid., p. 51.
22. Ibid., p. 52.
23. Vide *IPS—I*, p. 73, n. 2.
24. Ibid., p. 74.
25. Ibid., p. 75.
26. Ibid., p. 76.
27. Vide *PEIP*, p. 25.
28. Vide ibid., p. 26.
29. *OIP*, p. 188.
30. *PEIP*, p. 26.
31. *EIP*, p. 58.
32. *OIP*, p. 195.
33. Ibid., p. 163.
34. Ibid., pp. 172-73.
35. Vide *R*, p. 79.
36. *EIP*, p. 73.
37. *OIP*, p. 137.
38. Ibid., p. 138.
39. Ibid., p. 143.
40. Ibid., p. 152.
41. Ibid.
42. Ibid., p. 153.
43. Ibid., p. 198.
44. Vide ibid., pp. 219-20.
45. Ibid., p. 221.
46. Vide *EIP*, pp. 82-83.
47. Ibid., pp. 82-83.
48. *OIP*, p. 221.
49. *EIP*, p. 83.

5

Metaphysics—Part Two

1. NYĀYA-VAIŚEṢIKA

We now take up the schools which are directly or indirectly based on the Veda. They are six in number, but they actually represent four different points of view in their understanding of the nature of reality. Between Nyāya and Vaiśeṣika, it is the latter that mainly goes into the ontological question of the nature of reality. Nyāya, generally following the same ontological point of view as Vaiśeṣika, emphasizes the epistemological question of how that nature comes to be discovered. Similarly, while Sāṅkhya is mainly metaphysical, Yoga, which mainly deals with spiritual discipline, has, except for some deviation, the same point of view as Sāṅkhya. We have then the metaphysical points of view of Mīmāṁsā and Vedānta, thus making four viewpoints in all.[1]

The point of view of Nyāya-Vaiśeṣika may be described as radical pluralism. The system postulates an infinite number of ultimate reals, which are absolutely different from one another. But they are not all disconnected, as they are classifiable under seven categories (*padārtha*). The first is *dravya*, which may be roughly translated as "substance." The rest are the various properties and relations of substance. The seven categories together explain the whole universe.

The *dravyas* are not all material. So Nyāya-Vaiśeṣika is not materialistic like Cārvāka. At the same time the system treats all *dravyas* alike, including the self. There are nine *dravyas*: earth, water, fire, air, *ākāśa*, time, space, self, and *manas*. The first five are the elements (*bhūta*). Their names refer to five kinds of atoms, which are partless, eternal, and infinite in number. Material objects are derived from atoms of earth, water, fire, and air. *Ākāśa* atoms do not produce anything. Time and space are conceived as objective realities. They are infinite and partless. Time is measured only indirectly by movements of objects, such as the sun. Similarly space is defined only in terms of objects in space. In other words, time and space are not of atomic structure. Points in space and instants in time are only conventional divisions of them. *Ākāśa* is not the same as space; it is what fills space.

The inclusion of the self under *dravya* shows that its conception here is not entirely spiritual. The self is many and each is eternal. Though theoretically omnipresent, for all practical purposes, the self is associated with a physical organism, where it feels, thinks, and acts. Knowledge (*jñāna*) is regarded as an attribute of the self, and that too, not as an essential, but only as an adventitious one. Dreamless sleep, where the self is not characterized by knowledge, is evidence of its adventitious nature. "The self thus differs from matter only in that it *may* become conscious and not in that it is itself mental in nature."[1] Desire and volition are two other similar attributes. The really mental, or spiritual, element, according to the doctrine, is not the self, but these three attributes which are all transient. *Manas*, which is the last *dravya*, is the link that connects the self with the senses and the body, through which we come to be related to the external world. It is the instrument of knowing. If the *manas* is inactive or otherwise engaged, no knowledge is possible whether of an external object or of an internal state. Though it helps in acquiring knowledge, it at the same time restricts the field of knowledge to select objects. It is incorrect to translate the term as "mind," for it is inert like any other sense and is separate for each self. Association with the *manas* is the basic cause of bondage, for, unlike the body and senses, it does not perish at death.

Dravyas serve merely as the framework of the universe. Their various properties and the relations into which they may enter are the other categories. These are *guṇa*, *karma*, *sāmānya*, *viśeṣa*, *samavāya*, and *abhāva*. *Guṇas* are attributes which pertain to one or more *dravyas*. Though dependent on *dravya*, they are altogether distinct from it. They are objective in status and can be known by themselves. They are not necessarily eternal. There are material and mental qualities. *Karma* represents various kinds of movement belonging to *dravya*. Infinite *dravyas,* however, are always stable. Like *guṇa*, *karma* too has independent ontological status. *Sāmānya* is a feature common to two or more things, in other words a universal, e.g., "cowness" in two cows. It is by virtue of *sāmānya* that objects are classifiable. *Sāmānya* is in all and in each. It can be apprehended only through a particular, e.g., "cowness" is known only through a cow. But though particular and universal appear together, they are distinct entities. Even things belonging to the same class are different from one another. Thus "cowness" belongs to two cows, but the two cows are different. *Viśeṣa* is the differentia of ultimate things which are otherwise alike. For example, two atoms of earth or two selves resemble each other in their intrinsic form. If they are yet distinguished as two, there must be a distinctive feature in each. That feature is its *viśeṣa*.

Samavāya is necessary relation, for example, the relation between substance and quality, say a rose and its redness, which are distinguishable but not separable. This is contrasted with the relation between two entities which are merely together, like a table and a rose placed on it. The latter is called *saṁyoga,* or conjunction. Yet both relations are conceived as external, consistent with the pluralism of the school. That *saṁyoga* is external, is evident. But the system regards even *samavāya* as external. This is because the necessity involved is only one-sided. The red colour presupposes the rose, but the reverse does not hold good. In *saṁyoga* both the terms related are equally independent, but in *samavāya* one is independent. "...relation, as conceived here, is not a bond of unity; it is rather a sign of difference."[2]

The last category is *abhāva,* or negation. Nyāya-Vaiśeṣika is realistic. It believes that all knowledge by its very nature points to an object beyond it and independent of it. The recognition of *abhāva* as a category is the result of its realism. If knowledge of an object points to the existence of the object outside it, equally so the knowledge of its negation should point to its non-existence apart from such knowledge. As in the positive sphere, so in the negative, knowledge must be different from the known. In other words, "absence of an object is not the same as the knowledge of its absence."[3] However, by absence of an object (*abhāva*) is meant only "the negation of something somewhere and not absolute nothing (*śūnya*), which the Nyāya-Vaiśeṣika dismisses as unthinkable or as a pseudo-idea."[4] We may speak of the negation of a jar in a room, but never of negation itself. It shows that *abhāva* is relative to *bhāva*, or presence. Thus, unlike the other categories, this is a relative concept. It corresponds to the predicate in a negative judgement, like "the lotus is *not* blue." Four varieties of negation are mentioned: (i) *prāgabhāva,* e.g., the absence of a jar before production, (ii) *dhvaṁsābhāva,* e.g., its absence after destruction, (iii) *atyantābhāva,* e.g., the bare ground with no jar on it, and (iv) *anyonyābhāva,* or mutual negation between two things, e.g., between a jar and a cloth. The last is the same as *bheda,* or difference.

We may briefly state the theory of causation in the system as it also illustrates its pluralistic and realistic character. The system believes that causation is the production of something new (*ārambhavāda*). It means that the effect is non-existent prior to production (*asatkāryavāda*). This does not mean that the effect can exist apart from the cause. The effect inheres in the material cause as a quality may be said to do in a substance. It is a relation of *samavāya*. Another point to be noted is that all such products are impermanent. That is to say, just as the non-existent comes to be, the existent product later ceases to be. Unlike Buddhism, Nyāya-Vaiśeṣika maintains that a product will last at least for two instants—those of origination and persistence. Produced things abide not only in space and time, but also in permanent substances like atoms. Thus the universe consists of permanent things and changing things which depend on them. This view of change is different from that of Buddhism and Jainism. To the former, change alone is real. To the latter, change takes place to an enduring substance. But here change is only an addition to permanence, though dependent on it.

The atoms which Nyāya-Vaiśeṣika postulates are mere abstractions, and the system fails to reconstruct concrete wholes out of them. The existence of atoms is deduced from the known divisibility of material objects. They are the uncaused cause of all that is transient in the material universe. The origination of objects takes place by a process of conjunction of atoms and their destruction, by their disjunction. It is in this connection that the idea of God enters into the system. It seems to be a later addition. When the question arises how inert atoms combine at all to make the world, it is said that it is an all-powerful God that initiates the process by suitably disposing the atoms to combine. God not only creates the world in this sense, but also protects it and in due course destroys it to create it again. The guiding factor in the whole process is the past *karma* of individual selves, which are to be born in a particular *kalpa*.

The idea of God is not fully developed in the system. He is not the Supreme Being of Vedānta. He is classed under *ātman* and described as *paramātman* to distinguish him from the *jīvātman*, or individual self. Further, the existence of God is established through inference and not through revelation as in Vedānta. But in trying to do so, one of its thinkers, Udayana, takes full advantage of the lack of any proof to the non-existence of God. He shows that none of the *pramāṇas* can be adduced to make out that God does not exist. Though a dialectical device, this has some force against atheism. He also says that the universality of the belief in God is sufficient proof of it.

The goal of life is conceived in this system in a negative way. It consists in escaping from pain (*apavarga*). Freedom from pain does not mean the attainment of happiness. The doctrine believes that pain and pleasure are so inextricably bound with each other that the avoidance of pain necessitates avoiding pleasure as well. So *mokṣa* is a state where there is neither pleasure nor pain. Such a state is attainable because pleasure and pain are adventitious to the self as evidenced by sleep. In fact, all experience is accidental to the self and comes only by its association with the body and senses. Bondage arises from the wrong notion that pleasure and pain are necessary features of the self. Knowledge of its intrinsic nature as devoid of both is the means to *mokṣa*. From being a reasoned conviction it must become an intuition. For this, the practice of *yoga* is necessary. Such a conception obliterates the difference between soul and matter and is hardly attractive. But a conception of *mokṣa* has to be judged not by what it is said to be after life for an enlightened person, but by how he lives after enlightenment and before death. Such a person, according to the school, though he is not free from pain and pleasure, would have learnt to endure pain and ignore pleasure and lead a life without selfishness, narrow love, and hate.

2. MĪMĀṀSĀ

The Mīmāṁsā point of view is pluralistic like that of Nyāya-Vaiśeṣika, but not radically so. Of the two branches of Mīmāṁsā, that of Kumārila is more influential, and this admits of what may be called "sectional synthesis." It believes in the existence of a plurality of souls and a multiplicity of material ultimates. But it also effects relations in portions of reality. We shall mainly deal with Kumārila's doctrine.

Of the seven categories formulated by Nyāya-Vaiśeṣika, Mīmāṁsā accepts only five, viz., substance, quality, action, universals, and non-existence. *Samavāya* and *viśeṣa* are rejected as arbitrary assumptions. In explaining relations between two entities, instead of *samavāya,* the system adopts the principle of identity in difference (*bhedābheda*).

Substance (*dravya*) and attribute (*guṇa*), e.g., a rose and its redness, are not totally distinct as in Vaiśeṣika; they are distinct and, at the same time, identical. Each taken by itself is an abstraction; it is their concrete unity that is real. Thus the relation is not external as in Vaiśeṣika but internal. If the two were entirely different, they should be separable; but they are not, as even Nyāya-Vaiśeṣika admits. They together form an identity in difference (*bhedābheda*), a conception which is found in Jainism and Sāṅkhya-Yoga also. The relation is termed *tādātmya*. The word, of course, means identity, but all identity, according to Kumārila, is identity in difference. It is because they are identical that we are able to predicate qualities of substances. It is not right to postulate absolute difference just because the notion of *two* arises, or absolute unity just because the notion of *one* does. "This way of viewing things, it is clear, compromises in a large measure the pluralism of the doctrine, and shows that it is not radically pluralistic as the Nyāya-Vaiśeṣika is."[5]

Another evidence of such partial synthesis in the system is in reference to universals. Universals not only represent common features of corresponding particulars, but actually link up those particulars. Two or more cows form a unity in diversity—again a relation of identity in difference. Thus there are synthesized groups of particulars instead of independent particulars as in Vaiśeṣika.

According to Nyāya-Vaiśeṣika, the ultimate units of all physical objects are atoms, which are indivisible and super-sensuous particles of matter. Kumārila admits that the basis of the physical universe is plural, but in tracing the ultimate entities, he stops at sensible particles such as the motes seen in the rays of the sun. The Nyāya belief in atoms is based not on perception, but on inference and the insight of seers. Mīmāṁsā does not recognize individual insight as a *pramāṇa* and regards the use of inference against the facts of perception as unjustified. According to it, the only authority on supra-sensuous matters is revelation; but revelation is silent on the existence of atoms. Like Nyāya, Mīmāṁsā also holds that the ultimate particles of the four elements, viz., earth, water, fire, and air, combine to produce the various objects of the world. The relation between these objects, which are wholes, and the ultimate particles, or parts, which make them is again conceived as *tādātmya*, or *bhedābheda*. Thus whole and parts are not absolutely distinct, but distinct while being the same.

The relation between the particles and the objects which they compose leads to the wider question of the relation between material cause and effect. The Kumārila school believes in *satkāryavāda*. The effect is existent in the material cause before production, though not in the same form. It manifests itself by a transformation of the material cause (*pariṇāmavāda*). It rejects the Nyāya view that a substance (*dravya*) can be produced anew. Every substance is eternal, though its attributes, or modes, may change, and the substance endures through these changes. The clay becomes a pot or a jug and so on. But the same material persists in all of them. The relation between the material cause and the effect, according to this theory, is one of identity in difference (*bhedābheda*) and not *samavāya*. In this view of causation the system agrees with Sāṅkhya-Yoga.

So far we have seen how aspects of the physical world are synthesized in Kumārila's Mīmāṁsā on the principle of identity in difference. But the system stops with such partial synthesis instead of extending its principle to unify the whole of physical reality. Even so, it gives a more satisfactory solution to the problem of the one and the many than Nyāya-Vaiśeṣika. Prabhākara, in contrast, recognizes *samavāya* as a category and, in so doing, completely rejects the relation of *bhedābheda* admitted by Kumārila. As a consequence, substance and attribute, universal and particular, and material cause and effect come to be conceived as altogether distinct as in Nyaya-Vaiśeṣika.

The conception of the self in Kumārila's system is also superior to that of Nyāya. Knowledge (*jñāna*) is not an adventitious quality of the self; it is an innate phase of it. The self, thus, is by itself spiritual. Knowledge represents a process (*vyāpāra*) in the self, and implies that the self undergoes modal change while knowing objects. Though undergoing modifications, the self is regarded as eternal. According to Kumārila, change does not militate against permanence. Experience shows us many things that change almost constantly, but yet maintain their identity. The senses including *manas* furnish the external conditions which induce change in the self constituting knowledge. According to Nyāya, in sleep there is total absence of knowledge. But Kumārila holds that though knowledge is not manifest then, the self is characterized by the potency to know (*jñāna-śakti*). The relation between the self and *jñāna* is explained as one of identity in difference (*bhedābheda*). In the conception of the self Prabhākara more or less sides with Nyāya-Vaiśeṣika.

Nyāya recognizes a supreme self, or God, in addition to individual selves. But Mīmāṁsā as a whole rejects the idea of God. In fact, elaborate arguments are adduced by Kumārila to show that there is no such entity. We cannot, for example, satisfactorily account for the presence of misery in the world if it were created by an omnipotent and benevolent God. Indian doctrines usually explain this by reference to the past *karma* of individual selves. But Mīmāṁsā contends that if *karma* has to be cited to explain misery in spite of recognizing God, it can as well be taken as the full explanation of it (as in Jainism). As a consequence of rejecting the idea of God, Mīmāṁsā looks upon the world as self-existent. Neither had it a beginning nor will it have an end. The system thus rejects the theory of cycles put forward by many other Hindu schools. Origin, growth, and decay characterize only individual things in the world; the world as a whole "was never other than what it is now."[6] Just because it denies God, the system cannot be equated with materialism, for it believes in surviving souls and in the theory of *karma*. In fact, it lays greater emphasis on the ethical side of the universe than theistic doctrines with their reliance on divine grace.

In its earlier phase Mīmāṁsā regarded *dharma* as the highest value. The concept of *mokṣa* is a later addition, and, with this, *dharma* comes to be subordinated to *mokṣa*. The conception of *mokṣa* in Mīmāṁsā is similar to that in Nyāya-Vaiśeṣika. It is a negative state of escape from suffering and along with it from pleasure. The only difference is in regard to the means to *mokṣa*, which is *karma* here instead of *jñāna*. Abstention from optional and prohibited deeds and the performance of obligatory ones secures freedom from rebirth.

3. SĀṄKHYA-YOGA

Sāṅkhya is frankly dualistic. It recognizes two ultimate and separate entities, nature and spirit. They are termed *prakṛti* and *puruṣa* respectively. The system has a more synthetic understanding of nature than Kumārila's Mīmāṁsā. Kumārila's synthesis of nature is half-hearted. He applies the principle of identity in difference (*bhedābheda*) to explain only select aspects of nature. But Sāṅkhya extends the same principle to the whole of nature by bringing it under a single head, *prakṛti*, which, though one, contains the many. All things in the physical world are evolved out of *prakṛti*. Accordingly, nature ceases to be discontinuous as in Nyāya or Mīmāṁsā. The whole of the physical world forms a unity in diversity. Though, as we shall see, the same principle of synthesis is not extended either to the realm of *puruṣa* or between *puruṣa* and *prakṛti*, the system has a clearer perception of the spiritual nature of the self than even Kumārila's Mīmāṁsā.

Prakṛti, which is a primal entity, is not directly perceived. Its existence, like that of atoms in Nyāya, has to be inferred. Effects presuppose a cause. The world objects must have a source, and that source is *prakṛti*. Generally speaking, Sāṅkhya prefers a rationalistic explanation in support of its conclusions, instead of invoking the aid of revelation. *Prakṛti*, though one, is complex in nature. It is constituted of three factors, each of which is described as a *guṇa*. The term *guṇa* here does not mean "a quality" as it commonly does, but "a constituent" of *prakṛti*. The three constituents are distinct in nature, but they are interdependent, so that they can never be separated from one another. They form "a unity in trinity." The three *guṇas* are *sattva*, *rajas*, and *tamas*. Each of them stands for a distinct aspect of physical reality, *sattva* signifying whatever is pure and fine, *rajas*, whatever is active, and *tamas*, whatever is stolid and offers resistance. To the experiencing mind they are respectively the sources of pleasure (*sukha*), pain (*duḥkha*), and bewilderment (*moha*). Though they are thus somewhat antagonistic in their nature, they act in harmony. Consequently, the physical world is an orderly whole with its own laws. Everything that emerges from *prakṛti* is also constituted of these three *guṇas*, for, according to the doctrine, the effects are essentially identical with their material cause. In fact, it is the common and enduring features of things that give us an idea of the nature of *prakṛti*.

The three *guṇas* are in a state of equilibrium in *prakṛti* until it begins to differentiate itself into the various things constituting the world. The diversity in these things is due to the diverse proportions in which the *guṇas* enter into their make-up. "Though only three in number, the *guṇas* thus really stand for a manifold of distinctions."[7] *Prakṛti* is thus not only complex, but also all-pervasive. Further, *prakṛti* is undergoing evolution (*pariṇāma*) perpetually while maintaining its identity as long as it lasts. A period of evolution (*sṛṣṭi*) is followed by a period of dissolution (*pralaya*), when the whole diversity of the world becomes latent in *prakṛti*. Thus the process of *prakṛti* is cyclical.

The things that emerge from *prakṛti* are predominated by one or other of the three *guṇas*. Most of the things of the material world as well as our physical frame are such that *tamas* predominates in them. They are objective. Those in which *sattva* predominates are of fine structure and comprise the psychic apparatus by the aid of which external objects get revealed to the spirit, or *puruṣa*. Of this group, the most important member is the *antaḥkaraṇa*, or the "internal organ." Its chief function is to receive impressions from outside and suitably respond to them. It is assisted by the senses, which also belong to this group. The whole psychic apparatus is specific to each individual and accompanies him through all his lives as his "subtle body" (*liṅga-śarīra*). It is cast off only when freedom is achieved.

On the relation between the material cause and the effect, the view here is the opposite of what is found in Nyāya-Vaiśeṣika. The effect is supposed to be in the material cause always in a latent form. Nothing can come into being afresh or pass away finally. This is called *satkāryavāda*. What is latent becomes manifest by a change of form (*pariṇāma*). Thus material cause and effect are not quite distinct; they form an identity in difference. Sāṅkhya-Yoga recognizes efficient and final causes also. The final cause, or purpose, in the evolution of *prakṛti* is providing for worldly experience (*bhoga*) and release (*apavarga*) to the *puruṣa*. The efficient cause is conceived in the system in a negative way. It is useful only in removing obstacles to the manifestation of the effect from the cause. *Prakṛti* has the potency for evolution, but its direction to the final end requires an efficient cause, or stimulus. According to Sāṅkhya, this initial stimulus is the mere presence (*sannidhi*) of *puruṣa*. Such a solution is far from satisfactory. Why the stimulus should come only at a particular point of time when both *puruṣa* and *prakṛti* are eternal and omnipresent, is one difficulty. Another is the real meaning of *puruṣa*'s presence when *puruṣa* is said to be manifold.

The existence of *puruṣa*, like that of *prakṛti*, is reached through reason. If *prakṛti* exists, *puruṣa* too should exist to know it. *Prakṛti* lacks the very element by which its awareness is possible, viz., sentience. It is *puruṣa* that represents this. Objects point to the subject, the non-sentient to the sentient. Another argument is based on the design found in the physical world. Instances show the presence of purpose in various objects. The adaptation of the bodily organism, for example, suggests that it is meant to serve a definite end. It is thus concluded that the entity which all the adaptations and contrivances in the world serve is *puruṣa*. In other words, nature evolves *for the sake of* spirit. Thus the character of common things is the basis for inferring both *prakṛti* and *puruṣa*. It points to *prakṛti* as their *first* cause and to *puruṣa* as their *final* cause.

Puruṣa is manifold, unlike *prakṛti*. The plurality of *puruṣas* is deduced from the fact observed that persons differ in their endowments and temperaments. But the system fails to see that what is true in their empirical condition need not be true in their essential nature. The system itself admits that in the liberated state there is no difference between one self and another. But in that case we fail to see how they could be many instead of being one. The logical conclusion to be drawn from this is that if a single *prakṛti* points to the existence of *puruṣa*, that *puruṣa* should also be one—"cosmic nature enshrining a cosmic self."[8]

The nature of *puruṣa* is the very opposite of that of *prakṛti*. *Puruṣa* is not complex, but simple; it is passive, a mere "looker on" (*sākṣin*), while *prakṛti* is ever active. By itself it is only an experient (*bhoktā*). It serves as an agent (*kartā*) and a knower (*jñātā*) only when it is associated with and assisted by the internal organ and its adjuncts. This association is false, a result of the ignorance of one's true nature. When so associated in the empirical condition, it is more properly called *jīva*. There is in it the true self and also the internal organ, which is a product of *prakṛti* falsely associated with it. In what is called self-knowledge what we really know is only this non-self, or knowable element which is included in the *jīva*. This does not mean that the self is unaware of itself, for it is regarded as the essence of sentience. In thus distinguishing the non-spiritual aspect of our personality from its true spiritual aspect, the system makes a sharp division between *puruṣa* and *prakṛti*, which are entirely opposed to each other.

The exact manner in which these two disparate entities come together remains a difficult question in the system. But whatever the explanation, it is admitted that they cooperate and virtually act as one. It is a matter of experience that a spirit needs a body to operate and a body requires a spirit to activate it. However, this complex of nature and spirit is only the empirical self (*jīva*), and not the true, or transcendental, self (*puruṣa*). The product of *prakṛti* that most intimately enters into this union is the internal organ, and next in order are the senses and the body. "…spirit without nature is inactive and nature without spirit is blind."[9] Each finds its complement in the other, and the defects of both are made good. This association of the two is found not only in ordinary life, but also in *jīvanmukti*, in which the system believes in a literal sense. When the *jīvanmukta* departs this life, *puruṣa* which is immortal, remains in itself, wholly emancipated from nature. That condition is described as *kaivalya*, which means "isolation," or "aloofness," to distinguish it from *jīvanmukti*.

The empirical self, which is not a detached entity like *puruṣa*, is subject to the tendencies acquired in the course of its past lives. And these render its apprehension of an object selective. Its knowledge does not interfere with the nature of the thing apprehended, but owing to subjective limitations, a person at any particular time happens to know only some or other features of it, omitting the rest. The nature of the selection made in the case of any object depends on the past life or character of the person apprehending it. This is the reason why a thing that attracts one may repel another. The aspect under which an individual perceives the world is thus intimately personal to him. This does not mean subjectivism, for the different world-views point to an objective world which is common to all and is real in its own right. The chief argument in support of this realistic position is that, in spite of differences among men in their views of things, there are points of agreement among them in regard to their existence and nature. Thus the system avoids both bare realism and extreme subjectivism. Neither are things precisely as they are apprehended nor does the mind make its own things. "It is *we* who know, just as truly as it is the *world* that is known."[10]

Knowledge as commonly known to us is thus personal and fragmentary. The *whole* world is presented to no person at one and the same time. And so far as knowledge is not recognized to be thus partial, it becomes an error. It is an error of omission (*akhyāti*), though not of commission (*viparīta-khyāti*). Such a view of knowledge teaches humility about one's own view and regard for the views of others. "In one word, it bespeaks toleration which, as a matter of fact, is a striking feature of all Indian thought."[11] Ordinary knowledge being thus imperfect, truth consists in comprehensive knowledge, which lays appropriate emphasis on all aspects of the object known. The question arises whether such knowledge is possible. The internal organ, being essentially of the nature of *sattva*, is capable of revealing all that is. But as a matter of fact, *rajas* or *tamas* predominates it in life and renders knowledge partial. He who has succeeded in subduing these two factors and has restored the internal organ to its *sāttvika* nature acquires intuitive vision of the whole of *prakṛti* as it is. In that state one sees through *prakṛti* and realizes its absolute distinction from *puruṣa*. It is the knowledge of this distinction (*viveka-jñāna*) rather than that of the world as it is, that is stated to be the means to release. *Prakṛti* itself has a part to play in this fulfilment. "It is designed for this end and exists solely for it."[12] Worldly life is a necessary preparation for this consummation. All alike have to pass through the experiences of common life (*bhoga*) before their mind is turned towards the final goal (*apavarga*). "It means that the true ideal does not suggest itself to anyone that has not seen for himself the imperfections of *saṁsāra*."[13]

The discipline that leads to this goal is long and is fully described in the allied system of Yoga. The discipline comprises what are described as the eight limbs (*aṅga*) of meditation (*yoga*). We may refer to only one point in it which marks a departure from Sāṅkhya. It is the recognition of God in Yoga. Sāṅkhya is rationalistic. Even the design of the world is cited by it not to point to a designer (God), but to one whose end it is meant to serve, viz., *puruṣa*. But Yoga introduces the concept of God on practical grounds. Devotion to God is regarded as one of the virtues to be cultivated (*niyama*) as a step in the practice of *yoga*. Again, such devotion (*bhakti*) is suggested as an alternative to the elaborate path of *yoga* to attain the *viveka-jñāna* alluded to earlier. However, the conception of God here is nowhere near that of Vedānta. *Īśvara* here is *one* of the *puruṣas*, though a perfect one. Though omnipresent, he is not all-comprehensive. He is not responsible for the creation of the world, which is the spontaneous work of *prakṛti*. All that he is stated to do is to prompt, in a way, the evolution of *prakṛti* by bringing about its connection with *puruṣa*.

4. PRE-VIEW OF VEDĀNTA

The idea of the ultimate reality becomes a prominent feature of Vedānta as the principle which unites the realm of nature and the realm of selves. We here pass from dualism to monism. The whole of the objective universe as well as the individual selves are traced to the ultimate reality designated as Brahman or *ātman*. The doctrine thus not only integrates the physical reality like Sāṅkhya, but also establishes the unity of all things, physical and spiritual. "Brahman constitutes the continuant element, and the *jīvas* as well as the multifarious forms of nature its changing phases."[14]

Sāṅkhya unifies all physical things under the concept of *prakṛti*, which is said to be self-evolving. But here *prakṛti* itself is traced to Brahman as its basis. And it is Brahman that is the source of the multifarious things of the world. Brahman thus comprehends the entire universe. In all the other doctrines outlined above, nature and spirit are conceived as entirely distinct. Here on the other hand nature is conceived as but a form of spirit. Thus Vedānta is not only monistic, but also idealistic.

Bhartṛprapañca, who lived before Śaṅkara, stops here and represents this all-comprehensive principle called Brahman as the sole reality. Brahman viewed thus as comprehending the universe (*saprapañca*) is also characterized by attributes (*saguṇa*). The individual self, it is said, is not separate from but intimately connected with Brahman so conceived. Thus Brahman involves both identity and difference. But Śaṅkara does not agree with this. According to him, identity and difference, being mutually contradictory, cannot be predicated of one and the same entity. It makes the nature of the thing in question self-discrepant; and self-discrepancy, according to him, implies that the thing is an appearance. Brahman must, therefore, be not involved in the world (*niṣprapañca*). Since such a reality cannot be described in terms of attributes (*nirguṇa*), it can only be indicated in negative terms, such as "*neti neti*," as taught in the Upaniṣads.

But if we represent reality thus, it may seem that it is unknown and unknowable and hence as good as non-existent. So it is pointed out that the negation of features is only a part of the teaching. The other and more important part is the final identification of the individual self with Brahman. Nobody can deny his own self or plead ignorance of himself. And to show that the self of man in its essence (*ātman*) is nothing but Brahman is the final assurance of Brahman as the sole reality. Our ordinary awareness of ourselves is not sufficient for us to claim that we have realized Brahman, but it is adequate to give us a "conjectural insight" into the nature of reality.

Thus from the beginning, the monism of Vedānta takes two lines: one that denies all differences with regard to reality, and the other which, in some manner or other, accommodates difference in its conception. Śaṅkara's Advaita is the sole representative of the former. But the latter appears in more than one form in the history of Vedānta. Bhartṛprapañca accords equal status to identity and difference. Brahman is both one and many. This view went into oblivion after Śaṅkara severely criticized it. But it was sought to be revived with slight modifications by later thinkers like Bhāskara and Yādavaprakāśa; but their views also soon faded away. In view of their commonality in regard to the question of the relation of the world and souls to Brahman, the name Bhedābheda comes to be applied to all these schools. The name stands for the belief that *bheda*, or distinction, and *abheda*, or unity, can coexist in intimate relation with each other. This view will be dealt with in this chapter with reference to Bhartṛprapañca, who is its foremost exponent. Among other schools of Vedānta that find a place for difference in the scheme of reality without sacrificing the spirit of monism, Viśiṣṭādvaita and Dvaita are prominent. Each in its own way seeks to avoid the logical contradiction of equating difference and identity by re-interpreting the concept of identity. Rāmānuja takes the idea to mean inseparability. The world and souls, though distinct from Brahman, are inseparably related to him. To Madhva, identity signifies only that the world and souls, which are different from Brahman, are dependent on him. In sum, Rāmānuja seems to accord greater weightage to the principle of identity than Bhartṛprapañca, for he accommodates difference within the concept of identity instead of equating it with the latter. Dvaita emphasizes the concept of difference and links the different entities through the concept of dependence. A distinguishing feature of both Viśiṣṭādvaita and Dvaita is that both of them are theistic, looking upon Brahman as Viṣṇu, unlike Advaita or even Bhedābheda, for which Brahman is the impersonal reality. But we shall concentrate on the philosophical pattern of these schools, omitting their theistic commitment. The type of theism which they represent, viz., Vaiṣṇavism is not a necessary component of their philosophy, for we find Śaiva schools also which are parallel to them in their philosophy.[15]

5. BHEDĀBHEDA

The main problem on which Vedānta schools diverge is, as already pointed out, that of the relation which the physical world and the individual souls bear to Brahman. The Upaniṣads are vague on this question. Though there are statements about their identity with Brahman (*abheda-śruti*), there are also statements that distinguish them from Brahman (*bheda-śruti*). The most obvious way of reconciling these two sets of statements is to accord equal validity to both and hold that the world and souls are at once identical with and different from Brahman. This is the line that Bhartṛprapañca takes. "Brahman, according to him is one; but its unity is such as includes variety. Its conception is thus of a one-many."[16]

Brahman comprehends an infinite number of selves and diverse physical objects. This variety, which is implicit in Brahman, becomes explicit in the process of creation (*sṛṣṭi*). Creation is thus not origination of new things, but the evolution of what subsists in Brahman (*brahma-pariṇāmavāda*). Dissolution (*pralaya*) succeeds creation, when the variety returns to Brahman. Creation and dissolution succeed each other endlessly. The attribution of both identity and difference to Brahman is thus justified by introducing the concept of change (*pariṇāma*) in Brahman.

With reference to the two stages in creation, unmanifest and manifest, Brahman is spoken of in two ways. When variety is implicit, Brahman is called *para*, or the higher. When it becomes explicit, Brahman is described as *apara*, or the lower. The distinction made here is not on the same lines as in Advaita. Śaṅkara regards the acosmic Brahman as *para* and the cosmic Brahman as *apara*. The cosmic Brahman, which is the lower form, is an appearance (*vivarta*) of the higher and, therefore, not of the same order of reality. Hence the relation between them is also unreal. But Bhartṛprapañca, whose conception of Brahman is only cosmic, makes the distinction between *para* and *apara* within this conception. The cosmic Brahman, which is *para* before manifesting the universe, becomes *apara* when it unfolds the universe. Thus both are real and in the same sense, and their relations also is real. The relation is one of identity in difference (*bhedābheda*), where the *para* Brahman stands for the principle of identity and the *apara*, for that of difference. This idea is conveyed by the example of the serpent and its coils, hood, etc. or of the sun and its rays.

To Śaṅkara, the *jīva* is Brahman in disguise and is purely the result of a misconception (*avidyā*). But to Bhartṛprapañca, the *jīva* is, like the physical world, a real transformation of Brahman. He too recognizes *avidyā*, but it accounts only for the lapse of Brahman into the *jīva* condition of finitude and not also for its worldly life. In fact, the *jīva* is the result of two conditions—*avidyā*, or ignorance, and *asaṅga*, which means the attachment arising from selfish impulses. *Avidyā* delimits the *jīva*; *asaṅga* modifies it. Brahman at all stages being recognized as one-many, when the individual soul attains liberation, it is not lost in Brahman. It continues to retain its individuality, though that individuality is not the same as in ordinary life, i.e., manifest.

A peculiar feature of this school is that it accords equal importance to *jñāna* and *karma* in the means to liberation. Liberation is not attained by adherence to moral and religious duty alone or by the acquisition of right knowledge alone, but only by a combination of both (*jñāna-karma-samuccaya*). *Karma* helps the cultivation of detachment by purging the soul of its selfish impulses (*asaṅga*), and *jñāna* leads to liberation by dispelling its ignorance (*avidyā*) regarding its ultimate oneness with Brahman. Other schools of Vedānta also utilize *karma* as a means to release, but they assign to it a relatively subordinate place in the scheme of discipline.

The theoretical basis for the combination of *karma* and *jñāna* in the school is its attitude to the two portions of the Veda, the *karmakāṇḍa* and the *jñānakāṇḍa*. Mīmāṁsā regards the former as the real teaching of the Veda and looks upon the latter merely as supportive of the former. Schools of Vedānta generally accord to the *karmakāṇḍa* a place subordinate and subservient to *jñānakāṇḍa*, which they regard as the central teaching of the Veda. But Bhartṛprapañca assigns equal importance to both the parts and tries to coordinate the teachings of both. Both *karma* and *jñāna* are to be regarded as the means to *mokṣa*, for both alike are prescribed in scripture. We may, therefore, conclude that among Vedānta schools, systems like that of Bhartṛprapañca come closest to Mīmāṁsā in their attitude towards *karma*.

Bhartṛprapañca recognizes what has been described as *pramāṇa-samuccaya*, by which it is meant that the testimony of common experience is quite as valid as that of the Veda. The former shows the presence of variety in reality and the latter, of unity. Perception not only presupposes variety, but also validates it, for what is properly ascertained by a *pramāṇa* cannot but be true. Scripture itself confirms the truth of diversity. There are portions in the Upaniṣads, like those describing creation, which refer to diversity. At the same time the Upaniṣads emphasize the unity which we miss in common knowledge. Hence

Bhartṛprapañca concludes that Brahman should exhibit both the features and be a unity-in-diversity (*dvaitādvaita*).

The problem presented by the Upaniṣads is how the world and souls stand in relation to Brahman—whether they are ultimately different from Brahman or identical with it. Following Kumārila's Mīmāṁsā, this school argues that difference (*bheda*) and sameness (*abheda*) are intelligible only if taken together, for each is a mere abstraction taken separately. Existents like substance and quality or universal and particular can neither be wholly different from each other nor entirely the same. If they were entirely different, they should be separable. If they were absolutely the same, we would not speak of them as "two." Hence the relation between them can only be *bhedābheda*. Similarly, the relation between Brahman and the realm of variety, which evolves out of it, can only be one of identity-in-difference. But, as Śaṅkara points out, to say that they are both different and identical is nothing more than a mere restatement of the problem in a new form. Being mutually contradictory, difference and identity cannot be predicated of one and the same thing. It makes the nature of the thing self-contradictory; and self-contradiction, according to Śaṅkara, points to falsity. If unity and diversity be each an abstraction taken separately according to Bhartṛprapañca, their combination also is an abstraction according to Śaṅkara. Hence, in Śaṅkara's view, reality transcends both and, at the same time, explains them.[17]

6. VIŚIṢṬĀDVAITA

The manner in which Rāmānuja explains the relation of the world and souls to Brahman is unique. By common usage we often identify things that are distinct. We identify substance and quality when we say "The rose *is* red," though they are not the same. In "I *am* a man" one identifies a surviving soul with the mortal human form. This intimate relation is termed *apṛthak-siddhi*, which means "inseparability." "It connotes that one of the two entities related is dependent upon the other in the sense that it cannot exist without the other also existing, and that it cannot be rightly known without the other also being known at the same time."[18] The relation between Brahman on the one hand and the world and souls on the other is of this type.

Matter (*acit*), soul (*cit*) and God (*Īśvara*) are equally ultimate and real. Yet the first two are absolutely dependent upon the last and, therefore, inseparable from it. This relation of inseparability (*apṛthak-siddhi*) is the pivot on which the whole philosophy of Viśiṣṭādvaita turns. It is parallel to, but not the same as, *samavāya* in Nyāya-Vaiśeṣika. In both, the relata are quite distinct and real; but while *samavāya* is an external relation, *apṛthak-siddhi* is an internal one. This view is also different from the *bhedābheda* view, for it does not admit that things that are taken to be distinct can lose their distinction at some stage.

The idea that the world and souls are inseparably related to Brahman, though distinct from Brahman, is conveyed by the analogies of body and soul, substance and attribute, and so on. The world and souls are the body of which Brahman is the soul. The body is defined by Rāmānuja as that which the soul controls, supports, and utilizes for its own ends. Matter and souls, as the body of God, are directed and sustained by him and exist entirely for him. In other words, God is the central principle of both the individual and the physical world. Brahman is an organic unity in which matter and souls are the subordinate elements. The subordinate elements are termed *viśeṣaṇa* and the predominant element, *viśeṣya.* The complex whole, which is Brahman, is described as *viśiṣṭa.* And this is the sole reality. Hence the name Viśiṣṭādvaita.

Another illustration of the relation is that between substance and attribute. In a blue lotus, the blueness is quite distinct from the lotus, for a quality cannot be the same as a substance. At the same time blueness as a quality depends on the substance, lotus, for its very being, and cannot, therefore, be external to it. The complex whole of the flower is thus a unity. The identity of substance and attribute is not a bare identity, but one that does not rule out difference. Another example that suggests such identity is that between substance and its modes, e.g., between clay and jar. "In fact, it obtains wherever we have inseparable correlatives."[19] Of two such entities, the major member is designated *prakārin*, and the minor, *prakāra.*

Thus, though Brahman, the soul, and the physical world are all different and equally eternal, they are at the same time inseparable. It is important to remember that the three entities are different, although they stand in a peculiarly close relation to one another. The name Viśiṣṭādvaita applied to the doctrine should not be taken to mean the obliteration of these differences. Souls and matter are not identical with Brahman or with one another. "What is meant by describing the doctrine as *advaita* (monism) is not that the complex of these three elements is a synthesized unity of differences, but only that Brahman as embodied in or inspiring the souls and matter is one."[20] There is nothing outside this embodied whole. Whatever differences there are between souls and matter and between them and Brahman are within the one reality that is Brahman. A "blue lotus" is a unity in the sense that the substance of the flower, which is characterized by "blueness" and "lotusness," is one. Similarly a person who was once a youth and is now old is the same in the sense that his soul is the same. And likewise Brahman, who is qualified by the world and souls or who is embodied in them, is one, though these qualities or bodies are different from him while being inseparable from him. "...it is the qualified or the embodied that is one, while the factors qualifying or embodying it are quite distinct, though inseparable from it."[21]

According to Rāmānuja, the central point of the teaching of the Upaniṣads is the unity of Brahman in the above sense. In support of this view, he cites the two kinds of coordinate propositions that occur in them—one affirming the identity of the soul with Brahman and the other, that of the world with Brahman. To understand his interpretation, it must be known that, according to Rāmānuja, all things that exist are eventually forms, or modes (*prakāra*), of God. Similarly all names are his names; every word becomes a symbol of God and finally points to him. In the statement *tat tvam asi*, the term *tvam*, which literally stands for the *jīva*, really points to God, who is the *jīva*'s inner self (*antaryāmin*) of whom the *jīva* and, through it, its physical body are modes. The term *tat* stands for God as the cause of the universe. The identity meant by the statement is of these two complexes—God as the indweller of the *jīva* and God as the source of the world. It means that though the world and souls are real and distinct, Brahman in whom they are included is one. In Advaita the distinction due to adjuncts between *jīva* and *Īśvara* is rejected as but an appearance. Here the distinction is not denied; but at the same time the organic unity of the whole is affirmed.

There is no doubt that this is a very plausible way of getting over the difficulty which the Upaniṣads present by speaking alternately of both difference and identity when they relate the world and souls to Brahman. Where they distinguish these from Brahman, the Upaniṣads give expression to a fact of common experience. Where they identify them, they only mean that they are inseparable from Brahman in the sense explained above and not that they are one and the same. But it is difficult to believe that such an interpretation is consonant with the spirit of the classical Upaniṣads taken as a whole. There is only one section which seems directly to support it, viz., *Bṛhadāraṇyaka Upaniṣad,* III.5, where God is described as other than, and yet as the "inner controller immortal" of, both the individual soul and the world. But this teaching is of Yājñavalkya, whose conception of Brahman, as set forth in other portions of the same Upaniṣad, is monistic in the literal sense of the term. "The section in question may, after all, signify nothing more than the transcendent and immanent character of ultimate reality...."[22]

We have so far considered the general structure of Viśiṣṭādvaita. We shall now go into some details. Rāmānuja acknowledges only two categories; substance (*dravya*) and non-substance, or attribute (*adravya*). By substance is meant whatever serves as the substratum of change. It means that Rāmānuja accepts *pariṇāmavāda*, or *satkāryavāda*. But it is the attributive elements (*viśeṣaṇa*) alone that change, though for this reason the complex whole (*viśiṣṭa*) is also spoken of as undergoing modification. The substantive element (*viśeṣya*) in itself is changeless. There are six *dravyas*, but we shall confine ourselves to four of them.

Prakṛti is the dwelling place of the soul and, through it, of God himself. *Sattva*, *rajas*, and *tamas* are not the constituents of *prakṛti* as in Sāṅkhya, but its essential attributes. The whole physical world, with all its variety, evolves out of *prakṛti* under the guidance of God. The relation between *prakṛti* and its evolutes, or modes, is *apṛthak-siddhi*. Rāmānuja designates this as *satkāryavāda*, but not in the sense that the effect was already in the cause before it became manifest. It is *satkāryavāda* in the sense that it is *sat* itself, or the already existing reality, that is conceived as effect by reason of the transformation of its modes. The material cause, say "clay," is not a bare substance without modes. The cause is clay characterized by a mode (lump) and the effect is clay which has another mode (pot).

A special feature of Viśiṣṭādvaita is the postulation of knowledge as an essential attribute of God and soul. It is called *dharmabhūtajñāna* to distinguish it from knowledge as the essence of both entities (*svarūpajñāna*). The Upaniṣads insist on the changeless nature of spirit (*ātman* or Brahman). The reason for postulating two kinds of *jñāna* might be to show that spirit in itself is changeless according to the present doctrine and thus to harmonize it with the teaching of the Upaniṣads.[23] *Dharmabhūtajñāna* is reckoned as a substance (*dravya*), since it can assume different forms according to the nature of the object to be known. It is all-pervading in the case of God and the liberated souls and accounts for their omniscience. But in the case of the bound soul it is contracted, and this explains its finite knowledge.

The *jīva*, like *prakṛti*, is different from God, but not independent of him. It is described as a *prakāra*, or mode, of God in the sense that it is an accessory to him, and not in the sense of being a transformation of him. It is the body of God inasmuch as God is immanent in, acts upon, and guides it from inside. Its physical body is derived from *prakṛti*, but God is its indweller, controlling it without interfering with its freedom of action. Like God, the *jīva* is of the essence of sentience and changeless; it apprehends things through changes in its *dharma-bhūtajñāna*. Souls are many, but all are alike, being of the nature of sentience. The soul is not merely sentience, but also of the essence of bliss. But the bliss is more or less obscured in bondage and becomes fully manifest only in liberation.

The term *Īśvara*, in Viśiṣṭādvaita, is understood in two senses. First, it stands for the all-comprehensive Brahman, who includes in himself all material and spiritual elements. Though comprehending all, Brahman is unaffected by the evil and suffering which belong to the souls and the changes that matter undergoes. He is not merely the efficient cause of the world. He is also the material cause, since *prakṛti*, from which the world is said to emerge, is not external to him. Thus he is the *sole* cause of the world. In fact, in this all-comprehensive sense, *Īśvara* may be thought of in two stages—as cause and as effect. In dissolution (*pralaya*) he subsists as the cause with the world and souls latent in him. In creation (*sṛṣṭi*) what is latent becomes manifest. Subtle matter becomes gross; and souls enter into relation with physical bodies appropriate to their past *karma*. Since *Īśvara*, so to say, *grows* into the entire universe, he is called Brahman. This would suggest change in Brahman, which is against the teaching of the Upaniṣads. But Rāmānuja explains that the change is only to be secondarily understood. In himself, God does not suffer change; he is said to change only through changes in the entities comprising the whole of which he is the inspiring principle. "But it is not easy to see how he can be said to remain changeless when his inseparable attributes are changing."[24] However, it is this *Īśvara* in himself, regarded as the unchanging centre of the changing universe, that is the other meaning of the term *Īśvara*. In this sense *Īśvara* is the *antaryāmin* who dwells within the entire universe of nature and souls.

The above view of *Īśvara* is philosophical and is based upon the Upaniṣads. But it is intertwined with details of a theistic creed of the Bhāgavata type. In the latter phase, God is conceived as completely personal. He is known as Nārāyaṇa, or Vāsudeva. He is not only the Supreme Being (*Para*) but also manifests himself in various ways to help his devotees. One such manifestation is as the *antaryāmin* of the soul. His presence within is common to all souls and as such he guides them like a friend. It should be distinguished from the *antaryāmin* of the entire universe of matter and souls, referred to earlier.

It is one thing to claim that the conception of the ultimate reached in philosophy is the same as the ultimate conceived of in religion. It is quite another to combine a particular philosophic doctrine with a particular religious creed. The theistic creed that finds a place in the system had developed a host of details not all of which could fuse with the philosophy of the Upaniṣads. As a consequence, there are some discrepancies in the doctrine resulting from the synthesis. We might mention just one of them, viz., the conception of Brahman. Rāmānuja admits several ultimate entities, but at the same time holds that Brahman is the sole reality. This position is justified by saying that while Brahman as the *viśeṣya* alone is real, all the rest which are attributive elements (*viśeṣaṇa*) derive their being from Brahman. But if all these entities are existentially one, it is difficult to see how the distinction among them can be ultimate. It is precisely because the elements of diversity lack independent being, that the Advaitin denies reality to them in Brahman. The only other alternative is to grant that the relation between the elements of diversity and the Brahman which they constitute is one of *bhedābheda*. But such an explanation is unacceptable to Rāmānuja as logically unsound.

> The notion of *apṛthak-siddhi* on which the conception is based is as imperfect as that of the Nyāya-Vaiśeṣika *samavāya* which it is intended to replace. The only difference is that while *samavāya* tries to unite what are supposed to be distinct, *apṛthak-siddhi* tries to separate what is supposed to be one.[25]

The goal of life, according to the doctrine, is the attainment of the world of Nārāyaṇa and the enjoyment there, under his aegis, of perfect freedom and bliss. The means recommended is of two kinds. One is *prapatti*, or absolute self-surrender to God. Being a mental attitude, it is looked upon as a form of *jñāna*. The other is *bhakti*, or devotion. It involves training in three stages: *karma-yoga, jñāna-yoga,* and *bhakti-yoga*. The first is the doing of duty solely to please God; and the second is meditation on the true nature of the self as other than and subordinate to God. The third is loving contemplation of God for its own sake. It results in vivid recollection of God short of direct experience; and this in turn leads to absolute self-surrender (*prapatti*), which is directly resorted to in the other path. Actual liberation, which comes as an act of divine grace, happens only after physical dissolution.

7. DVAITA

The doctrine is more explicitly pluralistic than Viśiṣṭādvaita. Its pluralistic outlook is based on common experience. It also claims support for this view from the Veda, especially its earlier portions, viz., the Mantras and Brāhmaṇas. Even passages of monistic import in the Upaniṣads are interpreted here in a unique way in tune with the dualistic assumption. The notion of *bheda*, or difference, is fundamental to the system. It is said to be fivefold, between: God and soul, one soul and another, God and matter, soul and matter, and one form of matter and another. This, however, does not mean that the entities distinguished are independent. One thing may be dependent on another. For example, the physical body is dependent on the soul to which it pertains. Ultimately, everything is dependent on God. But God himself is not dependent on anything else. He is the only independent reality. What is independent is here defined as that which can, of its own accord, be, know, and act. Such an entity is God alone. Everything else exists, knows, and functions finally at God's will. This distinction in the case of God does not imply that God stands purely outside the universe as a mere spectator. He is not merely transcendent, but also immanent in the universe and controls it from within. Thus the unity which Dvaita believes in is not "numerical" but "teleological."[26]

It is on this basis that Dvaita explains Upaniṣadic statements of monistic import like "All this, indeed is Brahman" (*sarvaṁ khalvidaṁ brahma*). Thus Dvaita is not pluralistic in the ordinary acceptation of the term as Nyāya-Vaiśeṣika or dualistic like Sāṅkhya-Yoga. If it were, it would cease to be Vedānta, for it would then go against the very spirit of the Upaniṣads with their emphasis on Brahman as the central principle of the whole universe. The doctrine recognizes God as the supreme reality on whom all else depends; "and dependence, in its view, is as good as lack of separate status."[27]

God is the efficient cause of the world; and the material cause is *prakṛti*, which is conceived more or less as in Sāṅkhya. *Prakṛti* is eternal but insentient. *Sattva, rajas*, and *tamas* are neither its constituents nor its qualities. They are its first products. According to Rāmānuja, God is also the material cause of the world, as *prakṛti* inseparably belongs to him as his body. Such a view is regarded by Madhva as too intimate to be consistent with the transcendent majesty of God. God possesses all excellences. He is unknowable in the sense that he cannot be fully known. He is "apprehensible but not comprehensible."[28] He is the essence of knowledge and bliss. He not only creates and destroys the universe, but also controls it in each and everyone of its aspects. But being intrinsically perfect, he has nothing to gain by his activities. His entire creation is meant only to afford an opportunity to the souls for self-perfection.

Souls are many, but each soul is fundamentally different from the rest. Each has its own imperfections. Like God, the soul has sentience and bliss but on a much lower scale. It is on this principle of similarity that Madhva interprets the Upaniṣadic statement *tat tvam asi*. Souls are of three kinds: those that are bound but may become free; those that are confined eternally to the cycle of births and deaths; those that are doomed permanently to the misery of hell. The recognition of the last two classes is rather strange for a doctrine which is thoroughly theistic and places so much reliance on divine grace.

The prime source of *saṁsāra* is beginningless ignorance (*avidyā*). *Avidyā* obscures from man not only the true nature of God, but also of himself as dependent on him; and release consists in overcoming both these aspects of *avidyā* through knowledge. The mediate knowledge gained from scriptures has to be transformed into direct experience through meditation. But God's grace is the final means to liberation. It is attained through intensely loving devotion to him (*bhakti*). Liberation is possible only after death. *Karma-yoga*, which has to be practised till the end of life, prepares the ground for both knowledge and devotion.

As the concept of difference (*bheda*) is very important in the system, it needs some explanation. Advaitins reject the notion of difference. They say that it is relative and is not, therefore, intelligible without reference to the things that are different. The idea that A and B are different presupposes a knowledge of A and B. But since that knowledge points to them as *two*, it already involves the idea that they are different. Thus there is mutual dependence between the notion of difference and that of the things which differ; neither can be understood without the other also being understood. Hence the idea of difference is self-discrepant and, therefore, only of the nature of appearance.

The Dvaitin points out that the difficulty of mutual dependence arises because we wrongly assume that difference is something in addition to the terms it relates. But the fact, according to him, is that difference is nothing but the thing itself which is said to differ (from another); it is its very essence (*svarūpa*). In the above example, A is exactly what we mean by its difference from B; and similarly B, its difference from A. Since there are not two factors to be known—A *and* its difference from

B, or B *and* its difference from A—there is no question of mutual dependence. The outcome of the argument is that when we speak of difference between two or more things, we only mean that each of them is itself. "Everything is unique, and it is this very uniqueness that constitutes its difference from other things."[29]

Now, it may be asked how, in that case, we often talk of "the difference *of* A (from B)" as if the two, viz., "difference" and "A" were distinct. The Dvaitin's answer is that the identity claimed between a thing and its difference (from another) is a special kind of identity which allows itself to be expressed in a form that seems to differentiate between them. He describes it as "an identity associated with *viśeṣa*" (*saviśeṣābheda*). The concept of *viśeṣa* is as important to Dvaita as that of *apṛthak-siddhi* is to Viśiṣṭādvaita.

To understand the concept of *viśeṣa*, let us consider, for example, the relation between a substance and its permanent attribute, say between a coin and its weight. A substance necessarily possesses qualities. And a quality cannot exist by itself. Hence the relation between substance and quality is regarded as one of identity. But common practice distinguishes between the two. Thus we think and speak of the weight *of* a coin, which signifies a distinction between the two—the coin and its weight. To explain this discrepancy, the Dvaitin assumes something in the coin or in its weight or in both which makes possible a distinction between the two in spite of the fact that there is no actual difference between them. It is this "something" which the Dvaitin terms *viśeṣa*. Thus *viśeṣa* is what accounts for speaking of identical things as different. In each thing as many *viśeṣa*s are recognized as are necessary to account for such distinctions. It is on this basis that the Dvaitin explains the relation between a thing and its difference (from another). According to Dvaita, though the difference of one thing (from another) is identical with that thing, language permits us to make a distinction as when we speak of "the difference *of* A (from B)." It is *viśeṣa* that makes such a distinction possible.

Here is a new attempt to solve an old problem, viz., the problem of things which appear neither wholly identical nor wholly different. Jainism regards particular features and general features as two aspects of the same object. A cow is characterized by cowness and at the same time by its own colour, size, etc. The relation between the particular and the general is, according to Jainism, one of identity in difference. That is, the particular and the general are as such different; but as phases of the same substance, they are also one. It maintains this view notwithstanding the objection that contradictory features cannot be predicated of the same object. To avoid such a contradiction and in consonance with its realistic and pluralistic spirit, Nyāya-Vaiśeṣika assumes the unique relation called *samavāya* between substance and quality, particular and universal, whole and parts, etc. The relation of *samavāya* is a necessary one, since the relata are distinguishable but not separable. But, like *saṁyoga*, *samavāya* is regarded as an external relation, as the necessity involved is only one-sided. In a "red rose" the red colour presupposes the rose; but the rose itself need not be red. Coming back to Dvaita, we cannot say that the solution to the problem in terms of an assumed principle called *viśeṣa* is more satisfactory.[30]

8. ADVAITA

Central Metaphysical Position

Śaṅkara recognizes that there are two streams of thought in the Upaniṣads—one teaching the difference (*bheda*) of the world and souls from Brahman and the other denying this difference (*abheda*). But he thinks that the former is only a concession to empirical modes of thought, which take diversity to be real. The only teaching of the Upaniṣads, according to him, is the latter, which denies difference. It would be wrong to interpret the term *abheda* to mean unity, for there can be no unity apart from diversity, the two being relative terms. It means only "non-difference." Hence Śaṅkara's teaching is not to be described as monism but only as "non-dualism" (*advaita*).

According to Śaṅkara, the real (*sat*) is what is eternal; and Brahman is the sole reality of that type. The unreal (*asat*), according to him, is absolute nothing. The realm of diversity is neither real nor unreal in the senses defined. It is not real, for it is not eternal. It is not unreal, for it clearly appears to us as no non-entity, for example a hare's horn, can. Further, the realm of diversity possesses, unlike the totally non-existent, practical efficiency, or has value, as it is serviceable in life. It is, therefore, to be described as other than the real and the unreal (*sadasad-vilakṣaṇa*), or as an illusory appearance. "It is psychologically given (*prasiddha*), but cannot be logically established (*siddha*)."[31]

Now, although the realm of diversity as a whole is an illusory appearance, there is an important difference in the way in which the physical world on the one hand and the individual self on the other is so. This is explained by two kinds of examples relating to illusion. The physical world is an appearance in the sense in which a snake is an appearance where there is only a rope in the example usually cited. The appearance of the snake points to the existence of the rope. There can be no appearance without a real basis. But the dependence is one-sided, for while the disappearance of the rope necessarily means the disappearance of the snake, the reverse does not hold good. Likewise the physical world is an appearance in the sense that it depends for its appearance upon the higher reality of Brahman. All admit that the name (*nāma*) of a thing is conventional; but Śaṅkara points out that the "what" (*rūpa*) of it is also the same. The only true reality is what underlies the conventional particularity of common things.

The case of the individual self (*jīva*) as an illusion is different. We have to take a different example to illustrate this. A person looking at a white conch through a sheet of yellow glass, of whose existence he is not aware, takes it to be yellow. But a change in his standpoint, like the removal of the glass, will reveal to him that the yellowness belongs to the glass and not to the conch. The difference between this example and the previous lies in the later knowledge. A person may fancy that he sees a snake where there is only a rope. But closer scrutiny not only affirms the existence of the rope, but also contradicts the existence of the snake as which it appeared before. In the second example the later knowledge affirms the existence of the conch; what it denies is only an aspect of it, viz., its yellowness. The person who realizes his error in this case still sees the conch, but only adds that it is white and not yellow. The yellow colour really belongs to the sheet of glass, and but for its interposition there would be no illusion at all in this case.

> The illusion in the first case consists in mistaking a given object for another that is not given; in the second, it consists merely in attributing to an object which is given, a feature that does not really belong to it, though it also is presented at the time.[32]

These two types of illusion serve to illustrate the manner in which the same Brahman comes to appear as the physical world on the one hand and the individual self on the other. The experience of a *jīvanmukta*, which affirms the reality of Brahman, denies the world as such. The individual self is not illusory in this sense. It is Brahman itself appearing through the media of limiting adjuncts (*upādhi*) like the internal organ (*antaḥkaraṇa*). These *upādhis* are part of the physical world and are, as such, illusory. So, when Brahman is realized and these limiting adjuncts along with the rest of the world are shown to be false, what is denied is not the *jīva* as a spiritual entity, but only certain aspects of it like its finitude and its separateness from other selves. The *jīva* is, thus, reaffirmed as Brahman.

The difference in the explanation brings out clearly what is meant by the identity of the *jīva* and Brahman, which is of fundamental importance to the doctrine. The *jīva* is not illusory in the same sense as the world so that it is lost in Brahman when the final truth is revealed. If it were, there would be none to be saved and the teaching of liberation would be meaningless. But at the same time the *jīva* is not preserved as such in liberation, for it is only as Brahman that it continues to be, losing its limitations, which are false. In empirical life these limitations, which really belong to its physical adjuncts, appear transferred to it, just as the yellowness of the glass appears transferred to the conch in the example cited. We may, therefore, say that while the physical world is an appearance of Brahman in the first degree, the *jīva*, or ego, is an appearance of it only in the second degree.[33]

> Brahman is the sole reality, and it appears both as the objective universe and as the individual subject. The former is an illusory manifestation of Brahman, while the latter is Brahman itself appearing under the limitations which form part of that illusory universe.[34]

Before going into the details of the doctrine, it is desirable to explain the Advaita view of causation as it throws fresh light on what has been said in the foregoing. The view will become evident if we consider the relation between the material cause and the effect. On this question there is direct opposition between Nyāya and Sāṅkhya. Of the views of these two schools, the Advaitin prefers the latter. If the effect, as Nyāya holds, were not existent in the material cause before production, it would mean that any effect could be produced by using any material cause. But since we need particular causes to produce particular effects, the effect must be pre-existent in its cause, the two forming an identity in difference as Sāṅkhya believes. But the latter view is, according to Advaita, correct only as between one material object and another, e.g., between the lump of clay and the pot made out of it, as both have the same ontological status. It cannot hold good between Brahman, the reality, and the world of objects, which is an appearance. Between the clay and the pot, the relation is actual, as both are appearances of Brahman. But the relation between Brahman and the world or anything in it can only be false. Hence, according to Advaita, the concept of causation is wholly empirical and without any ultimate significance. "The causal relation holds between one phenomenon or appearance and another, but not between phenomena and reality."[35] Belief in it, no doubt, forms an important implication of all practical life, but it is not defensible when applied to the relation between Brahman and the

cause or as effect according as diversity is latent or manifest. This is the lower (*apara*) conception of Brahman in contrast to the higher (*para*), which is *nirguṇa*. It is the cosmic parallel to the *jīva*. Each is Brahman itself with an unreal adjunct. *Māyā*, which is the adjunct of Saguṇa Brahman is all-comprehensive. Individual selves have as their adjuncts parts, or phases, of *māyā*, the adjunct of each *jīva* being specially called *avidyā*. Just as the whole world is the effect of *māyā*, the portions of the world like the physical body and the internal organ, which accompany a *jīva*, are derived from the *avidyā* of that particular self. It shows that the distinction between the *jīva* and Saguṇa Brahman (and between one *jīva* and another) is entirely due to their adjuncts. In themselves the *jīva* and the qualified Brahman are not distinct. This is the import of the Upaniṣadic statement *tat tvam asi* ("That thou art"). The *jīva* and the qualified Brahman are not *as such* one, but only as bereft of their respective adjuncts.

Saguṇa Brahman, when personified, becomes the *Īśvara*, or God, of Advaita. The difference between *Īśvara* and the *jīva* is again entirely due to the adjuncts—cosmic in the one case and finite in the other. It is the finite nature of the adjuncts that explains the evils of the self such as narrow love and hate, which are absent in *Īśvara*. In popular language, *Īśvara* is the creator of the world, and *māyā* is the power (*śakti*) that helps him create. In this form he is the material as well as the efficient cause of the world. *Īśvara* is also compared to a magician, and the world is regarded as his magic, since, like a magician, he is not deluded by what he creates. However, we must not forget that what is ultimate is only Nirguṇa Brahman and not either Saguṇa Brahman or *Īśvara*. These latter conceptions are only stepping stones to understanding the true nature of Brahman.

Jīva

Like Saguṇa Brahman, or *Īśvara*, the *jīva*, or ego, is also complex in character, being a blend of the self and the not-self; the not-self is *avidyā* in the case of the *jīva* and *māyā* in the case of Saguṇa Brahman. In deep sleep the *jīva* is associated with *avidyā* alone. In dream it is associated, not with *avidyā* as such, but with the internal organ (*antaḥ-karaṇa*), which is an off-shoot of *avidyā*. In the waking state it is conjoined not only with the internal organ, but also with the physical body, which is another product of *avidyā*. This wrong identification of the self with the not-self is called *adhyāsa*; and it is from this that all the confusions and troubles of life arise. The self imagines that it is a knower of objects, a doer of action, and an experient of the results of action. It is again in this complex form based on *avidyā* that the self undergoes transmigration. This fact implies that liberation, which depends upon the conquest of ignorance, is transcending the notion of the ego. "Thus, paradoxical as it may seem, man, truly to be himself, must get beyond himself."[39]

An insight into the true nature of the *jīva* as identical with Brahman is provided by the conception of the *sākṣin*, or "witness," in Advaita. "It is the *jīva* viewed in its *true* character—not as one with or even as related to any of its adjuncts, but as aloof from all of them."[40] We may describe it as the transcendental ego to distinguish it from the *jīva*, or the empirical ego. It is pure consciousness, or consciousness in itself (*svarūpa-jñāna*). It is thus the "seeing light" and is virtually identical with Brahman. It has to be distinguished from knowledge as it is familiar to us (*vṛtti-jñāna*), which is a state of the *jīva*, or empirical subject. Knowledge of external objects takes place when the internal organ streams forth and assumes the form of the object, this modification being called *vṛtti*. Knowledge of internal states like pain and pleasure also takes place by a *vṛtti*, but without the internal organ having to stream out. Thus *vṛtti-jñāna* changes with changes in the internal organ according to the nature of the object to be understood. But *svarūpa-jñāna* only witnesses these changes without itself undergoing any change. All change is *for* this consciousness, not *in* it. The witness is thus implied in all empirical thought, but not identified with it. Its existence is deduced from the analysis of self-consciousness. The Advaitin believes that what knows must be other than what is known. Kumārila explains that in self-consciousness the self as subject knows itself as object. This is a contradiction in terms. The Advaitin points out that nothing can be the subject as well as the object of the same action. The eye can see other things, but not itself. In what we call self-knowledge what we know are only the knowable and non-spiritual elements of the *jīva* like the body and the internal organ. "In reality, it is not the 'I' but the 'me' that we know."[41] The true self cannot be known as an object; but this does not mean that it remains unrealized, for it is self-revealing.

The *sākṣin* as such is not Brahman. The word *sākṣin* means "witness," or a disinterested looker-on. It implies something to be looked at. The conception is thus relative. What it observes are the states of the internal organ as they unfold themselves. It appears never by itself, but always in association with the internal organ either in its latent or in its manifest form. The reverse is also true—no internal organ is conceivable without involving a reference to some *sākṣin* or other. Thus it is only the unity of the passive *sākṣin* and the active *antaḥkaraṇa* that knows, feels, and wills. In this complex form it is known as the *jīva*, or the empirical self. Such a conception satisfactorily accounts for the double character of subject and object which one and the same *jīva* exhibits in so-called self-consciousness. The *sākṣin* and the *jīva* are thus not identical, though at the same time they are not quite different either. While the *jīva* may become the object of self-consciousness on account of the objective element it includes, the *sākṣin* is the pure element in all knowing. It is not knowable but reveals itself as the ground of all knowing. "...the *jīva* is spirit immanent in the *antaḥkaraṇa*, while the *sākṣin* is spirit as transcendent."[42]

The existence of the *sākṣin* is also evident from the analysis of sleep. In waking and dream, when the internal organ is active, one is aware of oneself as knowing something. This is the notion of the *jīva*, or the empirical ego, in other words, one's sense of individuality arising from the identification of consciousness with the internal organ. In dreamless sleep, when the internal organ is inactive by being merged in its cause, viz., *avidyā*, one loses one's sense of individuality even as there is no object to be known. What obtains now is only the *sākṣin* (not the *jīva*) and the *avidyā* with which it is associated. This makes the experience of deep sleep quite unique, though it occurs normally and almost daily. Individuality does not become totally absent then, but it remains dormant owing to the presence of *avidyā*. That is why a person recalls his own sleep. The uniqueness of the experience is that *avidyā* operates only partially. It obscures the non-dual reality, but it does not project diversity as in dream and waking. This is shown by the later reminiscence that one did not know anything while asleep. All distractions being absent, there is also the experience of bliss, which is the true nature of the self, and this survives for a while even after waking.

Nirguṇa Brahman

The concept of Nirguṇa Brahman is the most distinguishing feature of Advaita on the theoretical side. Brahman may be represented as the infinite consciousness (*cit*) which underlies empirical knowledge or as the infinite being (*sat*) presupposed in all finite existence. But in neither way can it be represented in its purity, for empirical knowledge and phenomenal existence have appearance superadded to reality. In fact, this is the case with all empirical things. While they are not apart from Brahman, they cannot either singly or in combination stand for it. That is why Brahman is described as *nirguṇa*.

The term *nirguṇa* does not mean that Brahman is a substance without attributes, but only that it transcends the distinction between substance and attribute. It means that "nothing which the mind can think of can actually belong to it."[43] Whatever we think of is for that very reason objective (*dṛśya*), but Brahman is never presented as an object (*dṛk*) to a subject. So the familiar categories of thought are all inapplicable to Brahman, and no direct description of it is possible. This is the implication of the negative formula for Brahman used in the Upaniṣads—*neti neti* ("not this, nor that").

It may be objected that such an entity is a sheer abstraction. The objection would be valid only if Brahman is purely objective, as conceived in Sattādvaita, a monistic view prevalent at the time of Śaṅkara.[44] "If an objective reality be negatively described and all knowable features are abstracted from it, we may conclude that there is nothing of it left behind."[45] The Brahman of Śaṅkara is not objective, but at bottom identical with the individual self. Hence, the view here is Ātmādvaita. Such an identification carries the maximum certainty to the reality of Brahman, for nothing can be more certain than one's own existence. The very act of doubting one's own being would affirm its existence. Such a view does not mean that the self is known to us completely. But it is not wholly unknown either.

Though Brahman cannot be described directly, we can point to it utilizing the appearances as aids: "for an appearance, which can never be independent, necessarily signifies a reality beyond itself."[46] In this way every percept and every concept can be made to indicate Brahman. The Upaniṣads draw our attention to Brahman by analysing the external world as well as ourselves. But they prefer the latter route. External objects reveal Brahman as *sat*, but the subject which cognizes them reveals it not only as *sat*, but also as *cit*. Terms like *tvam* or *aham* denoting the subject afford a better clue to its nature besides dispelling all doubt about its existence. When such terms are combined with another like *tat* denoting Brahman in an assertive proposition like *tat tvam asi* or *aham brahma asmi*, the reference to Brahman becomes ensured.

Brahman is not merely indefinable; it cannot be known either, for the moment it is made the object of thought, it becomes related to a subject and, therefore, determinate. Such is the nature of the Saguṇa Brahman, or *Īśvara*. It is Brahman in an "empiric dress"—the Absolute as it appears to us, and not as it is in itself. It is Brahman as *jñeya*, or that can be known. In itself, Brahman excludes all relations, including that between subject and object, and is, therefore, unknowable. But though it cannot be known, it can be realized.

One should be careful in understanding what the Upaniṣads mean by describing Brahman as indefinable and unknowable. It is not beyond the reach of words at all. To suppose that it is so would be to deprive the Upaniṣads of their very purpose. Even granting that a negative description is the only possible one, it does not follow that Nirguṇa Brahman is a blank, for negation necessarily has its own positive implication. As a matter of fact, Advaitins assign only a secondary place to negative statements like *neti neti*; the primary place is given to positive statements like *tat tvam asi*, which point to the reality in us as the Absolute. The idea is that a negative statement is not to be understood in isolation, but along with positive ones. "Negation is only a preliminary to affirmation."[47] What the Upaniṣads deny is only a purely objective conception of the Absolute—as one merely inferred from outer phenomena—the implication being that it reveals itself within us. Such an interpretation alters totally the significance of the negative description, "for we are thereby constrained to admit not only its positive character but also its spiritual nature."[48]

Thus it is not a bare, or contentless, being for which Nirguṇa Brahman stands. Nirguṇa Brahman is not the negation of Saguṇa Brahman, but its very truth, and underlies every aspect of it. It is true that it cannot be regarded as an object of knowledge, but we can "know" Brahman by being it. The whole course of practical discipline in Advaita is oriented to this consummation. Though the ideal of Saguṇa Brahman is not the ultimate, the Advaitin does not regard it as useless. It furnishes an ethical and devotional ideal by following which the disciple can acquire the moral fitness for the Advaita experience. Even from the purely theoretical point of view, it is not without a value, as it provides for a method for teaching Advaita. The method starts with the diverse worlds given in individual experience and arrives at a unity in terms of the idea of Saguṇa Brahman as the origin and end of the universe. Since the idea of unity in diversity, or identity in difference, is logically self-discrepant, the teaching suggests the apparent nature of the universe and goes beyond it to arrive at the idea of Nirguṇa Brahman as the sole reality. "The contradictions and anomalies of ordinary experience have at first to be resolved at least in the seeming orderliness signified by the ideal of Saguṇa Brahman, if we are to reach the advaitic ultimate unerringly."[49] Thus the Advaitin's criticism of the concept of the qualified Brahman is only to show that it is not adequate and not to signify that it is valueless. In fact, it is the general Advaita position that "practical utility need not rest on metaphysical validity."[50] Thus there are "two grades" of teaching in Advaita—the higher one relating to Nirguṇa Brahman (*parā vidyā*) and the lower one concerning Saguṇa Brahman (*aparā vidyā*).

> All philosophy starts from experience. But it is usually assumed that the data of experience, if they are to lead to right conclusions, should stand for actual facts or be valid. This is not admitted by the Advaitin as necessary.... That is, the Advaitin attaches no necessary ontological significance to the data that serve as the bases of reasoning. He begins his inquiry, taking them at their face value, and leaves their validity or invalidity to reveal itself in the course of the inquiry or as its result.[51]

Practical Teaching

The goal of life according to Advaita can be deduced from its conception of the nature of the individual self. The *jīva* is Brahman itself, and its supposed distinction from it is due to the illusory adjuncts with which it identifies itself out of *avidyā*. Therefore liberation consists in realizing one's true nature as Brahman. The identity of the self with Brahman is not something to be newly attained; it is already there and has only to be realized in one's own experience. All that is needed is to remove the obstacle of *avidyā* that keeps the truth concealed from us, and the means for this is right knowledge (*jñāna*). It is, therefore, only in a negative sense that we can talk of achieving *mokṣa* here. As in other doctrines, the achievement of the goal here also means effecting a change; only the change here is in the realm of thought, not in the realm of being. "...man has to alter totally his standpoint towards himself and the world in order to become free."[52]

The discipline prescribed consists of two parts—the first meant for cultivating detachment (*vairāgya*) and the second for acquiring knowledge (*jñāna*). The former part consists in performing one's duty without any desire for fruit, as taught in the *Bhagavad-gītā* (*karma-yoga*). This helps to purify the affections and fit the aspirant to pursue seriously the ultimate truth. "...*karma* is not here conceived as the cause of *mokṣa* or even of *jñāna* which is its means, but of a true desire to know (*vividiṣā*)."[53]

The latter part of the discipline is threefold as set forth in the Upaniṣads. Through the study of scripture (*śravaṇa*) the disciple comes to know the identity of the self with Brahman. But this knowledge, being only communicated by another, cannot be fully convincing, as it is so much in variance with common experience (*asambhāvana*). Personal reflection (*manana*) based on examples taken from ordinary life assists the disciple in convincing himself of the correctness of Advaita teaching. As Brahman transcends common life, these examples can only indicate the probability of the Advaita truth and cannot establish it independently of revelation. The knowledge acquired so far is only mediate, and meditation (*nididhyāsana*) on the Advaita teaching is required to transform it into direct experience. The way it does this is by the removal of old habits of thought which are incompatible with the new knowledge (*viparīta-bhāvanā*). When the truth of the statement "That thou art" dawns upon the mind, the intrinsic bliss of the self is also released in its wholeness.

The need for reason is recognized in Advaita as shown by the position assigned to *manana*, though as an aid to scripture. Even scripture is not the ultimate means to *mokṣa*. Scripture can convey only mediate knowledge; but the goal is to realize the ultimate truth in one's own experience. Thus the aim is finally to get beyond both reason and revelation and rest in direct experience (*anubhava*). Revelation itself goes back to the intuitive experience of the seers. So it is that experience which is to be corroborated by the disciple. The person who has realized the final truth even while in the body is a *jīvanmukta*. "He is in life and yet lifted out of it."[54] He is free from all sense of obligation, but this does not mean that he grows indifferent to the world. He helps others, but his service will be the spontaneous expression of his felt conviction regarding the oneness of all. When his body drops off, he is said to be freed in the final sense (*videha-mukti*), though he is already free. In accordance with the teaching of the Upaniṣads, Advaita also recognizes liberation in stages (*krama-mukti*) in the case of those who advance on right lines but lack right knowledge.

REFERENCES

1. *OIP*, p. 230.
2. *PEIP*, p. 102.
3. *OIP*, p. 237.
4. Ibid.
5. *EIP*, p. 131.
6. Ibid., p. 135.
7. *PEIP*, p. 53.
8. *EIP*, p. 115.
9. *PEIP*, p. 56.
10. Ibid., p. 57.
11. Ibid., p. 58.
12. Ibid., p. 59.
13. Ibid.
14. Ibid., p. 105.
15. Vide *EIP*, p. 175.
16. Ibid., pp. 152-53.
17. Vide ibid., p. 154.
18. Ibid., p. 177.
19. *OIP*, pp. 400-401.
20. *EIP*, p. 178.
21. Ibid.
22. Ibid., p. 179.

23. Vide *OIP*, p. 389.
24. Ibid., p. 407.
25. Ibid., pp. 409-10.
26. *EIP*, p. 190.
27. *R*, pp. 205-6.
28. *EIP*, p. 191.
29. Ibid., p. 189.
30. Vide ibid., p. 194.
31. Ibid., p. 156.
32. Ibid., p. 157.
33. Vide ibid., p. 158.
34. Ibid.
35. Ibid., p. 159.
36. *OIP*, p. 339.
37. *EIP*, p. 161.
38. *OIP*, pp. 372-73.
39. *EIP*, p. 165.
40. Ibid.
41. Ibid., p. 166.
42. *OIP*, p. 344.
43. Ibid., p. 373.
44. Vide *EIP*, p. 162.
45. *OIP*, p. 375, n. 3.
46. Ibid., pp. 373-74.
47. Ibid., p. 375.
48. Ibid., pp. 375-76.
49. Ibid., p. 377.
50. Ibid.
51. *IPS—I*, p. 100.
52. *EIP*, p. 169.
53 Ibid., p. 171.
54 Ibid., p. 173.

6

Values—Part One

1. VALUE IN GENERAL

The Nature of Value

The meaning of "value" can best be indicated by contrasting it with the meaning of "fact." The immediate purpose of all knowledge is to acquaint us with facts. A fact may be known directly as when we look around and perceive some object or other. It may be known indirectly as when we hear a sound and connect it with a possible source. A fact need not be a present existence, like these examples; it may be what existed in the past like yesterday's rain or what will exist in the future like tomorrow's sunrise. Again, the object known need not necessarily be certain; it is enough if it appears to be so for the moment. All that is required is that at the time of being known it should not be known as unreal.

In everyday life a knowledge of a fact does not stop with the satisfaction of theoretic curiosity; it *ordinarily* leads to action. Action involves a desire, either to attain the object which we like or to avoid an object which we dislike. If the desire is positive, the object desired (*iṣṭa*) becomes a value; if it is negative, the object not desired (*dviṣṭa*) is the opposite of value, or disvalue. Hence, we may define value as "that which is desired." A value judgement like "I like sugar" is more than a judgement of fact like "sugar is sweet."

> Indian thinkers commonly speak of two functions of knowledge—one which is theoretical, viz., revealing the existence of objects (*artha-paricchitti*), and the other which is practical, viz., affording help in the attainment of some purpose in life (*phala-prāpti*). The results of these two functions of knowledge are respectively what we mean by "fact" and "value."[1]

A thirsty traveller, who happens to come upon a water source, discovers a fact; and when he quenches his thirst, he realizes a value. These two functions are closely connected with each other, since the knowledge of a fact usually leads to the pursuit of some value.

Value has usually a reference to the future. A fact is something given (*siddha*). It has, therefore, only to be apprehended. But a value, which is an object of final interest, does not usually exist already, but has to be brought into being, or realized by effort (*sādhya*). However, there are exceptions to this. When a value has already been realized, effort is required only to preserve it. In this connection there arises the question whether values are feasible, or possible of achievement (*kṛti-sādhya*). Ordinarily speaking, the possibility of their achievement need not be certain. But this does not affect their status as value, for it is enough if, at the time of their pursuit, they are not definitely known to be impossible of achievement.

It has been represented above that the cognition of a fact could lead to a desire for it, and desire makes it a value to be realized. Thus it may appear that the feeling of desire precedes the sense of value. Actually, however, the arousal of desire is itself mediated by the idea of value in the object. The cognition of a fact suggests the idea of some value, and it is that idea which awakens a desire and leads to action for realizing it. But it is not the bare idea that leads to desire. The idea of value, according to Indian thinkers, is always associated with a feeling of pleasure, owing to the past experience of the valuing subject. In fact, a value is entitled to be called so only when it carries with it the pleasure of appreciating, or prizing, it. (This, however, is not to identify value with pleasure.) It is because there is a feeling of pleasure in valuation that the idea of a value kindles a desire for realizing it. Thus, though we have defined value as an object, or content, of desire, implying that desire leads to the idea of value, psychologically speaking, the act of valuation precedes desire. But still the definition is not wrong, because what desire leads to is the fulfilment of the same value which prompts it. "It begins with an idea of value which, being tinged with a feeling of pleasure, arouses a desire for it; and that desire by prompting, in its turn, appropriate activity culminates in the realization of the value."[2] Thus all the three aspects of the mind—cognition, feeling, and will—are involved in the process of value-realization, each aspect functioning predominantly at a different stage in the process.

The inquiry so far shows that fact and value are distinct but closely connected with each other. The idea of value presupposes the knowledge of some fact. And every fact of which we become aware puts us in mind of some significance for it in life. Though thus interconnected, the appeal of each is predominantly to a different side of our mind. Facts appeal primarily to the cognitive side, and value mainly to the conative side. "If a fact is given and is to be apprehended, a value is appreciated and requires to be achieved."[3]

We have earlier said that the end aimed at, or object desired (*iṣṭa*), is termed a value. But it is not always so. The means to it (*iṣṭa-sādhana*) also are often described as value as a matter of courtesy. Thus a value is either intrinsic or instrumental. The former is regarded as value in the primary sense, i.e., as what is sought for its own sake. The latter is described as value in the secondary sense of what is sought for the sake of another. Thus wealth is an instrumental value, while the fulfilment of any of life's needs by means of wealth is an intrinsic one. An intrinsic value does not admit of the question "why," but an instrumental value does. However, the distinction between the two is not always hard and fast, for the one may take the place of the other as a result of a change in the attitude of the subject. Thus a miser may come to regard money as an end in itself instead of as a means. Contrarywise, the satisfaction of hunger may first be looked upon as an end in itself, but at a later stage of life, as a means to bodily health and well-being.

The Locus of Value

We clarified that the idea of value in an object precedes the desire for it, and desire leads to effort for realizing the value. But in view of the connection between value and desire, there is a controversy on whether value is prior to desire or desire prior to value. It relates to the locus of value. Do we desire an object because it possesses value, or do we value it because we desire it? If the answer affirms the latter question, value is subjective; if it affirms the former, it is objective. There are arguments for both these views. Indian thinkers generally take the objective view. To understand this, it is necessary to examine the subjective view.

Values, it is argued, are subjective because they are entirely dependent on the changing opinion of the valuing subject. Men have likes and dislikes, and they project them on outside objects which, in themselves, are valueless. There is no difference between one object and another as objects. So there is no standard of value except individual taste. Such a view has the direst consequences for the welfare and progress of humanity in the absence of any agreement as to what is true, right, and so on. But leaving aside this practical objection, it could be seen that this view is not supported by facts. The appeal of many values, especially the higher ones, is as much to others as it is to any particular individual seeking them. In other words, they are trans-subjective. Truth, for example, must be the same for all. "It has a certain coercive power, which precludes all dissents from it."[4] It may not be so easy to prove the objectivity of the other higher value, viz., the good. But this does not mean that it is subjective and its judgement left to individual fancy. When a person admires another for performing his duty at great self-sacrifice, he expects that such a deed will evoke admiration from all others also. In other words, we recognize the binding character of the deed on all agents who may find themselves in similar circumstances. There is no doubt a subjective element in such cases. But this is confined to the *response* of the individual to this sense of universal obligation and does not extend to the moral value itself. Thus it can be shown that at least the higher values do not depend for their validity upon individual caprice, but upon their acceptance by many, if not by all.

The lower values, *artha* and *kāma*, have reference to particular external objects. So the question whether these values are objective or subjective depends for its answer on the place of external objects in value situations. Some among Indian doctrines recognize that external objects are in themselves valuable. Nearly all the other Indian doctrines also admit a trans-subjective standard in judging values, though they differ in regard to the exact place of external objects in value situations. But at the same time there seems to have been a view that external objects are neutral in respect of values and so they are entirely relative to the individual.[5] Their argument is as follows. If external objects are held to be valuable in themselves, their appeal, being based on their intrinsic nature, should be the same in the case of all persons. But it is a notorious fact that it is not so. A thing which satisfies one may repel another. It may not satisfy even the same person at another time. For example, food, which satisfies a person when he is hungry, fails to do so when he is not. Hence external objects do not possess any intrinsic value, and the conception of value depends entirely upon the subject and his mental processes.

The reply to this subjective view comes from the realistic doctrine of Nyāya. It is admitted that at anyone time the appeal of an object differs according to individuals and that the same object may not give the same satisfaction to the same person at different times. But from this it does not follow that no contribution at all is made by the object to the value situation. When it is said that value belongs to the object, what is meant is that it is fundamentally a feature of the objective factor and not that it exclusively belongs to the object. As a matter of fact, valuation is a complex process involving more than one factor of which the object is certainly the central one. But how far it contributes to value realization depends on the whole objective situation in which it appears. The factors that enter into this situation are the space-time context in which it appears, the presence of aids that are helpful to the realization of its value, and the absence of hindrances to it. To this situation we must add the character of the valuing subject as one of the determining conditions. The situation taken along with the subject furnishes the context in which the valued object operates. It is only with reference to that context that we have the complete explanation of the appeal that the object makes as a value or fails to do so. That is, though the object is essential, its final appeal is determined by its context. It is clear from the position assigned to the subject as just one of the determining factors, that all valuation must reckon with the primacy of the objective factor. Our definition of value as what is desired may make it appear that it is subjective, but it is really not so. Desire is recognized here only as an indication of the presence of value in the object, not as the cause of value.

Another argument may be advanced against the subjective view and to show that value is objective. Whatever be the value, whether lower or higher, a suitable means is required to realize it. The end is thought of first at the time of planning. In actual execution the reverse takes place—the means is sought first and the end reached through it. The idea of the intrinsic value serves as the *final* cause of desire. For the desire to issue in activity (*ceṣṭā*), a knowledge of the appropriate means to it (the instrumental value) is indispensable. The appropriateness of the means depends on two factors: (i) a belief that it is fitted to lead to the desired result (*iṣṭa-sādhanatā-jñāna*) and (ii) a belief that the result is possible of achievement (*kṛti-sādhyatā-jñāna*). Now, it has to be admitted that the means anyway is objective.

We may, therefore, conclude that subjective and objective factors are both necessary and involved in value realization. The existence of the value is objective, but the response to it is subjective. Subjectivists mistake the response to value for the locus of value. It is as impossible to think of value in abstraction from objective factors as it is to think of it in abstraction from the valuing subject. The one is as integral to the value situation as the other.

The Idea of Puruṣārtha

It is necessary to see the difference between men and lower creatures in the pursuit of ends. We have stated that the idea of value precedes the pursuit of it. It means that we have a definite awareness of what we seek. This is a very important difference between men and animals. Animals too strive to satisfy their desires. But we have not sufficient evidence to show that they have an *idea* of the satisfaction they are seeking. They do not seem to have a conception of the past or the future and appear to be guided in their present behaviour by mere instinct. Man can not only transcend the world given at the moment, but also conceive of an ideal world which is fixed and independent of it. Thus the distinguishing feature of values as pursued by man is that his activities are consciously directed to ends. Hence human values are values in the true sense of the term. The Sanskrit name *puruṣārtha* stands for "what is desired by man."

So far as biological ends like food, sleep, and so on are concerned, man shares them with the rest of the animal world. But there are other ends like knowledge and virtue which are special to man as a reflecting subject. And it is these that strictly deserve to be called *puruṣārthas*. Even the lower ends which man pursues in common with animals may be called *puruṣārthas* in so far as man understands their significance in life, though pursuing them often unconsciously. It is the conscious pursuit of them that transforms them into *puruṣārthas*. Thus even the ends which man shares with animals may become *puruṣārthas* provided they are sought knowingly. The first element (*puruṣa-*) in the compound, accordingly, restricts, not the scope of the ends sought, but only the manner of seeking them. The implication of the other element (*-artha*) is that the end is not existent (*siddha*) at the time it is cognized as worth pursuing and is still to be accomplished (*sādhya*). It, therefore, demands effort from the person who seeks it. When we speak of *puruṣārtha* as something yet to be accomplished (*sādhya*), we usually have in mind an intrinsic value. This is *puruṣārtha* in the primary sense (*mukhya*). Now, the pursuit of an intrinsic value presupposes a knowledge not only of that value, but also of a suitable means to its realization, an instrumental value. The means (*sādhana*) is also called *puruṣārtha*, but in a secondary sense (*gauṇa*). It may be existent already (*siddha*) or is itself to be secured (*sādhya*). "We may thus define a *puruṣārtha* as an end which is consciously sought to be accomplished either for its own sake or for the sake of utilizing it as a means to the accomplishment of a further end."[6]

From what has been stated so far it may appear that an intrinsic value (*mukhya-puruṣārtha*) is something which does not already exist, but is to be produced anew. But this is only to take the word *sādhya* in a positive, or direct, sense—of what is "not yet" but "yet to be." In fact, the early Mīmāṁsakas took the stand that no existent object can by itself be an intrinsic value. It can, at best, be only of an instrumental nature. But there were others who contended that an intrinsic value need not necessarily be *sādhya* in the above sense. The word *sādhya* may be understood in a negative, or indirect, sense also to represent an intrinsic value. In this sense an intrinsic value appears in two forms. (i) The end sought may be already present, and yet we may not be able to realize it owing to some obstacle or other as, for example, in the case of a buried treasure. Here the achievement of the value consists merely in removing the obstacle, and the activity is directed solely towards this end. (ii) In the above example the hindrance is physical. It may even be mental and consist merely in our failure to realize that what we seek is already in our possession. For example, a person may be searching for his eye-glasses though actually he may be wearing them. Here the attainment of the value consists in the person overcoming the delusion either by discovering the glasses himself or by being apprised of the fact by someone else. This shows that knowledge, like action, can be a means of achieving values. In these two cases nothing new comes into being. Still, the achievement of value in both cases, as in the earlier case, involves a change in the existing state of things. Only, in the first of them the change is in the realm of being; in the second, it is in the realm of thought.

Values—Lower and Higher

We may now examine how man comes to entertain higher values. That man is able to pursue his ends with a previous knowledge of them implies that he is aware not only of the object he seeks, but also of himself as aware of it. This capacity to be self-conscious is a great gift, because it enables man to review his thoughts, feelings, and actions and pass judgements of approbation or disapprobation upon them. Such self-criticism necessarily points to the awareness of a standard by which he judges. That standard can be nothing short of absolute perfection, which in Indian terminology is the ideal of *mokṣa*. The reason is that self-criticism is bound to continue until complete freedom from imperfection is reached. Man would not feel he was imperfect unless he had such an ideal, latent though, in his mind, which makes him a spiritual being.

Man is also actuated by lower impulses, which he has inherited from the past. This lower nature prompts him to pursue inferior ends and often prevents him from responding fully and uniformly to the call of his innate ideal of perfection. This double nature results in an internal conflict between the flesh and the spirit, or as they are called, the lower and the higher selves. Fortunately, man's higher nature is such that it is bound to assert itself sooner or later. Man cannot be at peace with himself until he chooses to obey it, overcoming all obstacles. It is with reference to his higher nature that man conceives of higher values like knowledge and goodness. The difference between the lower and the higher values is a difference between what man feels he *is* and what he feels he *ought to be*. The lower values are those which man feels naturally inclined to seek, and the higher, which he feels are really worthy of his pursuit. But the pursuit of the higher values does not mean that the lower ones are to be shunned and abandoned. In fact, some of them like food and drink cannot be avoided. They are needed for preserving life and form the very basis of all activity. They are, therefore, described as survival values. They are a necessary precondition for the pursuit of the higher values. There are others, like wealth, which are used as means to the survival values. These may be used as means to the pursuit of the higher values also, though they are not indispensable in this case. But their whole character will get transformed if they are sought as means to the higher. Thus to make a distinction between the lower and the higher values does not mean that the lower are to be given up. It only means that the primacy of the higher should never be forgotten in the pursuit of the lower. In any case, their pursuit should not come into conflict with that of the higher ends.

> ...the conception of value involves not only the distinction between good and bad, but also that between better and worse. This idea of gradation is basic to the conception. The first axiom of a philosophy of values, it has been stated, is that some things are preferable to or worthier than others.[7]

We have hitherto used only modern terminology for the different values. The Indian terms for them, though not precisely their equivalents, generally correspond to them. Among the lower values, the needs felt by man in common with the rest of animal creation, which may be summed up as self-preservation and race-preservation, are all brought under the head *kāma*. *Kāma* is an end in itself because it is natural and does not admit of the question "why." The means of satisfying these needs are infinite in number, and they are all brought under the head *artha*. *Kāma* represents what is agreeable and *artha* what is useful.

A little reflection will show that the lower values are not finally satisfying. The instrumental values coming under *artha* are precarious (*ānaikāntika*). There is no certainty in regard to many of them, if not all, that they will secure the end (*kāma*) which is sought to be attained through them. What was fruitful once or for one person may not be so at another time or for another person. The intrinsic values comprising *kāma* are unstable (*anātyantika*). The satisfaction derived through *artha*, even when it proves useful, is only provisional, in that it is sooner or later replaced by a desire for some other mode of satisfaction. This irony of life makes us ask whether there are any values that are not vitiated by these defects. The Indian answer to this question is that there are two such values, viz., *dharma* and *mokṣa*. Between them, *dharma* is the means and *mokṣa* is the end. *Dharma* never fails to fetch its fruit; and *mokṣa* is eternally satisfying. They represent what have been described as the higher values. *Dharma* corresponds to the good, and *mokṣa*, as we shall see later, has an implicit reference to the true.

These are the four well-known *puruṣārthas—artha*, *kāma*, *dharma*, and *mokṣa*. They are not of equal rank. They admit of being arranged in an ascending scale, and the determination of their relative status is the chief problem of philosophy as conceived in India. To begin with, we may describe the first two as secular, or empirical, values, and the last two as spiritual. Philosophy is concerned with the higher values of *dharma* and *mokṣa* and the right means to realize them. In fact this is the sole purpose of the Veda. But philosophy considers the other two also in order to show how they are inferior. Hence philosophy, as conceived in India, is "a criticism of values."[8] Other branches of learning may deal with single values, as for example, *arthaśāstra* and *dharmaśāstra*. But the comparison of values and the discussion of their superiority and inferiority does not occur in them. According to the majority of Indian thinkers, there is no opposition between the two sets of values. So the lower ones need not be abandoned for pursuing the higher ones. When they are made to subserve the latter, they become totally transformed.

Though all the four are ordinarily reckoned as values of life, early works like the *Rāmāyaṇa* and the *Mahābhārata* mainly refer to the first three, as these works are chiefly addressed to common people for whom *mokṣa* is of little immediate interest. This does not mean that they ignore *mokṣa*, which ideal is as old as the Upaniṣads. This distinction between the group of three (*trivarga*) and *mokṣa* is also a convenient one for the treatment of values. Leaving aside *mokṣa* for the time being, we shall see how the pursuit of *artha* and *kāma* has to be in consonance with *dharma*.

Artha and *kāma* are common to men and animals. The only difference is that man can seek them knowingly, though often he also, like animals, follows them instinctively. And in so far as he seeks them consciously, they become *puruṣārthas*; otherwise they just remain values. The case is quite different for *dharma*, for its appeal is restricted to man. Man is innately aware of it. The term may be rendered as "moral value." In orthodox systems its scope is much wider, for it includes also the religious values mentioned in the ritualistic portion of the Veda. But even here there is no harm in interpreting *dharma* as moral value, for it is admitted in ritualism that its basis is moral virtue. As to the relation of *dharma* to the lower values, it is enough if we discuss its relation to *kāma*, since *artha* is ordinarily only a means to *kāma*. *Kāma* stands for pleasure, and we cannot help desiring our own felicity. But every pleasure desired is not desirable at all times, for example delicious food for a sick person just because he longs for it. Thus *kāma*, though appearing to be a legitimate value, may sometimes prove to be a disvalue. *Dharma* furnishes the criterion to distinguish between these two kinds of *kāma*, the desirable and the undesirable. "That variety of *kāma* is a true value which is in accord with the requirements of *dharma*, but not any other."[9] In thus helping to discriminate between good and bad *kāma*, *dharma* proves its superiority. This conception of *dharma* as a regulative principle is emphasized by all the philosophical and literary works in India—explicitly by the former and implicitly by the latter. It is this importance of *dharma* over *kāma* that Śrīkṛṣṇa means when he says: "I am *kāma*, not at strife with *dharma*." (*dharmāviruddha kāmo'smi*).[10]

The Higher Values

We have said earlier that the ideal of perfection is latent in man ever urging him to strive for reaching a state in which he may rest with a feeling of contentment. However, since the ideal is not explicitly known, the ends which he actually pursues often fall short of the final ideal. These are the well-known ideals of truth, goodness, and beauty. This trinity of values is universally recognized, though each tradition may have its own conception of their nature. The Sanskrit terms *dharma* and *jñāna* easily reveal the place of goodness and truth in Indian philosophy. The recognition of beauty in it is not so evident. But, as we shall see later, its place in the Indian philosophy of values cannot be denied. What is special about the final Indian conception of these three values is that neither individually nor collectively can they be regarded as the ultimate in value. The highest value is only *mokṣa*, and truth, beauty, and goodness can only be subordinate to it. They have limitations which indirectly point not only to the need for *mokṣa* as the highest ideal, but also to its general nature. There is another point about the Indian attitude to these values. It admits that it is quite permissible to pursue these values for their own sake, for they are, unlike *artha* and *kāma*, free from any taint of self-interest. But it recognizes that the highest service they can render is as handmaids to *mokṣa*. That is the central teaching of ancient India regarding these values.[11]

Let us consider the case of beauty first. There is beauty in nature as well as in art. The contemplation of a work of art leads to a state of mind which is absolutely impersonal. The appreciator forgets himself completely and is conscious of nothing except what is portrayed in the work. This attitude resembles *savikalpaka-samādhi* in *yoga*, in which one loses oneself in contemplative union with the object. As a consequence of this self-forgetfulness, man rises above common life and experiences a unique satisfaction such as in the realization of the ultimate ideal. Yet art experience cannot serve as the final ideal, for it lasts only as long as the art stimulus lasts; and that stimulus is bound to end as it arises from an external and fictitious situation created by the artist.

As for beauty in nature, assuming that beauty is immanent in the whole of nature, that beauty is beyond common human experience. Such of it as ordinarily comes within our experience is only the beauty of single objects like a smiling flower or a brilliant rainbow. It means that it is only a fragment of nature that is presented to us, and we cannot lose sight of the boundaries of what we appreciate. Beauty in nature as commonly known thus differs from a work of art, which is a world by itself and so self-complete as to absorb our entire attention. And in spite of natural beauty being real, so long as its appreciation is piecemeal, it cannot but be transient, because the fragmentary spectacle cannot be held before the mind for very long. Sooner or later it is bound to be replaced by another which may or may not be aesthetically appealing. Moreover, it is also possible that a beautiful spectacle in nature, for the very reason that it is real, may lose its aesthetic appeal and acquire a practical one even within the time it is kept in sight. A person admiring the beauty of a place may be distracted from the aesthetic attitude by the thought of making it a tourist attraction. No such diversion of interest is possible in the case of art because its object is imaginary. Thus the realization of beauty in nature can no more be the final ideal than that of beauty in art.

Finally, the pursuit of beauty, whether in art or in nature, while it appeals to the affective side of the mind, does not satisfy all the needs and aspirations of man. Man is a social being and cannot afford to be lost in self-complacency, cutting himself away from the joys and sorrows of common life. But there is nothing in aesthetic experience as such to guarantee against a life of self-centred satisfaction. For this reason also it cannot substitute for the final ideal. The ideal of perfection "cannot allow any side of human nature to be starved; and it will not therefore be ever divorced from sympathy for fellow beings."[12]

Goodness and truth have their own defects so that they too cannot serve as the final ideal. The idea of the moral good is based on man's social consciousness. It implies that man is aware not only of his own self, but also of others as having selves like his own and as subject to the same feelings of pain and pleasure as he is. That is to say, he realizes that he is a social being with obligations to discharge towards others admidst whom he lives. And from this realization arises altruistic activity signified by the golden rule that we should do to others as we would desire them to do to us. But we should remember that man is also a natural being with lower motives of a selfish kind to contend with. It shows that the pursuit of the good requires strenuous and continued effort to subdue and subordinate selfish considerations to social interests. So long as there is need for conscious effort, we cannot say that the final ideal of perfection has been reached, for that ideal implies that self-love is wholly overcome and altruistic service becomes the effortless expression of a permanent attitude of mind. It is true that long training in social morality establishes in us habits of right conduct. But such training, by its very nature, is guided by a general standard. Such a standard, though it may work in situations that conform to that standard, may fail us when new situations arise in life or when there is a conflict of duties. Such situations will again involve a tension of mind calling for a deliberate personal determination of the right action required. The contingency of tension and effort will wholly disappear and moral action will become spontaneous only when morality is informed by an intuitive understanding of the ultimate truth about reality. It only shows that goodness as a value depends for its complete realization on another member of the trinity, viz., truth, and that, therefore, it cannot by itself stand for the highest ideal.

Let us consider truth. This value does not suffer from the deficiencies of beauty. Beauty in art depends on a situation created by the artist. But truth has direct reference to reality. Beauty in nature as we commonly experience refers to parts of nature. But the truth sought in philosophy—unlike truth in common knowledge or in science—is all-comprehensive, its object being the whole of reality. Aesthetic experience, whether in art or in nature, is transient, considering the nature of the source in each case. But philosophic truth, bearing as it does on the whole of reality, ought to give stable satisfaction when discovered. Further, the pursuit of truth has the merit of being unselfish, as in the case of art and morality, for truth, in its pure and undefiled form, cannot be attained if it is vitiated by any personal motive like gain or glory.

With all this, philosophic truth has its own limitation. As such, it is necessarily mediate. Some modern philosophers hold that philosophy, like the pure sciences, must remain speculative and signify a purely theoretical understanding of reality. It should not, therefore, be expected to have a bearing upon life, which is the concern of religion and not of philosophy. But philosophy cannot be equated with the pure sciences. Even in its mediate form philosophy tends to influence life when once it has satisfied our reason and won our acceptance. Knowing a scientific truth like that the planet Saturn has a certain number of rings encircling it may have no direct relation to a person's mode of living. But a philosophic truth like that of the survival of the self surely tends to influence life—in one way if a person believes in it, and in another way if he does not. The reason is that, unlike pure science, philosophy is not confined to physical reality, but covers the nature of man and his place in the universe. It, therefore, contains a reference, latent or explicit, not only to values in general, but also to the final ideal of life, which, as an ideal, implies that man ought to aim at realizing it in fact.

To admit that philosophic truth tends to influence life is not, however, to claim that it *does* influence it. Though it refers to the final ideal, philosophy, taken as such, is only intellectual conviction about that ideal. The imperfections of life are a matter of direct experience. They can be removed only by a direct experience of the ultimate truth. Thus the truth of philosophy cannot substitute for the final ideal, the actual realization of which alone can transform life in the real sense of the term.

A common feature of beauty, goodness, and truth is that their pursuit is marked by disinterestedness. Any admixture of selfish aim is sure to contaminate them and detract from their position as higher values. For example, if a person tries to do good to others in order that they may do good to him, or even that he may enjoy the consciousness of his own goodness, he is not acting morally. It is chiefly because of this absence of selfishness that these values are termed "higher." Apart from this common feature, which may be termed negative, each value has its own positive excellence. The pursuit of the good signifies altruistic service; that of the beautiful affords relief from the tension of common life; and that of the true yields comprehensive knowledge, which, by removing all doubt and uncertainty, produces a stable conviction. But each has also its peculiar limitation. Goodness is necessarily characterized by strife, and can never be fully achieved in and by itself; beauty can be realized, but only for a limited time; and truth, so long as it remains mediate, may fail to influence life. Thus, though the realization of these values may overcome some of the deficiencies of common life, their limitations render them unfitted to serve as man's final ideal, the attainment of which alone can completely satisfy our spiritual nature.

We now come to another point. Although none of the three values is ultimate in the sense of an all-sufficing absolute value which leaves nothing further to be desired, all of them are fundamental in the sense that each appeals to a distinctive side of man's spiritual nature. Hence, though none of them by itself suffices to be the final human goal, each stands for some necessary aspect of it. No final ideal can exclude altruistic service or restful peace or a comprehensive knowledge of reality. All the three values are thus included in the final ideal. A far more important point about them is that, as shown by their description so far, they supplement one another. And for this reason, they are sufficient, when taken together, to indicate all the essential characteristics of the final ideal.

To begin with, disinterestedness should be a constant and outstanding feature of the final ideal. Further, it must contain the special excellences of the three values, but freed from their respective shortcomings. Conscious effort should disappear in the case of goodness, and moral action should become spontaneous and joyful. The restful peace resulting from the experience of beauty should not be provisional but constant; and this implies that it should be derived from the contemplation of reality in its wholeness. The complete knowledge of reality, again, for which philosophic truth stands, must not remain mediate, but should become a direct experience. To set free the three values of their respective defects means that they are totally transformed. Hence the final ideal is not a mere combination of the three values, but a creative synthesis of them. It thus not only includes the three values, but also transcends them. "This new ideal is, to characterize it in brief, a state of absolute unselfishness and of spontaneous joy that manifests itself always—whether one is engaged in outward action or is absorbed in inward contemplation."[13]

At this stage the question naturally arises whether such an ideal is at all feasible. There is a view that misery is a necessary feature of life and the only escape from it is in the imaginative realm of art. The real is bound to remain imperfect, and the ideal is always unreal. There is no harmony at all between the world of facts and the realm of ideals. That is pessimism, pure and simple. The outcome of this view is resignation. In such a state whatever help one renders to fellow-sufferers will be in pity rather than in love. It may be that this doctrine of despair cannot be logically refuted; yet the best thought all over the world is different. In India particularly, the majority of thinkers have all along believed in the possibility of realizing perfection. The chief argument in support of this belief is that man is not an alien in the universe, but a part of it. So there is no reason why the universe should be hostile to him in the pursuit of an ideal which is implicit in his very nature. Struggle, of course, is needed to overcome his lower self; but the nature of his higher self is such as will not allow it to be subordinated to the lower. Here is the necessity which impels man onwards until the ideal is fully realized. The progress may be slow, but it is not futile. Aesthetic experience is evidence of the possibility of achieving the final ideal. Far from being a mere escape from the troubles of life, it gives us a foretaste of the ideal state. Though unstable, it is of the same order as anticipated in the latter. And so we may well conclude from the fact of the one to the feasibility of the other.

We have so far seen how the three ideals, though not ultimate, point to the need for and indicate the nature of the final ideal. Their other significance is that they serve as means to reach that ideal. But there is an important difference between the way in which beauty serves this purpose and the way in which the other two do so. Being only analogous to *mokṣa*, the help which aesthetic experience renders is only incidental. By carrying us to the threshold of the ideal, as it were, and giving us a glimpse of it, aesthetic experience can only inspire us with a desire for realizing *mokṣa*. Unlike this, goodness and truth have a necessary role to play in leading us to the final ideal. We shall deal with the significance of each of these three values to *mokṣa* in the appropriate sections to follow.

Value and Pleasure

The old and familiar classification of values is as *dharma*, *artha*, *kāma*, and *mokṣa*. While granting this, the Nyāya thinker Udyotakara says that at bottom the only value is the attainment of pleasure (*sukha-prāpti*) or the avoidance of pain (*duḥkha-nivṛtti*). (We have already noted that the idea of value is always associated with a feeling of pleasure.) Value is defined as the object of desire (*iṣṭa*). And what is desired is always pleasure or freedom from pain. By implication, pain, or the loss of pleasure, is a disvalue (*dviṣṭa*). As this view also has come to prevail, it may appear that the Indian conception of value is fundamentally hedonistic. But examination will show that it is not so. "The generally ascetic character of Indian philosophic teaching shows that it is not hedonism."[14] (We are not including here the Cārvāka doctrine, which is avowedly egoistic, or hedonistic.)

There are two standpoints from which this question may be considered: whether pleasure is, as a matter of fact, sought by man and whether it is good and worthy to be sought by him. We shall take the latter for consideration first. The definition of value is merely that it is desired and not also that it is desirable, for what is desired need not always be desirable. So if the object of desire is always pleasure, the Indian view merely states the psychological fact that pleasure is desired. It does not signify that pleasure is in all cases worthy of being sought. In fact, the pursuit of certain pleasures is wholly disapproved. In the *Kaṭha Upaniṣad*, for example, *preyas*, which stands for common pleasure, is sharply distinguished from *śreyas*, or supreme bliss, which marks the final goal of life; and the former is discountenanced completely. Two kinds of pleasure thus come to be recognized, of which one alone deserves to be desired. "The criterion of preferability in regard to pleasure is thus something other than its pleasantness…."[15]

Such a view may appear to make a qualitative distinction in pleasure, but it does not. What distinguishes the higher from the lower pleasure here is whether or not its pursuit is prompted by right philosophical knowledge (*vidyā*) or ignorance (*avidyā*). To state the idea differently, the distinction is made on the criterion whether the pleasure is such as to help us forward in the attainment of the final goal of life. In itself, pleasure is qualitatively the same.

Thus the Indian conception of value does not advocate the pursuit of pleasure indiscriminately. Is it, then, hedonistic in the other sense, viz., whether it recognizes that what is sought is always pleasure? To judge from the manner in which value is defined, viz. that it is an "object of desire," the conception may seem to suggest that what is desired is always pleasure, but really it is not so. There are two reasons for this.

According to some systems of thought,[16] pleasure is the only end desired by man, but what they actually mean by pleasure is the supreme bliss of *mokṣa*, and not the pleasures which man commonly seeks. The latter invariably fail to satisfy him permanently. "They only arrest desire for the time being, but do not fulfil it."[17] If man yet seeks them, it is either because his conception of the ideal is extremely vague or because he is ignorant of the means to its attainment. Where neither of these is the reason, as in the case of a philosopher, it is the force of his former habits (*saṁskāra*) that accounts for such seeking. It should, however, be noted that this apparent good is not the same as "disvalue," for the latter, being of the nature of pain, never even appears to be good as this does. In fact, the very inadequacy of the apparent good serves as an incentive to seek the permanent good of *mokṣa*. Thus, according to this view, absolute bliss is the uniform motive behind the activities of different men and the several activities of one and the same person. It is that bliss which is altogether unmixed and from which there is no lapse when once it is attained. There is no question of such a view being hedonistic, for no pleasure as it is commonly known and is meant in hedonism satisfies this standard. "Indians seem to have been influenced by their doctrine of *mokṣa* in enunciating all value to be pleasure."[18]

Some other doctrines,[19] which recognize *mokṣa* as the final ideal, feel that even without reference to the supreme bliss, it is possible to reach the same conclusion on the basis of empirical pleasure. They admit that such pleasure is associated with all voluntary activity, but they explain its place in value situation in two different ways. Pleasure may be sought by a person directly for himself or it may be derived indirectly by him when he seeks the welfare of another. Let us consider two cases.

A person eagerly seeking some delicious food or drink finds it and then partakes of it. Here pleasure is a value in the sense that it is directly sought. But this does not mean that pleasure stands by itself abstracted from some object or other which occasions it. Though pleasure may be directly aimed at, one cannot set about realizing it until a suitable means to it is also secured. Hence pleasure cannot be the *only* value even when it is directly sought, and this view is not hedonistic.

In the following examples pleasure is not directly sought, but nevertheless enjoyed as a consequence of realizing some other end. A father performs the Vedic sacrifice called *vaiśvānareṣṭi* for the well-being of his male child. The father is not the recipient of the benefit (*phala*) of the sacrifice. Nevertheless, in thinking of the benefit that will accrue to his son, he is pleased, and this pleasure (*prīti*) is his reward. Similarly, a mother devoting herself to her child's care derives satisfaction if the child's well-being is ensured. Again, a person acquiring wealth, not for self-gratification, but for doing good to others, may derive satisfaction in the service that he renders. Since, in all such cases, pleasure is not the willed aim of the activity, it is not the value sought. Being merely a consequence of realizing another end, pleasure here is a sign of value rather than a value itself. If it is argued that, since eventually at least, pleasure is enjoyed and, for that reason, the Indian view is hedonistic, the reply is that, in that case, it is certainly not *egoistic* hedonism. There is such a thing as altruism, and man does value the good of another.

2. LOGICAL VALUE

The Psychology of Knowledge

There are two points of view from which the problem of knowledge may be approached—its psychology and its epistemology. The psychology of knowledge is concerned with the nature of knowledge as a fact of mental life, and its epistemology, with its validity as pointing to an object beyond itself. How knowledge takes place is only of indirect connection with metaphysics. Whether and how it comes to be valid is directly important for determining the nature of reality. Hence the interest of Indian thinkers in knowledge is mainly in the epistemology of knowledge. Still, their discussions have throughout a psychological basis, as it is necessary to know the nature of knowledge in the first instance. We shall, therefore, deal with the main features of this psychology.

The first requirement of knowledge is a conscious subject. To serve as the focus to which all experience may be referred, this subject should be characterized by a certain unity and continuity. This much is granted in one sense or another by all Indian thinkers including some of the Cārvākas. Nearly all schools also assume the existence of a soul, or self, which is usually termed *jīva*. These systems differ from one another in their conception of the ultimate nature of the soul. But all of them are agreed on the need for a self to serve as the subject of knowing, which we may describe as the empirical self as distinguished from the metaphysical self.

Closely allied to the conception of the empirical self is that of the *manas*. The *manas* is the means, we may say, whereby the metaphysical self comes to play the role of an empirical self. It is thus a constituent of the empirical self. It is this complex which is the empirical self that functions as the subject of experience (*bhoktṛ*) and the agent of purposive activity (*kartṛ*). The *manas* is usually regarded as physical in nature. This physical complement of the self is in some doctrines conceived as simple and atomic; in others, as complex and finite. In the latter it usually bears the name of internal organ (*antaḥkaraṇa*). According to many, the *manas* functions as an aid to inner perception, as for example, of hunger and thirst. It then serves as an internal sense. In the perception of external objects it serves as a common aid to the self, in addition to the specific external senses.

On the relation of knowledge to the knowing subject there are broadly three views. (i) To some schools like Nyāya-Vaiśeṣika, knowledge is a specific quality of the self, which arises in it when certain conditions are fulfilled, such as contact of a sense-organ with an object. (ii) To some like the Kumārila school, knowledge is a process which takes place in the self by virtue of which the object becomes known. Thus knowledge (*jñāna*) becomes a means to the awareness of the object (*saṁvedana*). The point conveyed here is that knowledge involves an activity and is not merely passive. (iii) According to some others like Sāṅkhya-Yoga, the self is of the essence of consciousness, i.e., it is sentience itself. Knowledge is neither a quality nor an activity in it. We speak of the occurrence of knowledge whenever this intrinsic nature of the self is revealed. The conditions under which this revelation takes place are explained differently by those who subscribe to this view.

The function of knowledge is to reveal objects to the self. As regards the manner in which this function takes place, there are two views. One is that objects are known directly; the other, that they are known only indirectly through psychic media, which in some way resemble or symbolize the objects in question. In either case, the internal organ cooperates with the self; only in the second, it also serves to link the self and the object which otherwise do not come together. The internal organ, receives the impress of the object presented, and it is through that imprinted form, or psychic addition, that the object is known by the self. This is the theory of representative perception as it is known to Western philosophy. There are obvious objections to this view, but we shall not go into them here.

Another point discussed in the Indian psychology of knowledge is the nature of the content of perception. Perceptual knowledge, it is admitted, is complex in character and is expressible in the form of a judgement. It is, therefore, described as determinate (*savikalpaka*). We are not only aware of a presentation, but also know something about it. That is, the judgement involves a reference to an object, its characteristics such as colour, and the relation between them. The important question is whether this is the primary form of perception. There are three answers to this question.

(i) Some schools like Nyāya-Vaiśeṣika assume that such perception must have been preceded by a stage in which the elements of the judgement should have been presented separately, on the principle that the complex presupposes the simple. This previous indeterminate (*nirvikalpaka*) form is not known to us, but has to be deduced from the fact of determinate perception. (ii) Others like the Kumārila school also speak of an indeterminate stage prior to the determinate. But here it is indeterminate for a different reason. This stage, like the determinate one which is to follow, itself represents the subject-object relation; but it is too vague and indefinite for the relation to be expressed in words. It gains clarity and definiteness only subsequently, when we are able to speak something about some object. Further, the indeterminate stage spoken of here is not a mere assumption, but a matter of perception, which is useful to activity such as in children and animals. (iii) Some other schools like Viśiṣṭādvaita agree that even the preliminary stage of perception is complex involving a "what" and a "that." Still, it may be called indeterminate for the reason that it represents the apprehension of an object, say a cow, for the first time. When the person perceives any cow for the second time, the cognition is accompanied by the revival of the former impression. And for this reason it is to be called determinate. If the first cognition is expressed as "This is a cow," the second is expressed as "This is also a cow."

How is knowledge itself known? According to some doctrines, Nyāya-Vaiśeṣika for instance, the fact that we know an object is itself known only subsequently to knowing the object. This subsequent knowledge (*anuvyavasāya*) may be a form of introspection or of inference. But the point to be noted is that knowledge, like the object, itself requires to be known. In holding that the object is known before its knowing is known, the view makes a distinction between knowledge and object, which is denied by other schools. The latter argue that knowledge not only reveals objects, but also reveals itself (*sva-prakāśa*). But the term "self-revealing" is understood in two ways. To some like the Yogācāra school, knowledge is knowable in the sense that it is knowable by itself instead of by another knowledge. But others like the Prābhākara school say that this view is unsound as one and the same thing cannot be both the knower and the known. Hence they say that "self-revealing" simply means "never requiring to be revealed," its presence being equivalent to its revelation.

All the features dealt with so far relate to the waking state (*jāgrat*). Indian thinkers also take into account the states of dream (*svapna*) and dreamless sleep (*suṣupti*), for they consider that, without a study of these states, neither the nature of knowledge nor that of the self can be properly understood. There is also sometimes mention of a fourth state (*turīya*). It stands for a "super-conscious" level of life, and its significance is not empirical, but transcendental.

The Means of Valid Knowledge

Epistemology is specially concerned with valid knowledge (*pramā*). The proximate means to valid knowledge is called *pramāṇa*; the object to which it refers, *prameya*; and the subject of knowing, *pramātā*. These are all cognate terms, and to consider the significance of anyone of them is also to understand the significance of the others. The consideration of *pramāṇa* is the best introduction to the Indian conception of valid knowledge.

The word *pramāṇa* comes from the root *mā* "to measure" and signifies "that by which we measure." Thus, etymologically, *pramāṇa* is the means of measuring, or ascertaining, the correctness of knowledge. Its need arises when a thing is known but its knowledge is still uncertain. The circumstances that led to this interpretation of the term *pramāṇa* are to be found in the later post-Vedic period when systems of philosophy were just emerging.[20] Philosophy had become a matter of conflicting tradition with its orthodox and heterodox streams, and the chief function of *pramāṇa* was naturally conceived as scrutinizing this tradition. The result of such examination would be the elimination of all that is opposed to concrete experience and is self-contradictory within a traditional doctrine. Therefore, the present view of *pramāṇa* means that non-contradiction (*abādhitatva*) is essential to the validity of knowledge, which accordingly comes to be included in the definition of valid knowledge.

Another view of *pramāṇa* which is equally familiar to Indian thinkers is as a means of discovering new truths. The earlier view implies that the thing in question is already known, though not for certain. But the later view implies that it was hitherto unknown. And a *pramāṇa* is a means of adding to our knowledge by revealing objects or aspects of them not hitherto known. Consequently novelty (*anadhigatatva*) also comes to be laid down as a criterion of valid knowledge. Indian logic, like any other, is thus a science of discovery as well as a science of proof. The two meanings of *pramāṇa* are closely connected, both being concerned with the truth of knowledge. "If the emphasis in the one case is on the cognitive side, it is on the probative side in the other."[21]

Incidentally, it must be remembered that whatever view they take of the exact nature of *pramāṇa*, Indian thinkers agree in holding that nearly all knowledge prompts the knower to act in accordance with it. Though the immediate aim of knowledge is the attainment of truth, its ultimate significance is the fulfilment of some purpose in life. But this pragmatic view of knowledge is far different from the view of modern pragmatism. Unlike the latter, Indian pragmatism does not identify the utility of knowledge with its validity. The validity of knowledge is determined by the nature of reality and the nature of the cognizing mind and is, so far, entirely independent of pragmatic considerations. Knowledge does not derive its validity from its success in action. "Practical activity is not constitutive of truth, but is only a consequence of it."[22] A more important indication of the difference of the Indian view from modern pragmatism is that all the Indian doctrines, as we shall see, recognize absolute truth in some sense or another.

There is much divergence among Indian schools concerning the nature, scope, and number of *pramāṇas*. Most schools agree in accepting three *pramāṇas*—perception (*pratyakṣa*), inference (*anumāna*), and verbal testimony (*śabda*). The inclusion of verbal testimony among the *pramāṇas* is a striking feature of Indian philosophy. The need for verbal testimony as a *pramāṇa* arises for knowing what lies beyond the sphere of perception and inference, which is based on perception. But Nyāya-Vaiśeṣika and Sāṅkhya-Yoga claim equal status in this regard for a variety of inference called *sāmānyato-dṛṣṭānumāna*, or analogical reasoning. It is necessary to say a few words on this.

There are two types of inference generally recognized in Indian philosophy. The first of them is *anumāna*, or syllogistic inference. It is illustrated by the example of deducing the existence of fire from the perception of smoke. The inference is based on the previously observed relation between smoke and fire. This type of inference is, therefore, applicable only to cases falling within the sphere of common human experience. The other variety of inference applies to cases that lie beyond it. In this, with the support of what is found in the sphere of sensuous objects, we reason about parallel cases in the sphere of the supersensuous. Hence it is called *sāmānyato-dṛṣṭa*, which means "seen from likeness." For example, we know that an instrument like an axe needs an agent to use it. Similarly, assuming that the *manas* is an instrument, we may conclude that it requires an agent, viz., the self, to explain its activity, though neither the *manas* nor the self is perceivable. The Nyāya-Vaiśeṣika argument for the existence of God is of this type. From the observed fact that an effect like a pot requires for its production a competent agent like the potter, it is concluded that the world, assuming it to be an effect, should also have been created by a competent being, God. Sāṅkhya-Yoga, again, uses this variety of inference to deduce the existence and nature of unmanifest *prakṛti* from the manifest things of the world.

The merit of this type of argument is that it is constructive, or creative, in character unlike ordinary inference. But it is not legitimate to claim for it, as the above schools do, the status of an independent *pramāṇa* on transcendental matters like revelation. The reason is, as Vedāntins point out, that its conclusion is at the most probable and not certain. Mere analogy is not the same as evidence. We are extending here a principle verified in experience to something beyond it; and such an extension is not legitimate, for in it we virtually jump from one particular to another, without passing through a general truth based upon actual observation, as we do in ordinary inference. Therefore the only *pramāṇa* on transcendental matters, according to Vedānta and Mīmāṁsā is the verbal testimony of the Veda. Such a conclusion does not mean that *sāmānyato-dṛṣṭa* is to be completely excluded from the consideration of transcendental matters. In so far as it can lend probability to a conclusion arrived at in scripture, it can be utilized as an aid to the latter. And where sufficient care is exercised, the degree of probability indicated by it may even be quite high. That is, "it may support the truth, though it may not establish it."[23] In fact, it is in this role that Advaita, for instance, utilizes *sāmānyato-dṛṣṭānumāna*. And in this ancillary form reason is designated here as *yukti*, or *tarka*.

Besides the three *pramāṇas* mentioned so far, there are three which are admitted variously in schools. *Upamāna*, or comparison, is admitted by Nyāya-Vaiśeṣika, Mīmāṁsā, and Advaita; *arthāpatti*, or presumption, is admitted by Mīmāṁsā and Advaita; and *anupalabdhi*, or non-apprehension, is recognized only by the Kumārila school of Mīmāṁsā and Advaita. Of these *pramāṇas*, the last needs special mention.

Schools of Indian philosophy like Nyāya-Vaiśeṣika, Mīmāṁsā, and Advaita recognize the concept of negative facts, or the non-existence of objects (*abhāva*), e.g., the absence of a jar somewhere. Negative facts, it is argued, are as much objects of knowledge as positive facts. "...knowledge of absence is not absence of knowledge."[24] The question arises how *abhāva* is known. According to Nyāya, a separate *pramāṇa* is not needed for knowing this. The non-existence of a perceivable object can be known by perception, just as its existence is known by it. The eye which reveals an umbrella which is presented to it also reveals its absence when it is not presented—provided every condition required for its perception excepting the presence of the object is satisfied. The non-existence of objects which are not open to perception, e.g. the absence of atoms in ether (*ākāśa*), is known by means of inference. But according to Kumārila, this view is wrong. As for the non-existence of a perceivable object, it is impossible to think that it is in contact with a sense organ—a condition admitted to be necessary to perception. As regards the absence of a non-perceivable object, inference is ruled out as it is eventually based on perception, which is out of question here. Hence Kumārila postulates a separate *pramāṇa* for knowing non-existence. According to him, all the other five *pramāṇas* are means of knowing only positive facts. But the absence of a fact is known only by the absence of the knowledge derived through any of these means, other conditions of apprehension remaining the same. It is this non-apprehension by any of the other means that Kumārila designates *anupalabdhi*. Advaita also recognizes this *pramāṇa*.

The Validity of Knowledge

The occurrence of doubts and illusions shows that knowledge is not always valid. From this fact arises the general question how knowledge stands in relation to its validity. The problem is twofold. One part of the question relates to the genesis (*utpatti*) of validity, or the conditions under which knowledge comes to be valid. The other part deals with the ascertainment (*jñapti*) of validity, i.e., the criterion by which we discover the validity of knowledge. There are four views in all in answer to this twofold problem, and we shall discuss them with reference to their chief representatives. The main contrast is between the views of Nyāya-Vaiśeṣika and Mīmāṁsā. We shall first compare them with reference to the origin of validity.

According to Nyāya-Vaiśeṣika, neither validity nor invalidity is inherent in knowledge. This does not mean that knowledge is neutral; it must be either valid or invalid. But the validity or the invalidity that characterizes it does not arise from the causes and conditions that give rise to knowledge. They arise from factors other than the causes and conditions, viz., their excellence (*guṇa*) or their deficiency (*doṣa*). No knowledge that arises will be valid unless the various causes and conditions of its emergence are possessed of particular excellence. For example, the presentation of an object is the cause of its sight, or visual knowledge, and the presence of light a condition for its sight. But the mere presentation of the object and the presence of light are not enough for its validity. The object must be presented sufficiently near and the place should be adequately lit for it to be seen clearly. These are the excellences. Similarly, no knowledge that arises will be invalid unless one or more of its causes and conditions are deficient, or possessed of *doṣa*. Thus the validity and invalidity of knowledge are extraneous in origin (*parataḥ*).

In contrast to this, Mīmāṁsā maintains that validity is inherent in knowledge, so that knowledge arising under normal circumstances is valid. If knowledge were not in its very nature valid, no external factor could make it so. Knowledge comes into being solely with a view to acquaint us with objects, and to question its validity will, therefore, be to question the very purpose of its existence. All that is necessary for knowledge to be valid is the absence of deficiencies (*doṣa*) in its causes and conditions. It is not necessary to import the presence of excellence (*guṇa*) to explain validity, as Nyāya does. The Nyāya theory is for this reason needlessly elaborate. Contrarywise, according to Mīmāṁsā, it is the presence of *doṣa* in the causes and conditions that explains why knowledge sometimes goes wrong. Thus validity occurs intrinsically (*svataḥ*) and invalidity through interference from another (*parataḥ*).

The same contrast exists between Nyāya and Mīmāṁsā in regard to the ascertainment of validity. According to Nyāya, since both validity and invalidity occur to knowledge *ab extra*, both are known only through extraneous factors. Though knowledge must be either true or false and never neutral, it cannot *by itself* be taken as either. Whether it is true or false can be known only after proper verification. Even in the absence of such verification, knowledge may have its bearing on practical life; but, so far as its logical character is concerned, nothing can be asserted. The external evidence called for may be either practical or theoretical; it may consist in putting the knowledge to some practical activity or "appealing to facts," as it is said. The main objection to the above view is this. What serves as the means of verification is another case of knowledge which itself needs verification; and to set about verifying it would be to apply this principle *ad infinitum*.

Mīmāṁsā takes the stand that since validity is intrinsic to knowledge in origin, it is also known intrinsically (*svataḥ*). That is to say, its validity is self-evident, or known simultaneously with its arisal. Left to operate by itself, knowledge necessarily leans to truth. Hence knowledge as such may be presumed to be valid. If sometimes it departs from truth and contradicts well-attested experience, it is because one or more extraneous factors have meddled with it. Only when there is any reason to suspect such interference, or when the knowledge in question is contradicted by another, it needs to be tested. That is, "it is not truth that needs explanation, but only error...."[25] And if the erroneous character of knowledge is then shown, it means that its invalidity becomes known through external evidence (*parataḥ*). Vedānta agrees with Mīmāṁsā in holding the doctrine of the self-validity of knowledge in origin and ascertainment.

Sāṅkhya-Yoga maintains that both validity and invalidity are intrinsic (*svataḥ*) to knowledge in its origin. The justification for this view lies in the school's theory of *satkāryavāda*, i.e., whatever manifests itself in something at any time must have been latent in it all along. And it is well known that knowledge assumed to be valid may sometimes turn out to be invalid. The doctrine again does not see any objection in contradictory features being present in the same thing, as it conceives of reality to be an identity in difference. Such a view, however, is quite indefinite. Similarly, in the matter of ascertainment also, it holds that validity and invalidity are self-evident (*svataḥ*) in knowledge, and do not require to be revealed by any extraneous factor. All that the view lays down is that both of them are not exhibited simultaneously to any one. But if all knowledge were thus known to be either valid or invalid even as it arises, there would be neither doubt nor illusion.

The last view, which belongs to Buddhism, holds that knowledge by its very nature is false (*svataḥ aprāmāṇyam*) and cannot be trusted without adequate evidence. It is this ultra-sceptical view that explains why even the realists among Buddhists deny being to much that is given in common experience. Such a view arises from the peculiar view taken of *pramāṇa* by all Buddhist schools. They recognize only perception and inference; and even perceptual knowledge involves, according to all of them, a subjective element. Such knowledge may have value for life by directing us to object-series, but it cannot reveal their real nature. Hence knowledge has no logical value and is described as valid only in the practical sense that it leads to successful activity. When it is not "valid" even in this restricted sense, it is conventionally spoken of as error. But at bottom all knowledge is erroneous. In other words, all knowledge, theoretically speaking, needs verification before it can be pronounced true. Thus validity depends on extraneous factors (*parataḥ-prāmāṇyam*). This view makes the position of experience quite precarious. If all knowledge is presumably misleading, the success of our activities, which are based on such misleading knowledge, becomes a matter of pure chance, and all life is reduced to a gamble.

Theories of Truth and Error

We have next to consider the nature of truth as conceived in the various schools. But the soundness of a theory of truth depends on the success with which it explains the occurrence of error. Broadly speaking, there are five typical explanations of error. Of these five theories, according to *akhyāti*, knowledge can never be false, while according to *ātma-khyāti* and *asat-khyāti*, knowledge can never be true. These are two extreme positions in regard to the attitude towards knowledge. Both the positions recognize the common distinction between truth and error. But they maintain that such a distinction has no logical value and is based purely on practical grounds. To that extent they fail to serve the ultimate purpose of a theory of error, viz., to evolve a proper criterion of truth. Only in *anyathā-khyāti* and *anirvacanīya-khyāti* is it clearly recognized that knowledge is sometimes true and sometimes false. And so a criterion of truth becomes meaningful only in them. Let us briefly consider the two extreme positions first.

To begin with *akhyāti*, the standard form of this theory is represented by Prābhākara Mīmāṁsā. Its other forms belong to an earlier phase of the same Mīmāṁsā, Sāṅkhya-Yoga, and Viśiṣṭādvaita. As the name indicates, the theory is that error is a lack of knowledge, rather than wrong knowledge. It is a case of non-apprehension and not of misapprehension. The non-apprehension is explained thus. (i) A white crystal placed by the side of a red flower may be wrongly regarded as a red crystal. Here there are two acts of knowing, each partial and valid so far as it goes. The crystal is perceived minus its true colour, viz., white. Similarly, the redness alone of the flower is perceived. The failure to notice that these are two separate acts of knowing results in the wrong notion of a red crystal. (ii) A piece of shell may be mistaken for silver. Here also there are two partial acts of knowing, but only one of them is perceptual, the other being recollection. The shell is perceived only with reference to its white and shiny features resembling silver. Actual silver is also recollected without realizing that it is only a recollection. And the failure to discriminate between the two acts results in the error of perceiving silver here and now.

Thus what is called error is only a matter of omission. The later discovery of the so-called error merely makes good this deficiency and does not cancel any part of what was previously known. It is a case of advance in knowledge, not one of "rectification of error." In fact, there is no error at all in this view, in the usual sense of a single *unit* of knowledge. "All knowledge is true in the sense that no portion of what it reveals is contradicted afterwards; and to question whether it agrees with reality in any particular instance is therefore to question its very nature."[26] But, then, we do commonly distinguish between truth and error. How do we explain this? It does not avail us to point out that error is partial knowledge, for human knowledge is always partial in one sense or another. So another explanation is given, and it is indirect. Though all knowledge is incomplete in so far as a given object is not grasped in its entirety, error is more incomplete than truth. And this *relative* incompleteness is shown by the fact that it fails to work in actual life. It does not produce the expected result as true knowledge does.

There is no doubt that the theory is simple and consistent in explaining the logical character of knowledge. But in denying the possibility of error from the purely logical point of view and in elevating error to the level of truth, it fails to evolve a proper criterion of truth as a theory of error is expected to do. Whatever distinction it concedes between truth and error is extraneous to epistemology and purely pragmatic. We may also note that a purely negative explanation cannot account for error. In terms of the theory, error is relatively incomplete knowledge. But speaking in these very terms, it is not enough for knowledge to be incomplete to go wrong; it should also be taken at the time to be complete or adequate, for surely nobody who knows that his knowledge is incomplete can be said to make a mistake when he takes it to be right. And in so far as what is incomplete is taken for the complete or the less adequate for the more adequate, there is misapprehension. "...all errors are therefore errors of commission. Errors of *mere* omission in the sphere of knowledge are strictly not errors at all."[27]

We now turn to *ātmakhyāti* and *asatkhyāti*. The former belongs to Yogācāra Buddhism and the latter to Mādhyamika. In these two theories also whatever distinction is recognized between truth and error is on practical rather than on logical grounds. But the reason for this failure is just the opposite of what we find in *akhyāti*. In the present cases truth is reduced to the level of error. No knowledge is true in the epistemological sense of the term. That is to say, knowledge can never reveal the nature of what is known. Such a conclusion arises from the Buddhist assumption that everything is momentary, the implication of which the upholders of these two theories take to its limits.

Even Vaibhāṣika, which claims that external objects are real and are directly known by means of perception, admits that what is perceived is not to be taken at its face value. Like Sautrāntika, Vaibhāṣika makes a distinction between determinate (*savikalpaka*) and indeterminate (*nirvikalpaka*) levels of perception. In the indeterminate stage, which is assumed as preceding the determinate, the passive mind has the bare sensation of an unrelated particular (*svalakṣaṇa*), say the colour blue. But at the determinate stage, which corresponds to judgement, the mind becomes active to elaborate the *svalakṣaṇa* and interpret it in terms of a relation (*sāmānya-lakṣaṇa*) such as between substance and attribute. It is thus that we have the perceptual judgement such as "this is blue," which is true only in so far as the particulars "this" and "blue" are concerned, but not of their relation. Thus, like Sautrāntika, Vaibhāṣika endows the perceiving mind with a constructive side on account of which reality becomes vastly transformed when it is experienced.

Starting from Vaibhāṣika, the place which Buddhism as a whole assigns to *jñāna* is very precarious. "Knowledge may have value for life, but its metaphysical significance is next to nothing."[28] The only criterion which such a view can offer to distinguish between truth and error is the fitness of knowledge to secure for us the object in question (*prāpakatva*) in actual life. That knowledge is true which confirms the expectation it raises. It should be noted, however, that even this practical verification of knowledge is held to be only approximate. Such an admission is rendered necessary by the unusual way in which reality is conceived. Going back to Vaibhāṣika, even in the *nirvikalpaka* stage, as Sautrāntika points out, the *svalakṣaṇa* which is actually given cannot be reached, for it ceases to be in a moment. So the utmost that knowledge can do is to direct us to the series of which the *svalakṣana* cognized *was* a member. Such verification is adequate to meet the demands of practical life, just as a person who sees only the lustre of a jewel stretches forth his hand and happens to secure it. Thus even the practical value of knowledge is only indirect. It is not, therefore, surprising that all knowledge should be regarded in Buddhism as presumably wrong, and where it is described as valid, it is only in a practical sense. *Ātmakhyāti* and *asatkhyāti* are avowed forms of this view.

Vaibhāṣika's theory of direct perception is irreconcilable with the notion of momentariness. Hence Sautrāntika holds that perception can only be representative. An object can be known only indirectly from the impressions it casts on the mind. Yogācāra argues that if all that we directly know are impressions, there is no reason to say that they are caused by external objects. Hence the only reality is the knowledge-series. The so-called outside world is but an illusory objectification of the mind, and hence the name *ātmakhyāti* to this theory. The analogy of dream, where the mental is mistaken for the external, is cited in support. The theory thus abolishes the distinction between truth and illusion, since in both alike there is no object outside knowledge. But it is evident that the analogy of dream is unsound. There is the important difference that while the object of dream is falsified sooner or later, the object of truth never is, so far as common human experience goes. The theory has been criticized on many other grounds also, but it is not necessary to go into all of them. But on the whole, the doctrine has no criterion of truth beyond a pragmatic one as in other schools of Buddhism.

Yogācāra denies the existence of external objects and affirms that cognition alone is real. Mādhyamika denies the existence of cognition also, holding that in the absence of an appropriate object, knowledge becomes inconceivable. The ultimate is thus void (*śūnya*). To Yogācāra all knowledge is erroneous as it consists in mistaking the mental for the external. To Mādhyamika all knowledge is false as it consists in mistaking what is totally non-existent to be existent. Hence the theory goes by the name *asatkhyāti*. Life itself is a delusion, and what is conventionally called "error" is only an instance of it. The conception of *śūnya* is ontologically untenable, but what matters to us here is the fact that the doctrine has no criterion of truth at all, as in the *akhyāti* view. In fact, there is no need for it in either—in *akhyāti* because all knowledge is true; in *asatkhyāti* because all knowledge is false. However, as a concession to ordinary life, the doctrine, like other schools of Buddhism, grants that the so-called truths serve the needs of action.

We now come to two theories which do make a distinction between truth and error primarily in terms of the purpose of knowledge, which is to acquaint us with the nature of reality. These are *anyathākhyāti* and *anirvacanīyakhyāti*. The most important representative of the first of these is Bhāṭṭa Mīmāṁsā. The same theory is offered with some modifications by Nyāya, Dvaita, and the realistic schools of Buddhism. We shall follow Kumārila's exposition, where it is specially called *viparītakhyāti*.

Anyathākhyāti is a correction to *akhyāti*. According to *akhyāti*, knowledge always corresponds with reality. The correspondence may be more or less adequate, but knowledge never completely fails to reflect the object. So the distinction between truth and error is only in the degree of correspondence. But *anyathākhyāti* holds that knowledge sometimes strays from reality and shows it "otherwise" (*anyathā*). Hence, true knowledge is defined as that which corresponds with reality, and false knowledge as that which does not. Thus Kumārila, unlike Prabhākara, recognizes error as such, and the distinction between truth and error becomes logically significant for him. This does not mean that Kumārila disregards the practical significance of knowledge. True knowledge is bound to lead to expected results. But utility is not a criterion of true knowing.

How does knowledge deviate from reality to become error? This is the result of partial misapprehension of what is given. All errors are errors of commission. As in *akhyāti*, here also it is said that error involves two separate acts of knowing. But while according to *akhyāti*, error results from failure to discriminate between them, according to the present theory, it is the result of a wrong synthesis between them as in the following examples. (i) When a white crystal is taken for a red one by its proximity to a red flower, the redness of the flower is mentally superimposed on the crystal, so that the crystal appears differently (*viparīta*) from what it is. This is the reason why Kumārila's theory is called *viparītakhyāti*. (ii) When shell is mistaken for silver, one of the acts of knowing, viz. of shell, is perceptual and the other, viz. of silver, one of recollection. And it is the wrong identification of the latter with the former that results in the notion that the object perceived is silver.

In terms of *akhyāti*, the discovery of error does not mean discarding any feature previously cognized, but only making good what is lacking in the cognition. The distinction between truth and error is thus logically inconsequential. But according to *viparītakhyāti*, when the mistake is rectified, a part of the cognition is sublated. For example, in the erroneous judgement "This is silver," the predicate "silver" stands corrected as shell, though the subject "this" remains. This means that erroneous knowledge, to that extent, suffers contradiction (*bādha*) by subsequent experience, whereas true knowledge does not. Hence the criterion of truth, according to Kumārila, is non-contradiction (*abādhitatva*). He lays down another criterion also for knowledge to be true—that it must point to an object not hitherto known (*anadhigata*). That is, truth must be in the nature of a discovery, novel. Even a temporal difference in two acts of knowing the same object will count for novelty. Thus the complete definition of truth is that "it is such knowledge as reveals an object or an aspect of it, not hitherto known, and represents it faithfully."[29]

The theories so far considered start with an ontological assumption that the object of error must be either real or unreal. Accordingly, it is usual to classify them under two heads: *satkhyāti* and *asatkhyāti*. The Mādhyamika theory is the only one of the second variety. The other three theories belong to the first group. To *akhyāti* and *anyathākhyāti* the object of error exists in one sense or another in the external world.

To *ātmakhyāti* also the object exists but only as an idea in the mind of the knower. But to start with any ontological assumption at all is to vitiate an epistemological theory at the beginning and render it dogmatic. The initial assumption leads each of these views to make further assumptions at later stages in the argument. If the problem of error is to admit of a solution at all, the effort should be free from such ontological assumptions. Epistemology, no doubt, must lead to ontology; but the two are not the same. The primary purpose of a theory of truth and error is to find out whether knowledge, in either case, has a content other than itself. Only if it has, does the further question arise whether its character is real or unreal. Epistemology is not called upon to decide this ontological question, though it necessarily follows upon the former question.

The *anirvacanīyakhyāti* of Advaita alone does not commit the mistake of mixing up ontology with epistemology. It starts straight from experience without laying down any ontological postulate, and identifies a content for erroneous knowledge distinct from that knowledge. Unlike Yogācāra, but like Mīmāṁsā, Advaita recognizes an objective content for error. To know is to know something, which is other than knowledge. The distinction between knowledge and the known is basic to knowledge. Error is not absence of knowledge, but wrong knowledge. Hence error points to an objective factor as surely as truth. It is only after settling this epistemological point that the Advaitin proceeds to discuss the ontological status of the object of error.

That the Advaita theory is free from any ontological bias can be shown from the fact that it refuses to accept either of the assumptions made in the other theories, viz. that the content of error must be either real or unreal. Their ontological predilections prevent them from thinking of two other possibilities, viz. that it may be both real and unreal or neither. In fact, in the theory of the later Sāṅkhya, called *sadasatkhyāti*, it is held to be the former. But as this merely combines the earlier two alternatives of reality and unreality, there is nothing new in it. Hence the only alternative is the last, which is unique to Advaita, viz., that the object is neither real nor unreal. The term *sadasad-vilakṣaṇa* is ordinarily used to describe this nature. The term as originally meant did not have a positive significance as representing a separate category; it was used merely as denying that the content is either *sat* or *asat*. The recognition of this alternative accords with the principle that epistemology should start from empirical facts as such and should not judge their ontological status till its inquiry is completed.

Before explaining the Advaita view of error, it is necessary to refute the views that the erroneous object is either real or unreal. Let us consider that a person mistakes a rope in the dark for a serpent. *Akhyāti* and *anyathākhyāti* hold that the serpent is to be reckoned as a physical existent because it is similar to the actual serpent experienced in the past. This is beside the point, because the problem is not about the serpent as such, but about the one that is presented here and now and is contradicted later. Those who give such explanations confound likeness (*sādṛśya*) with identity. The erroneous object may be similar to what was once experienced, but it need not be the same. The point is that the content here is a mere presentation and not that it is also physically existent.

If the erroneous content is a mere presentation, as stated above, it may be thought that it is either a memory image or an ideal construction as *ātmakhyāti* takes it. If it were a memory image, it would involve a reference to past time and a different place and would not be apprehended as immediately given. The mental impression left behind by past experience of a serpent is, of course, necessary as a basis for the present object being mistaken for one; but it does not follow from this that the serpent experienced now is itself a memory image. Nor is the so-called "serpent" an ideal construction, for in that case the serpent would either refer to the future or have no reference to time at all. In any case, the determinate position of the presentation in the objective sphere precludes its being merely a mental phenomenon. The fact that the erroneous object is actually presented, producing a reaction in the subject, runs in the face of *asatkhyāti*, according to which it is totally non-existent. The Advaitin points out that an unreal object is never presented at all. Nobody has seen or is going to see hairs on a tortoise shell.

Both reality and unreality being thus ruled out from the status of the illusory object, we are obliged to regard it as a unique presentation. Its uniqueness is that its nature cannot be fully expressed in logical terms as either real or unreal. The unique status has been indicated in both negative and positive terms. Negatively it is indicated by saying that it is impossible to conceive of the illusory object "as either the same as or as other than its ground."[30] The "serpent" can neither be identified with the "rope" nor distinguished from it. Such an explanation implies that its nature is not determinable (*durnirūpa*), or that it has no essence of its own. In other words, it is but an appearance. If it shows itself as real, that is due to the *being* of the ground, viz., the rope.

The above seems to have been the original explanation. But it has become usual to represent the illusory object as having a separate type of status which is not independent of the ground. In this connection the term *sadasad-vilakṣaṇa* has come to be used with a positive significance—as standing for a type or level of being midway between the real and the unreal, or a realm of "half reality." Such an expression would be meaningless only if *sat* and *asat* were the sole possible alternatives, which they are not, according to Advaita. Here is a realm of appearance of which self-discrepancy is the very essence. The reason behind this view is this: if the object in question were real, it would not be sublated afterwards; if it were unreal, it would never have been presented. "It means that error points to a thing that is precisely like what it appears, but is yet not characterizable as either *is* or *is not* (*sadasad-anirvacanīya*)."[31] This is the significance of the name *anirvacanīyakhyāti* to the theory. The *pramāṇa* for identifying such a status is *arthāpatti*. The essence of *arthāpatti* is "the construction of a suitable hypothesis to account for a proved discrepancy."[32] We are confronted with the clear inconsistency that what is vividly apprehended cannot be explained as either real or unreal. We are, therefore, forced to conclude that it must belong to a third order. "Hence 'false facts' must be admitted corresponding to wrong beliefs."[33]

Let us now consider the criterion of truth as it emerges from the above analysis of error. All knowledge, including error, has an objective counterpart. This does not mean that all the elements given on the objective side are equally real, but only that none of them is sheer non-being. Considering the whole content of erroneous knowledge, while some elements are necessarily real, others may be unique in the sense explained above. While the "serpent" in the example cited is sublated by later knowledge, the "this" element is not so contradicted. True knowledge, by contrast, is that whose content is free from such unique presentations. Accordingly, no part of its content has to be discarded as false or comes into conflict with the rest of our experience. Thus the criterion of truth, according to Advaita, is non-contradiction (*abādhitatva*).

The uniqueness of the objects of error is evident from the fact that they are "private" or "personal" to the person who cognizes them. The "serpent" which a person sees in the rope in twilight is special to him and may not be seen by others. Objects of illusion are not general or common to several, their presence not being vouched by collective experience. But objects of common knowledge, which are taken to be true, such as a real serpent, are "public," for they are cognized by others as well. A second difference is that while an object of illusion lasts only so long as its knowledge lasts, that of ordinary knowledge is more enduring. The latter already exists before it comes to be apprehended and normally continues to be afterwards as shown by its recognition later. The former, on the contrary, comes into being along with its knowledge and ceases to be along with the cessation of that knowledge. To denote these differences, objects of error are described as *prātibhāsika*, or apparent, and the objects of ordinary knowledge as *vyāvahārika*, or empirical. Dream objets belong to the former. This distinction shows how mistaken is the belief that Śaṅkara views the objects of everyday life to be false, or unreal.

To describe an object of error as "private" does not mean that it is a mere idea, or purely subjective, as in the Yogācāra theory. All that is meant is that it is cognized only by some individual and not by all. "No private object can indeed be conceived except as dependent upon a particular individual; the point to be noted is that it is not mental, but an object of mind."[34] It only shows that Śaṅkara claims some kind of reality even for objects of illusion. "To be perceived is for him *to be*...."[35] The Advaita theory has one great merit: it accounts for illusion as it occurs. "What we experience in it is that we *see* the serpent or silver; and this fact of knowing an object as present then and there is not explained, but is rather explained away in other theories of illusion."[36]

The Ultimate Significance of the Logical Value

All the theories discussed in the foregoing examine the problem of error and truth with reference only to perception (*pratyakṣa*). The reason is this. Of the various means to knowledge, the Veda has its exclusive sphere of the supersensuous, in regard to which it is believed to be free from error. Of the rest, which give knowledge of physical reality, *pratyakṣa* alone is not dependent on any other means. The other *pramāṇas*, viz., *anumāna*, *upamāna*, *arthāpatti*, and *anupalabdhi*, depend for their operation on the premises supplied by *pratyakṣa*. Consequently, the errors that are possible in perception could vitiate the material for the other four *pramāṇas*. Since the validity and invalidity of these forms of knowledge are, apart from other causes, eventually traceable to their perceptual bases, it is sufficient to discuss the problem of truth and error with reference to *pratyakṣa*.[37]

The discussion of validity with reference to perception relates only to the physical world and that too in one or other aspect of it. This means that common human knowledge is based on a distinction between the subject and the object, the knower and the known, and reaches forth for the truth of the object. Hence the truth with which epistemology is concerned is truth only in the relative sense. Truth in the absolute sense must comprehend the whole of reality, not excluding the self of the person that contemplates it. It must underlie not merely all that is known, but also the self that knows. Though the distinction between subject and object is involved in epistemology, it necessarily points to the ultimate truth which over-reaches the distinction. "Knowledge begins by assuming that they are different, but it culminates in the discovery of a latent harmony between them in which the difference is resolved."[38]

Even the ultimate truth, which is the goal of metaphysics, is not an end in itself, according to Indian philosophers. *Jñāna*, as we have termed it earlier, is not to be sought for its own sake, but as a means to liberation. "...Indian philosophy does not stop short at the discovery of truth but utilizes it for attaining something else which it holds to be more valuable."[39] In fact, all the three higher values—truth, beauty, and goodness—are regarded in India as subordinate to and subserving the goal of *mokṣa*. To look upon philosophic knowledge as an intrinsic value is to reduce it to the level of science, the only difference between the two being in the scope of knowledge. But such a view overlooks the important difference between the two in the impulses which they satisfy. "Science gratifies curiosity or wonder, if we prefer to put it so; but philosophy is meant to meet the deepest desire of man for peace of soul."[40] The true cause of man's philosophic quest is the restlessness consequent upon not merely intellectual doubts, but also the sorrows and sufferings of life.

Now, if philosophical knowledge is to serve as a means to liberation, it must undergo a radical transformation. By itself, philosophic knowledge, which is attained by study and reflection, is only mediate. But the imperfections of life are a matter of immediate experience owing to our congenital ignorance of reality. For example, most of us feel the empirical self to be the true self, while according to many systems, the truth is not so. What is immediately felt can be dispelled only by an opposite experience. A perceptual illusion, for instance, is removed only by a perceptual experience of the fact underlying the illusion. Seeing is believing. Hence if the imperfections of life are to be fully and finally conquered, our knowledge about reality must, instead of remaining a mere intellectual conviction, be transformed into an awareness which is equally immediate. The Sanskrit word *jñāna* is used indifferently to mean either mediate knowledge or direct experience. But sometimes the term *vijñāna* is used for the latter to distinguish it from *jñāna* when it means the former. The distinction between the two is in form rather than in substance. If *jñāna* stands for mediate knowledge of truth, *vijñāna* means the same but "as brought within or transmuted into one's own experience."[41]

To transform mediate knowledge into experience, all the Indian systems prescribe a course of practical discipline. The discipline consists of two parts—one for securing detachment from all personal interests (*vairāgya*) and the other for cultivating powers of mental concentration (*yoga*). The chief obstacle to the vision of the ultimate truth is egoism. Although that vision alone ensures the complete and final disappearance of egoism, to reach it itself requires a degree of unselfishness (*sattva-śuddhi*). In this act of cleansing the mind, the practice of goodness (*dharma*), in the spirit in which it is taught in the *Bhagavad-gītā*, becomes necessary. The removal of the obstacle is the negative requirement. The positive requirement for the transmutation of the mediate into the immediate knowledge is meditation (*nididhyāsana*). Meditation is the constant dwelling of the mind on the reality about the nature of which one has been intellectually convinced so that the conviction may gradually sink into one's own self and become a matter of experience.

REFERENCES

1. *QAP*, p. 101.
2. *ICV*, p. 4.
3. Ibid., p. 5.
4. Ibid., p. 13.
5. Vide ibid.
6. *PEIP*, p. 66.
7. *ICV*, p. 10.
8. Ibid., p. 16.
9. *QAP*, p. 104.
10. Vide ibid., p. 105.
11. Vide ibid., p. 34.
12. Ibid., p. 51.
13. Ibid., p. 56.
14. *IPS—I*, p. 133.
15. Ibid., p. 128.
16. Vide ibid., p. 129.
17. Ibid.
18. Ibid., p. 133.
19. Vide ibid., p. 130.
20. Vide *ICV*, p. 35.
21. *IPS—I*, p. 69.
22. *ICV*, p. 37.
23. *IPS—I*, p. 46.
24. Ibid., p. 140.
25. *OIP*, p. 260.
26. *EIP*, p. 145.
27. *ICV*, p. 65.
28. *OIP*, p. 209.
29. *ICV*, p. 72.
30. Ibid., p. 104.
31. Ibid., p. 105.
32. Ibid., p. 106.
33. Ibid., p. 106, n. 52.
34. *OIP*, p. 351.
35. Ibid.
36. Ibid.
37. Vide *IPS—I*, p. 19.
38. Ibid., p. 17.
39. *QAP*, p. 27.
40. Ibid., p. 28.
41. Ibid., p. 60.

7

Values—Part Two

1. ETHICAL VALUE

The Nature and Scope of Dharma

The idea of *dharma* has its origin and early development in the Veda. There are two important concepts in the Veda which later lead to the concept of *dharma*. These are *ṛta* and *ṛṇa*. The word *ṛta*, which frequently occurs in the Mantras, signifies both natural and moral order in the universe; and the guardians of both are the gods. The gods being the source of both natural and moral law, man must please them not only by offering sacrifices to them, but also by leading a morally pure life. In linking the moral order with the physical, two points are conveyed. One is that the good of the individual depends on the good of the universe. No man can live for himself; the individual should adjust his conduct to the nature of the world. The second is that there is a necessary relation between the world of fact and the world of value. We have here the germ of the belief of all Indian systems that ethics is based on metaphysics.

The term *ṛṇa* means "indebtedness." It occurs predominantly in the Brāhmaṇas. It stands for three obligations of man—to gods, to sages, and to ancestors. The first is fulfilled through sacrifices; the second, through study of the Veda; and the third, through family life. The first obligation is already implied in the concept of *ṛta*. The second and third are additional. But the more important point in the concept of *ṛṇa* is the explicit introduction of the idea of obligation. The idea of rewards is looked upon as the aim of sacrifices. But now the emphasis is on what ought to be done, and rewards become the mere consequences of what is done. The standard of conduct thus gets internalized. The motive shifts from gratification of desire to fulfilment of duty. One is not unconscious of the benefits of obligation, but one does not seek them specifically.

In the Upaniṣads and Epics we arrive at the concept of *dharma*. The word *dharma* literally means "what holds together." *Dharma* is thus the basis of all order in society. Social order cannot be explained by any external control exercised by rulers. The work of government will not go on smoothly until its orders are willingly obeyed. Therefore the new principle of *dharma* should be regarded as internal. "It should signify the sense of right and wrong which is a distinctive feature of man...."[1] Having a deeper basis in human nature than either *ṛta* or *ṛṇa, dharma* is the ultimate guide to right and wrong. The stability of society is traced eventually to the moral idea implanted in man. The sovereignty of *dharma* is accordingly greater than that of the state. It is universally binding, for it rules even the rulers. In short, *dharma* is the final authority in matters of conduct.

As the concept of *dharma* originates from those of *ṛta* and *ṛṇa,* it comes to include the idea of ritual, though predominantly it is a moral idea. Ritual is religious ceremonial, like sacrifice, which, operating in an unseen manner (*adṛṣṭa*), secures good to a person in the future, either here or hereafter. The inclusion of ritual does not underrate the importance of moral virtue. There could be virtue without any reference to ritual. But ritual necessarily has a moral significance. In the first place, the successful practice of ritual depends on the prior acquisition of moral purity. Ritual, in turn, contributes to moral purity, since its correct practice imposes so much self-restraint on the practiser. Thus the inclusion of ritual only enhances the moral content of *dharma.* Thereby *dharma* may be more than virtue, but not less. *Dharma* as morality is recognized by all schools, but *dharma* as ritual is special only to the Vedic schools. The association of ritual with morality is a consequence of the blending of philosophy with religion in India.

The Means of Knowing Dharma

Indian investigators (*śāstrakāra*) usually lay down a principle that inquiry into the nature of a thing presupposes that the thing is known in a general way and that only its particulars require to be known fully. The argument is that if it is altogether unknown, there can be no question of investigating it; and if it is all known already, there is no need to do so. According to this principle, *dharma* also should be regarded as known in general, if any inquiry is to be undertaken about it. Hence there are two sides to the question regarding the source of *dharma*-knowledge, viz., the source of its knowledge in general and that of a knowledge of its details. As regards the prior knowledge of *dharma* in general, this, as we have indicated earlier, lies in the fact that the moral idea is innate in man and not acquired. The notion of morality is universal, and even those who do not believe in a surviving self accept it.[2] Hence we have to consider only what the source is of our knowledge about the special forms of *dharma*.

The "enlightened" (*suśikṣita*) among Cārvākas maintain that the particulars of *dharma* are known through common experience. Restricting the scope of *dharma* to the present life, they explain the distinction between virtue and vice on an empirical basis. Individual experience is not always adequate for this. As moral acts generally have a bearing on others, it is the collective wisdom of the community that informs us what is right and what is wrong. Such empirical ethics has never appealed to the majority of Indian schools. It reduces *dharma* to mere expediency. The standard becomes utilitarian and relative. That conduct comes to be regarded as worthy of pursuit where the element of evil is relatively less. The idea of *dharma* as a means to what is wholly free from evil is absent here.

All the Indian schools excepting Cārvāka believe in a surviving self. And morality as conceived by them has a reference to a future life just as much as ritual has. Such an idea is a necessary consequence of the belief in the doctrine of *karma*. It is the belief that virtue as practised here has its reward in the hereafter. This places the conception of the moral good beyond the reach of common experience. Hence these schools appeal to a unique *pramāṇa* to guide conduct. Another circum-stance justifying reliance on such a *pramāṇa* is the need for the assurance that goodness will triumph, at all events, in the end. Without such an assurance, there will be little inspiration for moral conduct. No empirical experience can possibly give us this confidence. The existence of a social order and the perception of an ethical progress, if any, in it may indicate that moral effort is not futile. But from this we cannot be certain about moral justice, for we may well ask why such progress should not be followed by a set-back. The assurance that we desire is absolute; and this is the very purpose of recognizing a unique *pramāṇa* to know the details of *dharma*.

There are two views as regards this unique *pramāṇa*. According to schools like Jainism, the individual intuition of a seer (*yogi-pratyakṣa*) is sufficient authority on matters of *dharma*. But according to the strictly orthodox schools, the only *pramāṇa* for knowing *dharma* is the Veda, or *śruti*. The Veda is also the source of the knowledge relating to ritual. Here is another reason why in India ritual gets associated with morality. In connection with metaphysics we have seen why the orthodox schools did not agree that individual intuition is the final authority on matters spiritual and relied on the impersonal authority of the Veda. The same reasons apply to their dependence on revelation in regard to ethics.

The acceptance of the Veda as authority on matters of *dharma* may appear dogmatic, but it is not really so. First, the actual determination of particular *dharmas* requires a proper interpretation of the Vedic texts. Secondly, in practice, in addition to *śruti,* certain works on *dharma* which are described as Smṛtis, using the term *smṛti* in a restricted sense, are also invoked in this respect. The name *smṛti* here stands for "treatises which record truths about conduct that have been handed down from immemorial antiquity."[3] The Smṛtis are not independent of the Veda. Where they refer to the lower values of *artha* and *kāma*, they rest on common experience. But where they refer to the higher values, viz. *dharma* and *mokṣa*, these traditional treatises, or "moral codes," are believed to go back eventually to the Veda. Thus they represent not mere but sanctified tradition. Of course, in respect of some of the acts taught in the Smṛtis, their sources in *śruti* cannot be traced. Howsoever this may be explained, the authority of the Smṛtis is believed to rest finally on the Veda in every detail. But the Smṛtis as we have them, not only contain additions to *śruti*, but also sometimes contradict the latter. Where they contradict *śruti*, preference is to be given to the latter. The authority of a Smṛti is, therefore, final only where *śruti* is silent. A Smṛti may supplement *śruti*, but not supplant it.

There are two other sources for the knowledge of *dharma* mentioned in the strictly Vedic schools, but they are not independent of scriptural authority. These are (i) custom (*ācāra*) and (ii) self-satisfaction, or feeling at peace with oneself (*ātma-tuṣṭi*). They refer respectively to the customs observed and the feeling of self-satisfaction experienced by the cultured ones (*śiṣṭa*), not by all and sundry. Without such qualification, one might infer that they are in place in a code of empirical ethics, as the one recommended by the "enlightened materialist." *Ācāra* is traditional custom, or the habit of the community. To follow it, is to secure social approval for one's conduct. It is exemplified in the life of the best people of the community. It is the unwritten law of social tradition as distinguished from the codified tradition represented by Smṛti.

"If *ācāra* signifies social approval, *ātma-tuṣṭi* represents self-approval."[4] It is the acceptance of conscience as an authority on matters of morality. But, like *ācāra*, it is subordinated to the teaching of scripture. To ensure this, it is confined to the conscience of the good, as indicated in a well known observation of Kālidāsa in the *Śākuntalam*.[5] In any case, it ought not to come into conflict with scriptural teaching. Hence *ātma-tuṣṭi* stands for moral insight which is necessary in those matters of detail about which scriptural code and the practice of elders are both silent or are at variance with each other.[6]

Both *ācāra* and *ātma-tuṣṭi* are traced to a Vedic source in order to save *dharma* from individual idiosyncrasies and rest it on a community standard—and it is done on the belief that a group of enlightened people are less liable to wrong action than an individual. There was a time when each of them was held by some moralists to be self-sufficient. But that view has since been superseded. However, instead of being dropped, *ācāra* and *ātma-tuṣṭi* have been utilized as auxiliaries to scripture or as indications of the rightness of conduct approved by scripture.

The Doctrine of Karma

Karma means action, whether good or bad. The word *karma* is thus wider in significance than *dharma* and includes *adharma* also. What is known as the doctrine of *karma* signifies that nothing can happen in the moral world without sufficient cause as in the physical—"that each life with all its pains and pleasures is the necessary result of the actions of past lives and becomes in its turn the cause, through its own activities, of future births."[7] The Indian cannot think of a worse ethical view than one which countenances the play of chance in life. The belief in the *karma* doctrine is thus fundamental to the proper understanding of the Indian moral ideal. The doctrine has undergone many modifications down the ages, but its essence has remained the same.

The belief in transmigration, a recurring cycle of birth and death (*saṁsāra*), is a necessary corollary of the doctrine of *karma*. The fact is that virtue is not always rewarded in this life nor vice always punished. This forces upon us the belief in the continued existence of the self in a series of lives. Merely to assume that the soul is immortal is not sufficient to explain the discrepancy between virtue and well-being. Such an idea, moreover, involves the allotment of rewards and punishments for an endless period for the good or evil done in a life so brief as man's is. The Indians, therefore, believed not only in the immortality of the self, but also in pre-existence and reincarnation. This extended view of the self's existence gives greater scope for believing that man could succeed in his efforts to live rightly.

The doctrine of *karma* does not embody a *demonstrable* truth, as no philosophic doctrine does. However, its value as a hypothesis for rationally explaining the observed inequalities of life is clear. It has also its practical advantages. Belief in it assures a person that there are really no inequities in life and reconciles him to his lot. This explains the absence of any feeling of bitterness even among common people in India when any misfortune befalls them. "They blame neither God nor their neighbour, but only themselves, for it."[8] This power to bear misfortune without complaint is one of the most wholesome among the consequences of the *karma* doctrine. At the same time, the faith in *karma* conduces to charity in judging others. Though each man is himself responsible for the dispositions with which he is born, he has normally no control over them as he has over the ones he may acquire in this life. Therefore, when he commits wrong as a consequence of some initial disposition, it behoves others to judge him leniently, instead of blaming him outright. For the same reason, belief in *karma* has a chastening influence on those who succeed in life, because they will attribute their success more to what they had done in their past lives than to what they have done in the present one. Another advantage of the doctrine is that belief in it serves as a perpetual incentive to right conduct. Since what we did makes us what we are, what we do now will determine what we shall be; the future lies entirely in our hands. If the doctrine appears to teach fate, it is a fate of which man himself is the master.

The doctrine of *karma* is sometimes mistaken for determinism. But freedom does not mean total absence of determination, which would be mere caprice. To act from arbitrarily shifting motives would only disrupt social intercourse completely. Real moral freedom consists in being determined by one's own moral character. And this is exactly what the *karma* doctrine signifies. It would preclude self-determination only if we confine our attention to a single life. But in the wider perspective of transmigration, it becomes evident that man's present is traceable to nothing but his own actions done in past lives.

It is necessary to see how past actions influence the present life. Every deed that we do leads to a double result. Its direct result (*phala*) is the pain or pleasure following from it according to the nature of the deed done. Indirectly, it also establishes in us a disposition, or tendency (*saṁskāra*), to repeat the same deed in the future. So far as the former result is concerned, man's life is characterized by strict necessity; and he has to accept all the unpleasant consequences of his past actions as he does the pleasant ones. Whatever we knowingly do will, sooner or later, bring us the result we merit. What we sow, we must reap. Thus the *karma* doctrine signifies that there is absolute justice in the rewards and punishments that fall to our lot in life. "The law of *karma* accordingly is not a blind mechanical law, but is essentially ethical."[9] As regards the latter result, viz., the tendencies, they are within the possibility of man's control. Though by virtue of his past, he tends to act in a particular way, which is either good or bad, he is not under compulsion to do so. By regulating his tendencies at will, he can choose the activities in which he is to engage in such manner as will elevate his character. Here lies his freedom and his moral progress.

There is no contradiction in thus pointing to both freedom and necessity as the implications of the *karma* doctrine, for they refer to two different aspects of *karma*. Nor does the double significance of *karma* lead to any conflict in life's interests, for the sole aim of *all* our activities should be, according to all the Indian doctrines, ethical advance. Present endeavour need not conflict with experiencing the results of past actions, for we can become indifferent to the latter by fixing our attention on the former. In fact, enduring the results of past actions is not only not incompatible with pursuing future action, but could even be conducive to it. We have already referred to the retributive nature of rewards and punishments. But they are more than retributive; they also serve to educate man morally. They implicitly point to the direction in which we ought to grow.

We have said that previous lives predispose the mind to act in particular ways in the subsequent ones. It may, therefore, be asked when the disposition to act as one does was *first* incurred. But such a question is really inadmissible, because it takes for granted that there was a time when the self was without any disposition whatsoever. A self without any disposition is an abstraction as meaningless as a mere disposition without any reference to a self. It is this fact that is meant in the Indian exposition of *karma* that it is beginningless (*anādi*). No matter how far back we trace the history of an individual, we shall never arrive at a stage when he was devoid of all character. Thus at all stages, it is self-determination. One practical advantage of this belief in the beginninglessness of *karma* is that it dissuades man from wasting his time in seeking for its origin. It thereby signifies that he should concentrate on bettering his character instead of trying to find out why he is not what he ought to be. It should also be noted that the *karma* doctrine does not stand for an endless succession of births and deaths. All the systems believing in the doctrine acknowledge that there is a way out of the recurring series of lives, and this is to seek the final ideal of *mokṣa*.

The doctrine of *karma* may appear to modern scholars as a dogma that is merely taken for granted. That, however, is not the case, for there are arguments for it from early times, whatever be their worth. Before indicating them, we shall consider some of the objections raised against the doctrine. (i) We do not normally remember anything of our past lives and hence there is no sense of personal continuity accompanying those lives. The answer to this is that forgetfulness in this respect need not disprove the continuity of personality. For the past of a person to influence his present, it is sufficient that the thoughts and actions of the past, though as such forgotten, have left behind them their deep impression. (ii) The body is essential for the mental and moral life of the self. But the body does not transmigrate; it perishes at death. This objection overlooks the fact that Indian schools postulate as the support and condition of all psychical life, a physical vesture for the self which is other and subtler than the visible body, though its conception may vary. This subtle body (*sūkṣma-śarīra*) accompanies the self from birth to birth until the self finds release. Release, in fact, is release from it. It is in this vesture that the dispositions of former lives are stated to be treasured up. It is true that during a particular life the gross physical body is intimately involved in the experiences of the self, but as the subtle body is more enduring than this, the loss, or replacement, of the visible body will not affect the inner life of the individual. (iii) What is the justice of punishing a person for what he might have done in another life when he does not remember it? In the case of a human being, it may serve to reform him. But if the self is born as an animal, the punishment cannot serve any such purpose, since an animal is not self-conscious. The answer is that the purpose of *karma* discipline is twofold: reformation and retribution. In the case of a lower creature, punishment for wrong deeds done in a former life serves at least the purpose of retribution. The stringency of the moral law demands that evil-doers should reap the consequences of their deeds, no matter how they are born. The punishment also serves to deter others from evil conduct.

We shall now state in brief the arguments commonly found in Indian literature in support of *karma* and transmigration. One of them is that all men are born with certain predilections, and since they cannot be traced to the present life, they necessarily point to the experiences of another but forgotten existence as their source. And since the same argument can be extended to every preceding existence, there should have been for everyone an endless series of lives. Instances like the readiness to suck the mother's milk found in the new-born babe, man's innate fear of death, and so on are usually given to illustrate this conclusion. It does not avail us to explain these predilections in terms of heredity, for it leaves unexplained why a particular child should be born of particular parents. If the connection between the two is not a matter of accident, it can be accounted for only by assuming a certain affinity between them as a result of former lives. As regards the affinity of souls in previous births, Kālidāsa refers in the *Raghuvaṁśa* to the love at first sight between king Aja and his bride Indumati.[10] In the *Śākuntalam*, again, he refers to the strange fact that sometimes a person becomes melancholy at the sight of a beautiful thing or the hearing of sweet music, while normally such a stimulus should evoke joy. And the poet explains this as a consequence of recalling, though only subconsciously, some love or friendship of a former life.[11]

The Classification of Dharma

The main sources of information on this topic are the Dharmasūtras and the works on *dharma* which are described as Smṛtis, to which we have referred earlier. The Dharmasūtras are one class of Kalpasūtras, which came to systematize the teaching of the Veda on the practical side. The Dharmasūtras lay down the standard of *dharma*. Though they differ in detail, their common theme is threefold: rules of conduct (*ācāra*), penances (*prāyaścitta*), and law (*vyavahāra*). The Smṛtis, like those of Manu, Yājñavalkya, and Parāśara, are moral codes which come later. They amplify and add to the Dharmasūtras. The Smṛtis themselves have been commented upon. In the Smṛtis there is a tendency to differentiate between virtue and social conventions. The literature consisting of Dharmasūtras and Smṛtis goes by the name of Dharmaśāstra, which is reckoned as one of the main branches of learning in India. Usually, the *Mahābhārata* is also classed under this head.

There are three kinds of *karma* recognized by orthodox schools. They are obligatory deeds (*nityakarma*), prohibited deeds (*pratiṣiddhakarma*), and optional deeds (*kāmyakarma*). The first are actions whose performance does not depend on one's inclination, but are operative under all circumstances. There is another variety of obligatory deeds which have to be performed under special occasions (*naimittikakarma*). For example, in addition to the bath which is a daily duty, a special bath is prescribed under certain circumstances. Being obligatory like *nityakarma*, this special kind of obligatory deeds could be treated as part of *nityakarma*, taking the term in an inclusive sense. If the obligatory deeds constitute *dharma*, prohibited deeds stand for *adharma*, whose avoidance is as important as the performance of *dharma*. We have thus positive and negative duties. The third variety, viz., *kāmyakarma*, is explicitly designed to secure personal benefit to an individual here or hereafter. Their ethical significance is that they indirectly exercise a check on personal vagaries and thus promote self-discipline as well as social well-being. This check is of two kinds. (i) No one is allowed to perform a *kāmyakarma* to the neglect of obligatory deeds. (ii) No one is considered qualified for *kāmyakarma* if he indulges in any prohibited deed, like drinking. It only shows that desire as such is not bad, but it needs to be properly controlled.

Confining our attention to obligations and prohibitions, there is a twofold classification for each of them. (i) There are obligations and prohibitions of a general kind (*sādhāraṇa dharma*). They are binding on all. Virtues like truth-speaking and non-stealing are of this kind. (ii) There are those that are special, or relative, to one's social class (*varṇa*) and the particular stage (*āśrama*) that one has reached in life's discipline (*varṇāśrama dharma*). Thus, while contentment is commended in the case of a Brāhmaṇa, it is discountenanced in the case of a Kṣatriya. Several of them are of ritualistic character. But even they have a moral significance: they cultivate private virtues and promote common weal.

The *sādhāraṇa dharmas* have a bearing not only on human beings, but also on lower creatures, for, though the latter have no duties, they have certainly rights. In the higher stages of moral discipline the scope of the non-human life is extended even to plants in the belief that they too have feelings of pain and pleasure. Various lists of these general duties are found.[12] Most of these duties are negative; but this does not mean that they lack in altruism. They have a reference to others, and are not, therefore, mere abstentions. For example, non-stealing indirectly helps others. They are duties that generally point to the rights of others as their correlatives. "...self-denial is the very soul of morality."[13]

The special duties coming under *varṇāśrama dharma* cannot be neglected, but they are possible only on a wide foundation of general duties. A person who violates the ordinary duties is not entitled even so much as to talk of special duties. This is best illustrated in the case of Bharata who, though a Kṣatriya, refuses to take up the reins of government overlooking the rightful heirship of Rāma. The four classes (*varṇa*) together form an integral whole of society, and the cooperation of *each* is equally necessary for its well-being. Social solidarity is the essential aim of *varṇa dharma*. *Āśramas* are "stages of toil" into which the life of an individual belonging to the first three classes is divided. They signify a gradation in moral training based on a distinction in moral capacity. The aim of *āśrama dharma* is self-culture, but it is not without a social significance. The *āśramas* serve as a spiritual ladder to enable man to gradually reach the final goal of life.

What deeds actually constitute *varṇa* and *āśrama dharma*s is mostly determined by custom. Custom, though rigid in theory, is fluid in practice. The Hindu scriptures themselves recognize the need for change in the details of *dharma* according to the different ages. But what matters for us here is not so much *what* the deeds are as *how* they conduce to moral life. They are of a binding character, restricting human activity to certain courses, with the implication that man must not act as he wishes, but submit his will to the will of others and also listen to the voice of his higher self. They thus conduce to social welfare as well as inward uplift. It is the emphasis on either of these ends that changes between *varṇa* and *āśrama dharmas*. The *varṇa dharmas* are directly intended for social welfare, but indirectly help the individual also, who is a member of society. The *āśrama dharmas*, which are calculated to develop what are called self-regarding virtues, have undoubtedly their impact on the welfare of society also.

The Dharmasūtras do not merely contain particular rules of conduct; they also formulate the standard by which we may test the soundness of conduct as well as moral progress. Progress from one moral state to a higher one cannot be judged except by comparing both with an ideal best. The Sūtras are thus normative as well as prescriptive. The rules which they formulate are according to this moral ideal. The recognition of a standard results from the fact that rules are never exhaustive, and situations arise where appeal has to be made to the example of elders in society who are virtuous by instinct (*śiṣṭa*), or "moral connoisseurs." As they represent the moral standard, both orthodox and heterodox schools place great emphasis on their example. It is worthy of note that a cultured one (*śiṣṭa*) is defined as one free from selfishness (*akāmātmā*).[14]

The moral ideal has two characteristic features. One of them is the ascetic principle that governs the moral training as a whole. The principle, however, is not of the same rigour in the case of all persons. For example, while non-injury is required absolutely from a recluse, it is relative in the case of a householder in the sense that he must reduce injury to the minimum if he cannot avoid it altogether. This shows that the codes prescribed are eminently practical. The second feature is that, as a consequence of the belief in *karma*, the moral worth of the present life is judged in a perspective that extends far into the past and future lives of the individual.

The Purpose of Dharma

There are two main types of views on this question. One is that *dharma* is an instrumental value, and the other, that its value is intrinsic.

The first, again, is of two types, depending on the end for which *dharma* is a means. Thus, on the whole, there are three views. The discussion turns mainly on the significance of Vedic injunctions.

A very early view is that *dharma* is a means to attaining prosperity (*abhyudaya*) in this life or in the next or in both. This view is found in the earlier portions of the Veda, and it is later represented by the Kumārila school of Mīmāṁsā. It persists even today in the popular mind. A person who desires to enjoy bliss in heaven (*svarga*) in the company of the gods is called upon to perform the sacrifice called *jyotiṣṭoma*. Though the result is bound to accrue, he has to wait for the sacrifice performed in this life to bear fruit after death. The gulf is bridged by *apūrva*, an unseen power which is supposed to endure in the agent till the result is attained. This *apūrva*, not being mentioned in the Veda, has to be postulated (*kalpya*). Thus, for an optional deed (*kāmyakarma*), like the above, a result is explicitly mentioned in the Veda. But the present view holds that even an obligatory deed, like speaking the truth, is a means of attaining an end, though no result is expressly mentioned in the Veda in connection with it. Thus obligatory duties, whether coming under *sādhāraṇa dharma* or *nityakarma*, have the same significance as *kāmyakarma*. The reason put forward is that no voluntary activity is conceivable in the absence of an idea of a suitable end. The end involved in obligatory deeds is explained as the avoidance of some unwelcome result (*pratyavāya-parihāra*), which would follow if the behests were neglected. In other words, the result is negative, whereas in *kāmyakarma* it is positive. Thus, *all* voluntary activity, according to this view, is prompted by the desire for an end.

The above view is replaced in course of time by another under the influence of the concept of *mokṣa*, which all orthodox schools come to adopt as the ultimate goal. The view essentially retains the idea that *dharma* is an instrumental value (*iṣṭa-sādhana*), but substitutes *mokṣa* for heavenly bliss as the end of action. The way *dharma* fulfils this end is by producing "betterment of character"(*sattva-śuddhi*) as taught by the *Bhagavad-gītā*. According to the Indian conception, the *jīva*, or the empirical self, is complex in nature—consisting of a spiritual as well as a physical element. The latter is represented by the internal organ (*antaḥkaraṇa*). Being a product of *prakṛti*, it is constituted of all the three *guṇas*, but it is predominantly of the nature of *sattva*. Though essentially of *sattva*, in practice it is often contaminated by *rajas* or *tamas* and exhibits lower impulses. *Sattvaśuddhi* consists in restoring the internal organ to its primal character of *sattva* by purging it of the other two *guṇas* as far as possible and thus counteracting the power of evil. Complete elimination of these *guṇas* is impossible as all the three are interconnected. This is the direct aim of moral training, according to this view, the indirect and ultimate aim being *mokṣa*.

The focus of this view is on obligatory deeds (*nitya* and *sādhāraṇa*). Optional deeds are precluded, as they are avowedly meant for the personal end of earthly or heavenly bliss, which is not the same as *mokṣa*. Here also the end served by an obligatory deed is looked upon as negative as in the earlier one. But there are important differences between the two views in the nature of the negative end. (i) According to the previous view, the performance of duty only prevents the onset of future evil. In the present view, it results in the destruction of past evil (*durita-kṣaya*), because it is aimed at the eradication of evil tendencies themselves. (ii) The evil that is meant in the previous view is both ethical and religious, because it includes under the concept of duty ritualistic as well as moral deeds. But here it is moral evil alone that is meant. And that is why the performance of duty is said to better character. (iii) The negative end of duty, in the previous view, is final. Duty wards off evil consequences, and there its purpose ends. But in the present view, the cleansing of the mind, which is achieved by the performance of duty, is itself a means to another end, viz., *mokṣa*. Thus it goes beyond the previous view in recognizing that we cannot expect man to put forth his best efforts without an appeal to something positive. It is thus psychologically sounder than the previous view. It means gaining the larger life while leaving the narrow life behind. (iv) In the previous view, *dharma* is subordinated to a lower value, since even desire for *svarga* is a kind of *kāma*. But in the present view, the true character of *dharma* as a higher value is restored.

In thus serving as a means to *mokṣa*, *dharma* needs to be supported by *jñāna*, or the knowledge (in its mediate form) of what the higher self is. To be known fully well, the self has to be known in relation to the rest of reality, i.e., its social and physical environment. Like *dharma*, *jñāna* also thus becomes, in this view, a means to *mokṣa*. For mediate knowledge to be transformed into immediate experience, *jñāna*, in turn, requires the cleansing of the mind by the practice of *dharma*. Thus *dharma* and *jñāna* serve as complementaries in the effort for *mokṣa*.

The third view is associated with the school of Prabhākara. Prabhākara questions the assumption of the two earlier views that no voluntary activity is possible without a suitable end. He contends that desire takes away the very meaning of obligation. Any explanation as to why we should obey a moral law would only destroy the morality of the law. In fact, where desire operates, there is no need for a sense of obligation. The two are opposed to each other. And moral training consists in discharging one's obligations overcoming the obstacles that desire may place in the way. Moral obligations come to us as commands, and they need not have any connection with an end. They are meant to be discharged for their own sake. *Dharma* is thus an intrinsic value.

We may admit that the above explanation is convincing so far as obligatory deeds are concerned. People often act upon them as a matter of principle without thinking whether the results of the act are desirable or undesirable. This point was ignored by the advocates of the first view. But Prabhākara is wrong in extending this idea to optional deeds (*kāmyakarma*) also. According to Kumārila, an optional deed is meant to fulfil a desired end (*phala*). But Prabhākara argues that the *phala*, e.g., heaven in the case of the *jyotiṣṭoma,* is only a consequence of the act and not its goal. Unless the mandate of the sacrifice is first carried out, the result will not issue. Thus even what is called *kāmyakarma* is a command to be followed for its own sake.

According to Mīmāṁsā in general, the Veda reveals to us the kinds of duties we have to discharge and all the details concerning them. Thus it appeals to our cognitive side. The above information is conveyed to us through imperative sentences. Thus the Veda appeals to our will also. This is not all, according to the first two views. There is also an appeal to our feeling—directly according to the first view and indirectly according to the second—since both admit that no voluntary activity issues until the agent realizes that it will satisfy some desire of his. Now, Prabhākara denies the element of feeling in explaining the process of responding to a mandate and claims that the cognition that it is a mandate can by itself move us to act. Prabhākara's theory fails to be satisfactory, for it is wrong psychology to say that cognition alone can make us act. To insist upon such activity is to reduce life to meaningless drudgery.

We thus return to the second view that *dharma* is a means to *mokṣa,* which is the prevalent view. It combines the merits of the other two views, minus their defects. Like the first, it recognizes that moral duty needs the incentive of an ideal. The incentive, however, cannot be purely personal as the first view holds, since such a motive deprives duty of a sense of obligation, the need for which is pointed out by the third view. But while the third view wrongly claims that the sense of obligation is purely cognitive, the second traces it to our deeper longing for liberation. It thus answers to our higher spiritual nature, whichever strives to overcome our lower tendencies. The concept of liberation, of course, admits of different views and consequently the exact relation of *dharma* to it is also variously conceived. But the point to be noted is that ethics rightly understood cannot dispense with the idea of liberation. "The perplexities which ethics, as commonly dealt with, presents are mostly due to this divorce of ethics from the final ideal of life, which is wrongly regarded as a question *entirely* for metaphysics."[15]

Activism and Asceticism in Indian Ethics

From time immemorial two types of ethical discipline were known to the Hindus, and both were conducive to attaining the final goal of life. They are *pravṛtti* and *nivṛtti*, and they could be rendered as "activism" and "asceticism." In the *āśrama* scheme they are predominantly associated with the life of the householder (*gṛhastha*) and that of the recluse (*saṁnyāsin*) respectively. The positive and the negative paths, as they may be called, are not mutually exclusive ways of life as thought by some. One ancient view holds the householder's life as the norm and relegates *saṁnyāsa* to those who are unfit for it. Another, in contrast, praises the life of the recluse and regards the householder's life as an impediment to freedom.[16] But neither of these extreme views has survived. According to the final Indian view, only a combination of *pravṛtti* and *nivṛtti* results in a well-balanced life and makes for freedom. Kālidāsa, "who represents in a pre-eminent degree the genius of the Indian people," delights to depict in his works the harmony of the two paths.[17] But the question before us is how they are to be combined.

The older way of meeting the demands of activism and asceticism is to accommodate them in the sequence of the four *āśramas* in the life of an individual. These *āśramas* represent different stages in the moral advance of the individual; and the duties associated with each are in tune with the growth of his moral capacity. The normal course for one is to proceed from one *āśrama* to the next in the order in which the *āśramas* are commonly enunciated, viz. that of the Vedic student (*brahmacarya*), of the householder (*gārhasthya*), of the anchorite, or the one who has retired to the seclusion of the forest (*vānaprastha*), and of the recluse, or the one who has completely renounced the world (*saṁnyāsa*). This is known as the *samuccaya-pakṣa*, for it utilizes the training of all the stages. This practice was followed as early as the Upaniṣads, and it is current even now. Kālidāsa depicts his heroes as practising this course.[18]

The transition from *pravṛtti* to *nivṛtti* as represented by this scheme is not sudden. Even the life of *pravṛtti* involves numerous checks on natural impulses. So far, it implies *nivṛtti*. "*Pravṛtti* is not selfishness but restrained selfishness."[19] "In fact, no virtue is conceivable without self-restraint, and one of the main objects of the *āśrama* discipline is the imposition of restraint."[20] There are degrees of restraint indicating progressive development of *nivṛtti* and decrease of selfishness until the process culminates in *saṁnyāsa*. *Saṁnyāsa* stands for complete abnegation, which is the fulfilment of *nivṛtti*. "*Nivṛtti* is absence (i.e., total) of selfishness. So, there are no degrees of unselfishness."[21] Only we should add that complete abnegation in *saṁnyāsa* refers to the specific duties of the other *āśramas* and does not exclude the observance of general duties (*sādhāraṇa dharma*). These virtues have to be practised by the *saṁnyāsin* until they become a second nature (*lakṣaṇa*) with him when he realizes the final ideal. "Accordingly, when one assumes *saṁnyāsa*, one does not relax his sympathies, but rather widens and intensifies them."[22] Further, the *saṁnyāsin* has to discharge his own specific duties, which are mainly intended to perfect his spiritual nature.

Within the above view, a change took place. The revised view, like the older one, insists on Vedic study (*brahmacarya*) as the first stage. But it holds that in exceptional cases *saṁnyāsa* may be assumed immediately thereafter, provided the individual has sufficient detachment. This view is known as *vikalpa-pakṣa*, because it allows choice in the stage at which one may adopt *saṁnyāsa*. On the face of it, this teaching shortens the period of preparation for *saṁnyāsa*, but it implies that the individual in question must have undergone the antecedent stages of discipline in his former lives.[23] Thus, in any case, the adoption of *saṁnyāsa* presupposes the preparation of the previous stages. Hindu society discourages *saṁnyāsa* without full qualification. For this reason, the householder's life is praised as the one which combines the discipline of all the stages. So nothing can be further from the truth than to say that the Hindu outlook on life is predominantly negative.

The *āśrama* scheme combines *pravṛtti* and *nivṛtti* by associating them predominantly with the stage of the householder and that of the recluse respectively. But by doing so, the activistic ideal is subordinated to the ascetic, because the one is conceived as qualifying for the other. The relation between the two ideals so conceived is external, since the life of total self-denial is to begin only *after* the stage of active life. It does not amount to a synthesis of activism and asceticism. The question arises whether any attempt at such synthesis was made in ancient India. There were two such attempts, one in the *Bhagavad-gītā* and the other in the *Manusmṛti*.

How the *Bhagavad-gītā* synthesizes *pravṛtti* and *nivṛtti* in the concept of *niṣkāmakarma* has already been explained in detail in chapter Three. In brief, it consists in incorporating the spirit of *nivṛtti* into *pravṛtti*. This is done by the total exclusion of both personal and social interests from the performance of one's duties and their direction solely towards the spiritual end of self-purification. But *niṣkāmakarma* does not in the least reduce the importance of social life. It teaches that social life need not and should not be abandoned, but it must be pursued in a spirit of absolute detachment. Objective results for society do accrue from such performance of duty, but they are to be looked upon merely as the consequence of action and not as its end. Thereby the social significance of duty becomes implicit. Similarly the personal significance of the action becomes spiritualized, for particular objects of desire are replaced by the sole aim of self-purification. However, subjective purification is only the proximate end of duty. It is meant to subserve, along with philosophical knowledge, the higher aim of liberation.

All volitional activity permitted by the ideal of *pravṛtti* involves a negative and a positive purpose. The negative purpose is a measure of self-restraint. The positive purpose is either heavenly reward or earthly gain. The *Gītā* retains the negative aim, but renders it absolute in degree. The positive end of heaven or earth is replaced by that of salvation. It means that *pravṛtti* comes to lay as much emphasis on renunciation as *nivṛtti* does. *Pravṛtti* and *nivṛtti* thus come to be pursued simultaneously as it were instead of successively as before. Through this synthesis the new discipline elevates both asceticism and activism. "Asceticism thereby becomes much more than self-denial, and activity is freed from all egoistic motives."[24]

The synthesis of *pravṛtti* and *nivṛtti* we find in the *Manusmṛti* is different from the one found in the *Bhagavad-gītā* both in scope and in context. The *Gītā* teaching of *niṣkāmakarma* applies equally to all irrespective of their *āśramas*. But Manu's synthesis is enunciated with reference only to the stage of the householder. Again, it differs from the *Gītā* in regard to the type of action to which it refers. It is necessary to distinguish between actions that are prescribed (*vihita*) and those that are not. The former are a matter of obligation and should in any case be done. The latter are all the activities that issue from pure inclination to gratify selfish desire (*kāma*). Of these, again, some are explicitly prohibited (*pratiṣiddha*) and are, therefore, to be abstained from. It is to the remaining sphere of actions of a selfish nature that are not prohibited that the teaching of Manu applies. The *Gītā* is averse to all actions of a selfish

reveals two things: that the relegation of the field of art to the Ālaṅkārikas was perfectly justified and that the Indian philosopher, though not directly concerned with art, was alive to its exalted character and significance as a value.

Far from being a defect, the separation of the study of art from general philosophy has its own advantage. The content of a work of art does not belong to the real world. It is a product of the artist's imagination based on material taken from the real world. That it is imaginary does not mean that it is unreal or even illusory. The point is simply that ontological considerations are irrelevant to the nature of art. In fact, the aim of art is not to discover the nature of reality, but to secure for us a unique experience. The creation of art, of course, needs and accepts a provisional view of reality. But "it does not pronounce any final opinion on the tenability or otherwise of the view of reality it thus uses."[30] It is generally admitted that reality as represented in art is a unity in diversity. Even supposing that the representation is not necessarily this, but some other, it does not affect the purpose of art. The reason is that whatever representation art gives of reality is intended only to serve as a medium through which the aesthetic value could be realized, "art being concerned less with facts than with values."[31] On this ground, art may be described as alogical. While the study of art is closely connected with psychology, it regards epistemology and metaphysics as irrelevant to its pursuit.

To understand the nature of artistic beauty, we do not require any specific knowledge of reality. Whatever view we form regarding its nature is in no way determined by the metaphysical view we may hold. In fact, the application of a metaphysical standpoint to the study of art would result in conclusions not germane to art. Further, it is natural for different philosophers to hold different views about reality. Therefore, when philosophers undertake to inquire into the nature of artistic beauty, each is bound to impose his particular metaphysical view on it and try to evolve a theory of art that squares with his theory of reality. As a result, there will be as many theories of art as there are theories of reality as it has happened in the West. Indian thinkers have been of the view that while a diversity of views based on diversity in metaphysical thinking cannot be helped in the case of beauty in nature, such a diversity originating from metaphysical views would be unwarranted in the case of art. It is not that there is no diversity at all in the Indian treatment of the character of art. But the important point to be noted is that whatever diversity there is in this area is based on artistic considerations themselves and is, therefore, more genuine.

The wisdom of separating the inquiry from philosophy proper has been borne out by results. The Indian aesthetics of art, or Alaṅkāra-śāstra, has enjoyed a degree of freedom that has resulted in original discoveries. As an instance of this, we may cite what is called *vyaṅgyārtha*, or *dhvani*. It is a theory of meaning evolved by the Ālaṅkārikas themselves and sheds new light on the character of art which could not have been discerned by any approach from metaphysics. In fact, it is a theory of meaning which is not only recognized by any school of philosophy from the logical point of view, but is even opposed by some.

We have so far explained why the study of artistic beauty with reference to its character is generally avoided by philosophers in India. Even in regard to the significance of art, the philosopher's concern is not quite intimate. We can understand this if we remember that all the higher values are in India judged in terms of their utility for *mokṣa*. It is generally agreed among philosophers that as beauty in art is not essentially connected with reality, its pursuit cannot *directly* minister to the attainment of the final goal of life. Perhaps some among them thought that its pursuit might even distract men from that goal. The statement "all prattle about poetry ought to cease,"[32] represents their general attitude towards art. This over-Puritanic view of art is as old as Manu, who reckoned song, dance, and instrumental music among human weaknesses (*vyasana*).[33]

It may well be that the above view was not an outright condemnation of art, but a well-meant caution against the perversion of art as a means to selfish pleasure (*kāma*). In fact, the popular mind could easily commit the mistake. That this must have been the spirit of the view becomes evident when we come across other thinkers, who were neither less ancient nor less influential, who took an avowedly liberal view of the fine arts. Yājñavalkya, for instance, recommends music in view of its utility for salvation by conducing to concentration of the mind. In other words, it comes to be recognized by philosophers that, although art is not directly connected with *mokṣa*, it could serve as an indirect means to its attainment. "Art is a short-cut to the ultimate value of life, by-passing logic."[34] We shall deal with this significance in detail later. The point of interest for the present is that philosophers in India were not oblivious to the status of art as a higher value, but as it had no direct relation to *mokṣa*, they did not devote primary attention to its significance. Here, again, it was left to the Ālaṅkārikas to point out its exalted value. Though they deal only with poetry and drama, they imply a general theory of art.

Bharata speaks of his work, the *Nāṭyaśāstra*, which may be described as an encyclopaedia of all the fine arts, as the "fifth Veda."

Beauty in Nature

There is no lack of love for nature in the Indian mind from early times, and a variety of expressions are commonly used to describe beauty in nature. The Vedic gods, for example, are mostly gods of nature. When the Vedic poets praise the gods, they indirectly express their appreciation of beauty in nature. In later literature we find nature appreciation in a more direct form, for example, in the lavish and splendid descriptions of nature in Kālidāsa's *Meghasandeśa*. In the *Bṛhadāraṇyaka Upaniṣad*[35] the self, i.e., Brahman, is spoken of as the one object of all love; and if we admit that what is loved is necessarily lovely, beauty should be a prominent feature of Brahman. And since Brahman is there represented as finally the only object of love, it should indeed be perfect beauty. In the same Upaniṣad it is said that all other joy is but a particle of the joy that is Brahman. Here, we have a theory that natural beauty has its source in the Absolute and is a revelation of the one beauty that underlies all beauties. In theistic philosophies, again, it is common to find that God is described as the fountain-head of beauty. "He is the abode of beauty, as of all other perfections."[36] The *Bhāgavata* describes God as "the beauty of the universe" (*bhuvana-sundara*). In non-theistic philosophies, though explicit descriptions are hard to come by, there are certainly implicit views of beauty in nature corresponding to their conceptions of reality. These conceptions of reality may be divided into two classes: those in which evil is taken to be real, and those in which it is regarded as not ultimate, if not as an appearance. Corresponding to these metaphysical views, there are two theories of beauty in nature. We shall indicate them by taking Sāṅkhya-Yoga to represent the former and Vedānta to represent the latter.

When we speak of nature with reference to our ordinary experience of it, we mean only *parts* of nature, i.e., nature in particular objects and events. The whole of nature is not presented to our perception, and the discussion of beauty in it is possible, if at all, only with reference to the experience of a seer. There is no doubt that we come across beautiful aspects in nature. But there are other aspects in it which do not impress us in the same way. They are either ugly or just plain. Sāṅkhya-Yoga has an explanation for this discrepancy. The explanation is twofold. Everything, whether it belongs to the outer physical world (*prakṛti*) or to the inner psychic apparatus (*buddhi*) is made up of three factors, *sattva, rajas*, and *tamas*, the proportion of which is subject to change. Things in nature tend to impress us as beautiful only when they are predominated by *sattva*. And since matter is subject to change, things are not beautiful for all time. Apart from the constitution of the object, for the mind to respond to the presence of beauty, it must also be predominated by *sattva* at the moment. In its intrinsic nature, the *buddhi* is predominantly of the nature of *sattva*. But each individual *buddhi* has in itself, from the beginning, *vāsanās*, or acquired impulses, and these may modify its intrinsic *sāttvika* character and transform it into one of *rajas* or *tamas*. As a consequence, the same object may impress different people differently at the same time and the same person differently at different times. *Sattva, rajas*, and *tamas* also give rise to the effects of pleasure (*sukha*), pain (*duḥkha*), and delusion (*moha*) respectively. And since their dominance in the mind varies, what causes pleasure to one may give pain to another at the same time or even to the same person at a different time.

According to Sāṅkhya, the basic cause of this predicament is to be traced to a mistaken identification of the *puruṣa* with the *buddhi*. The mistake cannot be avoided until the *puruṣa* dissociates itself from the *buddhi* altogether as in *jīvanmukti*. He who acquires true knowledge realizes the intrinsic disparateness of *prakṛti* and *puruṣa*. Although the *jīvanmukta* perceives nature, he sees things not as related to him, but as related among themselves. Hence everything impresses him in the same way, whether it is beautiful or ugly, and he does not experience either pleasure or pain. According to Sāṅkhya, the distinction between beauty and ugliness is ultimate. Even the *jīvanmukta* perceives this. But he remains unaffected by it.

Vedānta agrees with Sāṅkhya that so far as common experience is concerned, nature presents us with phases of beauty and ugliness. It has no objection even to the explanation given by Sāṅkhya as to why we meet with this contrast in the parts of nature. But according to Vedānta, the whole of nature is in a sense beautiful. Such a view results from the Ātman doctrine of the Upaniṣads. The entire universe with all its variety is based on Brahman, or *Ātman*. As such, there is a basic unity underlying nature. We are commonly occupied with variety because of our fragmentary view of reality resulting from ignorance of the ultimate truth. But the *jīvanmukta* transcends this view. He may continue to perceive variety, but it ceases to have any significance for him. He merges in the unity which he realizes all separate existence including his own and enjoys perfect bliss. In this sense nature could be described as beautiful on the whole. This higher viewpoint is not possible for us while we are yet on the empirical plane. But whenever we are face to face with a beautiful aspect of nature, we transcend our narrow selves and feel delight, however short-lived it may be. We do not indeed realize then, like the knower, the unity of all that is, but yet we resemble him in one respect in that we lose sight of ourselves in the bliss that we enjoy.

Beauty in nature as we know it impresses us in myriad ways—sometimes as symmetry, sometimes as novelty, and sometimes as something else. And it is this variety that accounts for the almost bewildering number of theories of the beautiful in nature that we find in the history of Western aesthetics. But according to Vedānta, the beautiful things of nature, howsoever they may impress us, do not constitute true beauty at all. The true beauty of nature is the inner harmony of the universe, which is centred in Brahman. The particular things of beauty which we perçeive are only its outward and visible symbols. We may describe them as beautiful only in a secondary sense. However, as symbols of the ultimate beauty, the beautiful things of nature have this significance that, though diverse in themselves, they point to the same underlying harmony which constitutes real beauty. These "relatively greater glories of nature" are some of the distinctive manifestations (*vibhūtis*) of the Lord described in the *Bhagavad-gītā*.[37]

Both the above views of nature recognize the need for art. But the reasons are different. Whether we accept the Sāṅkhya or the Vedānta view, we have to admit that in our common experience both beauty and ugliness are part of nature, just as good and evil are part of life. Hence both pleasure and pain are inevitable experiences with reference to nature. According to Sāṅkhya, this is also the final truth of nature. The pure bliss of unmixed beauty can be experienced only in the imaginary creations of art. According to Vedānta, the world as a whole is beautiful; but this inner beauty is presented only to the knower. In his case art is superfluous, for he sees beauty in everything. Such ecstasy is a distant goal for the layman. He needs the provisional satisfaction of pure delight which art alone can give. Thus both Sāṅkhya and Vedānta recognize that man stands in need of art. But since the reasons are different, their perceptions of the significance of art also differ. To Sāṅkhya, art is an escape from the natural world, a "deflection," so to say, from reality and comes to satisfy the need—which somehow actuates all men—for relief from the struggles and perplexities of life. To Vedānta, art has a more positive significance. Though imaginary, it serves as a pathway to reality by catching for us intimations of the unity perceived by the seer, which we miss in our ordinary experience. To Vedānta, art reveals the best in nature, while to Sāṅkhya, it fashions something better than nature. But there is need for art in either case. "Here...we have another instance of Indian aesthetics transcending the differences that characterize the metaphysical schools."[38]

Beauty in Art (General Features)

To understand the place of art in life, we have first to examine the character of art. The beauty presented in a work of art rests on objects and events created by the artist's imagination. But imagination requires a real basis. So the artist has necessarily to draw material from nature and life. The artist is free to deal with this material as he pleases. But the classical Indian view is that the best type of art avoids two extremes. The artist neither alters the material to such an extent as to sever all connection with the actual world nor reproduces it as it is. In other words, he keeps clear of abstractionism and imitationism. The content of art is modelled upon the facts of the real world, so that it may be familiar to the appreciator. If it is totally unfamiliar, it would not evoke aesthetic interest. This does not mean that the artist's creations are exact copies of their actual counterparts. The reason is that we long to find in art what we miss in our ordinary experience of the world—a beauty that does not stand contrasted with ugliness and which evokcs uniformly disinterested joy. It is said of a famous painter that when somebody, on seeing a sunset painted by him, remarked that he never saw a sunset like that, he replied, "Don't you wish you could?"[39] This shows that the work of the artist involves a good deal of invention and mental construction. The attraction of art for us is its novelty. The art object surpasses in quality its counterpart in the real world. The artist selects out of the actual only such features as would be necessary to retain for his creations a resemblance to it, so that the object fancied is experienced by us *as if* it is being actually perceived. The rest are supplied by his fertile mind. The essence of art creation is imagination, or creative fancy (*pratibhā*). Its importance is brought out by the fact that in the art of poetry it is described as "the seed of poetry" (*kavitva-bīja*).[40] Its excellence is that it throws up an inexhaustible variety of ideas to go into the content of a fine art. In this sense the objects created in a work of art are described as "not of this world" (*alaukika*), and the artist himself is compared to the Creator (Prajāpati). However, the introduction of new features is not for their own sake. The artist is inspired by a total vision of what the created object should be; and it is in conformity with this vision that he resorts to innovation.

The essence of the artistic transformation of the actual is, according to Indian aestheticians, idealization, or *sādhāraṇīkaraṇa*. A particular object or event found in the actual world is invested with new qualities such that it is no longer a particular, but represents a general pattern, or universal idea. For example, though the sight of a particular old man might have inspired a painter, the old man in his painting would vividly represent the general idea of oldage with its pitiful frailty and decrepitude and the neglect which it usually suffers. Thus idealization is not merely presenting the actual in idea; it also signifies the sublimation of the actual.

The process of idealization gives to the artistic content two advantages. First, it renders the content wholly beautiful, the artist being at liberty to omit or alter such elements of his material as might mar the harmony of his theme. Hence the work becomes self-complete, every item falling in the right place and measure. Art deals in wholes, which admit of neither addition nor subtraction. Even those items that are displeasing when taken by themselves, like untimely death, blend with the general pattern of the work, a drama for instance, at the hands of the artist. This feature ensures the appreciator's total absorption in the object. The unity of the situation depicted "so satisfies the yearning in man for complete comprehension ... that it allays, for the moment, all his doubts and discomposing thoughts."[41] Secondly, the content being ideal in nature, the attitude which a work of art evokes in the appreciator is uniformly detached. Having its source in the artist's imagination, it appeals to the same faculty in the appreciator and not merely to his intellect. None but the simple-minded and unwary will mistake the objects of art to be real and behave as though they were real. In appreciating them, we are more concerned with their appearance than with their actual existence; we value semblance above reality. To say that they are not real does not mean that art objects are unreal, for in that case they would not have evoked interest. Nor are they illusory, neither real nor unreal, for, unlike illusions, the objects of art are not at one time wrongly believed to be real and later repudiated. In short, we do not look at them in terms of ontological categories. Neither believing nor disbelieving their reality, we merely "entertain them."[42] They hold our attention, but, having no relevance to the actual and the particular, they have no appeal to the egoistic self and carry no suggestion of anything to be done, for all activity is directed towards real objects.

Art objects, being impersonal in their appeal, become enjoyable in and for themselves. They thus appear the same to all. This does not mean, however, that the response will be the same in the case of all. It will certainly vary, but only according to the aesthetic sensibilities of particular appreciators and not according to their personal likes and dislikes. The complete detachment with which we are able to view such idealized objects makes for pure contemplation of them. But detachment does not mean that we have no interest in the art object. All that is meant is that our interest is confined to the object, and that it is not diverted by any thought of an ulterior use to which it may be put.

The pleasure derived from a work of art is quite unique. It is free from all the limitations of common pleasure. The pleasure of sense objects is uncertain. But a work of art is ever a source of delight. Again, common pleasure suffers from the duality of pleasure and pain. But the pleasure of art is absolutely pure. For this reason, it is described as higher pleasure (*para-nirvṛti*). And art will yield such pleasure not only when its subject-matter is pleasant, but even when it is not. That is why we enjoy a tragedy with its representation of unusual suffering. The facts dealt with by the artist, as parts of the actual world, may be a source of pain or pleasure; but when they are contemplated in their ideal form, they necessarily give rise only to pleasure. For this reason, pleasure (*prīti*) is represented in Indian works as the sole aim of art. Since common pleasure bears no comparision with it, this view of art is in no way hedonistic.

Art may have uses other than pleasure also for the appreciator. It is said, in the case of poetry for example, that it provides a correct understanding (*vyutpatti*) of the four *puruṣārthas*. But such uses are only remote and incidental to the appreciation. The immediate and primary result of the appreciation is the higher pleasure of which we have spoken (*sadyaḥ-paranirvṛti*). It should be noted that Indian works do not take this pleasure in the abstract. They consider it only as a constant and conspicuous feature of the total experience, or state of the self, during the contemplation of art. So, strictly speaking, it is the enjoyable experience as a whole and not the mere pleasure in it that is the aim and value of art to the appreciator. Again, a naive view takes the contemplation of art as the means and pleasure as the end. But, since pleasure cannot be separated from the contemplation, Indian writers make no such distinction. Pleasure can be described as the end only in the sense that the culminating stage of the process is marked by the repose of achievement.[43]

The dissociation of art from practical interests often leads to the misapprehension that its contemplation is quite passive. People take for granted that beauty is given readymade in a work of art, and that we have merely to yield ourselves to its influence. What is overlooked in this view is that a work of art is the expression of an ideal construction by the artist. Hence its appreciation demands a similar exercise of imagination from the aesthete. From the form of the work he has to reconstruct in his own mind the general idea implanted in it. It is only when thus ideally reconstructed, that the beauty of the work becomes actual for the appreciator, or "verified by his own heart." In this sense appreciation may be described as the reverse of creation. "...the beautiful as a value needs to be striven for and achieved (*sādhya*), no matter whether one approaches it as an artist or as a spectator."[44]

The implication of this finding is that the appreciator must himself be an artist at heart. That is, he must be of the same temperament as the artist, so that the artist's experience might find a ready echo in his heart. Indian aestheticians, therefore, describe the qualified appreciator of art as *sa-hṛdaya*, which literally means "one of similar heart" (*samāna-hṛdayaḥ*). This is not to say that he is equal to the artist. He lacks the original vision of the artist as well as his skill of expression. And that is why he is dependent on the artist for the same type of experience. But without this identity of temperament with the artist, a work of art will remain a closed book to one who approaches it. The identity of temperament means also a certain restriction in the circle of competent appreciators; there is no warrant for assuming that the aesthetic sense is universal and that all peoples are equally fitted to enjoy the pleasures of art.[45]

What is the significance of art? The question may be discussed from two standpoints—that of the artist and that of the appreciator. In each case, we find two main views in India, one put forward by Sāṅkhya and the other by Vedānta. In the history of Indian aesthetics the earlier writers generally followed the line of Sāṅkhya and the later ones that of Vedānta. The clue to the Vedānta view of the significance of art creation lies in its comparison of the artist with the Creator. In the view of Vedānta, the world is at bottom perfect. It is the peculiar glory of the artist that he often catches glimpses of the intrinsic beauty and joy of the universe. And in his works he constructs for us new situations through which we are enabled to see and understand this inner harmony of the universe. The various devices of art such as rhythm, symmetry, etc. serve not only to maintain concentration, but also to secure unity to the subject portrayed. Consequently, the appreciator realizes unity in variety in the work of art. This is like the knower realizing unity in nature's diversity. While in the one case what is realized is the truth of nature, in the other it is the truth of art, a lower truth. Nevertheless, in creating a new world of art, the artist indirectly reveals to us the inner significance of the world of nature. The conception of the artist as a revealer is implied in the Sanskrit word used for the poet, viz., *kavi*. "...*kavi* literally means 'one that shows,' and he who shows must necessarily have himself seen."[46] In this sense the word *kavi* is equivalent to the word "seer." And it is the vision of the true world that we get through the artist's work that constitutes the source of our satisfaction. If we adopt the Sāṅkhya point of view instead, the world is not perfect even ultimately; the mixture of evil and good, of ugliness and beauty, will remain permanent features of the world. In that case, the work of the artist is to fashion something better than nature, so that in his work at least man may find joy untainted by sorrow. According to both the views, the artist ought to be a creator. In the one case, the forms he creates disclose to us the truth of nature which, though hidden from us, is still there; in the other, they present for our contemplation something that is not in nature and is superior to it.

If such be the impulse behind the artist's creation, what is it that we as appreciators may expect from it? The answer is twofold as above. If we look at art from the optimistic standpoint of Vedānta, we seek it "to draw ourselves closer to the intrinsic truth and beauty of the universe." If we look at it from the pessimistic standpoint of Sāṅkhya, we go to it "to draw ourselves away from the sufferings and perplexities of actual life."[47] Nevertheless, in either case, we are transported, as it were, from our usual surroundings and, moving in a world of the artist's fancy, we forget ourselves. At this point we resemble the artist most, the only difference being that while he attains that condition spontaneously, we attain it only by his grace. It is this "migrating from our narrow self" that constitutes the secret of aesthetic delight. "The highest function of the poet who easily rises to this mood is to communicate the same to us."[48] Thereby he becomes our supreme benefactor.

In this delightful experience which we derive from art, Sāṅkhya does not recognize any connection with *mokṣa*. Such a view is held not because Sāṅkhya does not believe in *mokṣa*, but because its conception of *mokṣa* does not permit any connection of art experience with that state. According to Sāṅkhya, *mokṣa*, whether of the penultimate stage (*jīvanmukti*) or of the ultimate one (*videha-mukti*), stands merely for the complete absence of pain and does not denote the presence of bliss. For this reason, art experience cannot have any connection with the state of *mokṣa*. If anything, it resembles common experience, which, though one of pleasure mixed with pain, is experience (*bhoga*) anyway. The only value of art experience is that it gives us a temporary relief from common life. Art lifts us for a while out of this humdrum existence and refreshes our souls. In this sense art experience may be regarded as an intrinsic value.

The view that art experience has nothing to do with *mokṣa* experience is too negative for man to take abiding interest in art. Hence it is replaced by the positive view taken by Vedānta. Art experience resembles the experience of *mokṣa*. Like it, it is a state of complete unselfishness and pure bliss. As such, it serves as a significant pointer to the final experience. There are, indeed, important differences between the two experiences in the conditions that secure each. The ideal state is the result of inner transformation preceded by prolonged discipline, which is partly moral and partly intellectual, the culminating point of which is a direct experience of the whole of reality. Hence, when once attained, there is no lapse from it. On the contrary, art experience does not require as a necessary condition either comprehensive knowledge or moral worth. It can be brought about even in their absence "by the power which all true art possess." This is only a seeming excellence of it, for, being induced externally, it is woefully fugitive. But the enduring character of the final experience more than compensates for the trouble and exertion involved in attaining it. With all this difference, the quality of artistic delight, for which there is no comparison on earth, is such that it well serves as a foretaste of the bliss of *mokṣa*. It is of the same order as that of the ideal state; and the fact of the one points to the feasibility of the other. Art could thereby serve as a powerful incentive to the deliberate pursuit of that goal.[49] It must be noted that art subserves this spiritual purpose irrespective of its theme. Art is under no obligation to deal with any particular type of theme, spiritual or secular. Still, quite apart from its theme, art by virtue of its form as art can be of use to the spiritual aspirant.[50]

There is another respect in which art is useful to *mokṣa*. It serves as a training in mental concentration. According to all schools, mediate knowledge of reality has to be converted into immediate experience through continued meditation (*yoga*). Meditation is a difficult process, as the mind is known for its fickleness. To bring the mind to bear on the whole of reality, it has to be put through exercises involving particular objects, concrete and abstract, which develop the power of concentration. In this preliminary form of *yoga*, art could function as an excellent aid. Though art is not intended for *yoga*, it so happens that it serves that purpose. The contemplation of art involves the total absorption of the mind in the object. It has, therefore, been compared to the last lap in *yoga*, viz., *samādhi*. To reach the stage of *samādhi*, the *yogin* has to strain himself for long. But the fascination that the beauty of art can cast on the mind is so complete that it is gently weaned away from itself. Art could, therefore, be described as "the layman's *yoga*." A mind that is continually nurtured upon art cannot but acquire skill in concentration. On this significance, Sāṅkhya and Vedānta are agreed.

Beauty in Art (Special Concepts)

The content of a work of art is based on material taken from actual life. There is practically nothing in life that an artist may not resort to for his content. The only condition he has to observe is that whatever is drawn from life must be judiciously idealized so as to induce a detached attitude in the appreciator. While granting this general truth, Indian aestheticians came to distinguish between two types of themes, one of which they came to reckon as superior to the other. This contri-bution took place in the ninth century AD with particular reference to poetry and drama, two forms of the literary art. But the theory so evolved was eventually found to be equally applicable to all the fine arts. Consistent with its origin, we shall explain the theory with reference to poetry and drama without going into the details of its history.

A poet may choose to describe a situation (*daśā*), which may be either a scene in nature or a human activity. A situation does evoke human emotions and is also influenced by the expression of these emotions. But the poet's attention is mainly on external phenomena, and he refers to emotions only in passing. The *Ṛtusaṁhāra* of Kālidāsa may be cited as an instance of this type of theme. Here the poet describes in graphic detail the natural and human circumstances during the different seasons of the year. Emotions such as love run as an undercurrent in the narration, but the focus of attention is the situation. We have the other type of theme when the poet chooses not the situation as such, but some elemental emotion (*bhāva*), like love or pathos, that characterizes it. He is concerned with how the situation affects a human feeling and is in turn influenced by the manifestation of it. As an example of this type, we may refer to Kālidāsa's *Meghasandeśa*, where the poet describes the forlon state and anguish of a *yakṣa* deeply in love for his consort from whom he is separated through a temporary exile. That the poet's attention is centred on the emotion does not mean that he neglects the situation. In fact, he cannot afford to neglect it. The character of emotion is such that it cannot be conveyed except by delineating its causes and effects in the situation. But whatever attention the poet pays to the situation is only as a means to an end, not as an end in itself. In the former type of theme any detail that attracts the attention of the poet and is found fit for objective representation could be brought in. But here the choice of details is determined by their adequacy (*aucitya*) to convey the character of the emotion which the poet intends to convey. In fact, without such control, the situation could serve only to distract the reader from the emotion intended.

To bring out the relative importance of the situation and the emotion in it, the analogy of the body (*śarīra*) and the soul (*ātman*) is employed. The former is only the body of poetry; the latter is its true essence, or *ātman*. Thus the difference between the two types of themes lies not in an exclusive treatment of situation or emotion, but in the one or the other occupying the centre of the poet's attention and predominating the treatment. Emotions are classified as main and subsidiary. The former are elemental, or basic to human nature. Love, mirth, sorrow, anger, courage, fear, disgust, and wonder are examples. It is such emotions that are chosen as themes, as they admit of sustained treatment. The subsidiary emotions merely accompany the main emotions on occasions. For example, anxiety may sometimes accompany love. Such emotions are numerous. More than one basic emotion may find a place in a poem. But to preserve the unity of the work, one of them is chosen as the theme, and the others, which are not incompatible with it, are synthetically related to it.

Before we discuss the relative merits of the two types of themes, it is necessary to clarify two points with regard to the nature of the predominantly emotional type. (i) Only an emotion as idealized by the poet becomes the theme of the work. Either the poet's own emotion, felt at some critical point of life, or the emotion he has observed in another person would no doubt be the raw material for his work. But, when it becomes the theme of his poem, it belongs to no one in particular and is presented in its general form. It is an emotion that is not only "recollected in tranquillity," but sublimated as well.[51] That is why it becomes a source of pure delight to the appreciator. In actual life emotions are not uniformly pleasant. An emotion like sorrow is essentially painful. Even a pleasant emotion like love may have its painful phases. But when presented by the poet, every emotion becomes fully enjoyable because it evokes nothing but an impersonal, self-forgetful response from the reader. Incidentally, in being generalized by the poet, the emotion reveals its deeper significance for life. For instance, in Kālidāsa's *Śākuntalam*, love, which first appears as the manifestation of a natural impulse, is transformed before the play concludes into a "spiritual welding of hearts."[52] (ii) The idealized emotion is presented by the poet through a situation which is suitably idealized. An emotion cannot be directly communicated. What the feeling is like can be made known only indirectly by describing the situation in which it arises. To serve as a vehicle for the communication of the idealized emotion, it is understood that the situation also is an idealized one.

The predominantly emotional type of theme calls for a better type of equipment in the reader than the other type. In the first place, the reader's imagination has to be more penetrating. Where nature and man are described for their own sake, the reader's imaginative affinity with the poet enables him to get absorbed in the poet's description. But here, instead of getting lost in the depiction of outer phenomena, the reader is expected to catch a sense of the emotion implied in it. Secondly, the appreciation presupposes that the reader has previous experience of the emotion represented in the poem. And this past experience might have been gained either in this life or in some previous life. It is observed in actual life that a person cannot appreciate another's feeling unless he has himself felt it at some stage or other. Likewise, the emotion represented in poetry can be appreciated only by a reader who has himself had experience of it. It means that the emotion in the poem is apprehended by the reader only on the *basis* of his own past experience of it. In short, the reader must be "sensitive" to the poet's content as much as he is "sympathetic" to the poet's imagination.[53] The term *sahṛdaya*, which stands for a qualified appreciator of art, thus implies more for the emotional type of theme than for the other. The emotion chosen, being elemental, may be expected to be latent in all. But the degree of its past experience may vary among individuals, and that accounts for their varied response to different kinds of emotion. Some may like poems depicting love, others those depicting heroism, and so on.

The process of appreciation in the case of the predominantly emotional type of theme happens at a deeper level. Art appreciation in general is said to involve two stages. We may explain this first with reference to the type of theme where the situation predominates. To begin with, the appreciator's imagination is fascinated by the beauty of the presentation, and he gets mentally attuned to it (*hṛdaya-saṁvāda*). As a consequence of this attunement, the appreciator gets mentally absorbed in the object, or identified with it. Such identification (*tādātmya*), being a means to self-forgetfulness, naturally yields aesthetic delight. The appreciation of the predominantly emotional type also embodies these two stages, but they are with reference to the emotional content, the situation that bears it sliding into the margin of consciousness. The poet presents an emotion

appreciator amounts to a foretaste of *mokṣa.* And the process of contemplating the work is a form of training in *yoga.* Over and above these advantages, the *rasa* type of work has a moral significance. To appreciate this, we have to consider the general problem of the connection between art and morality. The problem of such a connection cannot arise when the artist describes nature, nature being a-moral. It arises only when he deals with human life.

Art is not intended to teach morals. The theme of art need not be moral in the sense that it should convey a moral lesson. Moral instruction is the business of the philosopher. In fact, art has no purpose at all. It is a spontaneous expression of an inner urge, for which the artist is free to choose his subject. The chief value of art is the delight that it affords. This recognition means only that art has no *direct* connection with morality. It does not mean that art has nothing to do with morality so that it could afford to go against moral considerations. The very urge for art as for morality (and truth) is the perception of evil in life. "It is the problem of evil that gives rise to art as well as to philosophy."[59] Only, while morality attempts to overcome evil, art either seeks to find an escape from evil (according to one view) or to represent what exists beyond evil (according to another). If art were unconnected with morality, there would be nothing to restrain an artist from portraying what is patently immoral. And in that case, it would cease to be a higher value, "and its recognition of evil as a fact of life would become virtually meaningless."[60] The pursuit of one higher value cannot be at the expense of another, for, then, they would not together appeal to the whole being of man.

Though art creation is spontaneous, it is certainly circumscribed by the condition that its theme must not be such as to degrade moral standards and corrupt the character of its votaries. However, this negative approach is not enough, for, then, art would be a selfish escape from the tedium of life—a course as blameworthy as pure asceticism is in ethics. "...art may prove so seductive to man that, in his zest for the pleasure it brings, he may grow negligent of his obligations to fellow-men."[61] Hence the best opinion the world over is that art should be more than being ethically neutral. It should influence the character of its seekers *indirectly.* "Art, correctly conceived, cannot be merely a selfish escape from life; it must also influence life permanently or, at least, tend to do so."[62] The practice of great artists, whose outlook is moral, is our support here. If the joy of the work is the indirect result of the artist's genius, its moral influence is the indirect effect of his innate goodness.

What is this indirect influence? It lies in the way in which the artist chooses his characters and portrays their significance in the plot. It is not what the characters *say* that counts, for that would be, again, direct instruction. What matter is what they *are* and what they *do*. Hence the artist must ensure that the implied outlook of his characters on life and the world is moral. They should stand for the higher and nobler aspects of life. It has been said that a true poem is that "which treats of the doings of the good and the great."[63] Even when the artist is obliged to bring in bad characters and the seamy side of life which they represent, his treatment should be such as to leave the unmistakable impression that they are warnings of what ought not to be. The conclusion to be drawn from these considerations is that "art should not have a moral *aim*, but must necessarily have a moral *view*, if it should fulfil its true purpose."[64] By serving in this indirect way as "a criticism of life's values," art could produce discriminative insight (*vyutpatti*) into them. In short, the creations of art must leave a moral influence on the spectator without his knowing that he is being so influenced.

While the indirect moral influence of art holds good for works dealing with any aspect of human life, those works that turn predominantly on one or other emotion are specially fitted for this service. Emotions are the basic springs of moral life. They supply the urge for conduct, even as reason gives it a direction. So moral training is essentially training of the feelings. A theme of art that concentrates on such a factor cannot but have a vital role to play in the moral improvement of appreciators. The right way to discipline the emotions is not to suppress them, but to sublimate them according to their true places in life. It is exactly this significance of an emotion for life that the artist shows when he idealizes it. And the process of appreciation in this case being inward-directed, the appreciator is enabled to live through the emotion in its idealized form, though for a while. Such an experience cannot but leave a wholesome effect on the character of the appreciator. Art of the *rasa* type is thus wonderfully suited as a means of emotional culture. It thereby becomes an aid to *dharma*. Its status as art renders this influence pleasant also. "...it can not only teach, but also please, and while it can successfully persuade, it can keep its persuasive character concealed from view."[65] Its moral influence has, therefore, been compared to the gentle persuasion of a devoted wife (*jāyā-sammita*). In the history of Indian aesthetics this became an additional reason for regarding the emotional type of theme superior to all others.

3. ULTIMATE VALUE

The Concept of Mokṣa

The idea of *mokṣa*, being central to Indian philosophy, has already been touched upon in its various aspects in earlier chapters. *Mokṣa* is the common goal and inspiration for Indian philosophy. Its feasibility is uniformly recognized by all shades of Indian philosophy (with the single exception of materialism); and the consideration of its nature and means is ultimately the uniform task of all of them. The recognition that *mokṣa* is possible even within the span of life serves as the meeting point of philosophy and religion in India; the total unselfishness issuing in loving service that characterizes that state constitutes the message of Indian philosophy. The higher values of truth, goodness, and beauty are not self-sufficient, but inevitably point to *mokṣa* as the highest goal. Knowledge and morality are, moreover, indispensable means to the realization of *mokṣa*. These ideas have been dealt with in chapters One, Two, and Six in appropriate places. In chapter Three the conception of *mokṣa* and its means both in the Upaniṣads and in the early post-Vedic literature occurs. And in chapters Four and Five the specific nature of *mokṣa* and the means to attain it as conceived in the different systems of philosophy, orthodox and heterodox, have been briefly included in the account of each system. Without much repeating whatever has thus been said earlier, we shall here review the concept of *mokṣa* chiefly with reference to its nature and means.

The essential features of what is described as the "ultimate value" are two. First, it must be an end in itself—not in a relative but in an absolute sense, that is to say, whenever it is chosen, it should be chosen for its own sake. Secondly, it should be all-satisfying. In other words, it should, in one sense or another, comprehend *all* the higher values. For this reason it must be one and eternal, or enduring and final (*ātyantika*). Only the concept of *mokṣa* fulfils these criteria.

All the Indian schools agree in holding that *mokṣa* is self-realization, or restoring the self to its normal condition, though the exact nature of the self is variously conceived. Since that condition is regarded as one of perfection, the ideal may otherwise be described as self-perfection, in which the lower self completely yields place to the higher. The same self endures throughout the process, and so the conception of *mokṣa* is "that of a consummation and not that of a means leading to an end."[66] We may speak of a distinction between means and end only in the sense that the process involves successive states that follow one after another in some definite order, so that the culminating state may be described as the end of the process. The point is that the members of the series of states belong to one and the same self and are, therefore, internally connected. Consequently, there is no end and means here as externally related to each other. The end, or purpose, if we can use that word for *mokṣa*, governs the whole process and is immanent at every stage of it. The end here is but the means realized, like the curds being the transformation of milk.

It is the emphasis on the self in the conception of *mokṣa* as self-realization that accounts for the common Indian name for philosophy, viz., *adhyātmaśāstra*, or "the science of the self." The usual objection that other things which are of equal importance are thereby neglected does not really apply here, since the self meant to be realized is the higher, or ideal, self. And so self-realization cannot be equated with seeking personal good. We may add here that in the theistic systems, whether pluralistic or monistic, self-realization is regarded only as a necessary aspect of *mokṣa* but not the whole of it. It is supplemented by the idea of God-realization, since, in some degree or other, a distinction is maintained between soul and God. This is the reason why *bhakti* is included by them in the means to *mokṣa*.

All schools are agreed that *mokṣa* is a state of restful peace, or absolute satisfaction. In fact, the realization of any value means satisfaction, or peace. In everyday life the satisfaction will be only provisional, for the desires fulfilled are only of some partial aspect of the self and not of the self as a whole. But in the fulfilment of *mokṣa* the satisfaction will be abiding, because it relates to the self as such. Beyond this feature, there is difference of opinion among schools on the exact nature of *mokṣa*. Some schools hold that in liberation there is only complete absence of pain, whereas some others aver that it is marked by supreme bliss.

The goal of life as first conceived in India was the attainment of unalloyed happiness in a future life (*abhyudaya*) by propitiating numerous deities. This was essentially seeking happiness for oneself. It was as a reaction to this hedonistic aim that various other schools adopted the opposite view of the goal as mere freedom from pain, which constituted, according to them, the true nature of *mokṣa*. This was the view advocated, for instance, by Nyāya-Vaiśeṣika and Sāṅkhya-Yoga. There was a reversion from this also later under the influence of Vedānta, which triumphed over all other schools. The new ideal was the positive one of bliss. This view does not replace the negative view, but includes and transcends it. The affirmation of complete bliss necessarily implies also the total absence of pain. Nor is this a restoration of the older hedonistic ideal, since the bliss of *mokṣa* is not a new acquisition by the self, which is what the older ideal means. It is simply the regaining of what is intrinsic to the self. Moreover, to say that liberation is bliss is not hedonistic, for the pleasure for which it stands is unmixed and eternal, but the pleasure which the hedonist has in view is neither.

The difference between the negative and the positive views of *mokṣa* arises from a difference in the conception of the self. Bliss is the intrinsic nature of the self, according to those who subscribe to the positive view; and this naturally reveals itself when the self is released from bondage. According to those who hold by the negative view, neither bliss nor its opposite belongs to the self, and, therefore, it is without either of them in the state of release when the true nature of the self is restored to it.

We now turn to another question. An intrinsic value, as we have said in Chapter Six, cannot be something that is already realized (*siddha*). To be sought for its own sake, the value has to be something yet to be realized (*sādhya*). (An instrumental value, on the contrary, could be either *sādhya* or *siddha*.) Now, the word *sādhya* may be taken either in a positive or in a negative sense. In the positive sense it means something to be newly produced, i.e., the achievement of the value concerned is a direct process. The attainment of happiness in heaven (*abhyudaya*) is a *sādhya* of this nature. No Indian school has taken *mokṣa* as *sādhya* in the positive sense of being generated anew, for what is produced, or effected, cannot be eternal. And all schools maintain that the ultimacy of *mokṣa* implies its eternality. The state of *mokṣa* is looked upon by all of them as, in one sense or another, normal to the self; and that of *saṁsāra* as a lapse from it. Hence, according to all of them, *mokṣa* is something yet to be in a negative sense of recovery, or restoration, of some sort; and the process of its achievement is indirect.

Now, if we take the word *sādhya* in the negative sense, there are two possibilities. In one the end sought may be already existent, and yet it may remain unrealized owing to some physical obstacle, as in the case of a buried treasure. Here the achievement of the value consists in physically removing the obstacle. It is not produced but rendered accessible. In the other variety also the end sought may remain hidden from our view and unrealized, but here the obstacle is not physical. It is mental, being merely our failure to realize that the end is already in our possession, as in the case of a person searching for his eye-glasses while still wearing them. The realization of value here consists only in overcoming our ignorance relating to it. Knowledge also can be a means for achieving value, like action. In both these negative forms of *sādhya*, the removal of the obstacle involves a change in the existing order of things. But while in the former the change is actual, i.e., in the realm of being, in the latter it is only mental, a change in our view of the object.

To most Indian schools, *mokṣa* is of the former type of negative *sādhya*. The true nature of the self is spiritual, and bondage consists in its lying concealed under real limitations. The achievement of *mokṣa* involves an actual change in the condition of the self to get rid of these limitations and restore it to its true spiritual status. We have to note that here, though *mokṣa* is not generated anew, it is an event which actually happens. We may say that it is a latent possibility that is made actual by a real change. Advaita, however, while agreeing with other schools that *mokṣa* is not newly brought into being, like *dharma*, differs from them in regard to the view that it is the result of removing actual obstacles. Its reason is that if *mokṣa* involves actual change, though with regard to its obstacles, it cannot be eternal as all schools maintain. Whatever is the result of activity, being dependent upon the aids to such activity, should necessarily be temporal. Hence, according to Advaita, *mokṣa* can be regarded as *sādnya* only in the second type of negative sense illustrated earlier. In its view, "the self has been and will ever be what it always is, viz., Brahman."[67] This truth is lost sight of owing to congenital ignorance. *Mokṣa* consists merely in getting rid of this ignorance; and simultaneously with this riddance, the self reveals itself in its true nature as Brahman. "It is in this special sense that *mokṣa* is to be described as *sādhya* and regarded as a value in Advaita."[68] The obstacle to be removed, viz., *māyā*, is here conceived as illusory. Hence in Advaita *jñāna* is regarded as thc sole and sufficient means to *mokṣa*, while in other doctrines *jñāna*, in someway, stands in need of *karma* to serve its purpose. If *mokṣa* means a becoming, or actual achievement, we may doubt whether it is or is not fully attainable. But here the question is inadmissible because, in truth, it is always attained. Strictly speaking, *mokṣa* is *siddha*, or ever accomplished. "The condition of *mokṣa* thus differs from *saṁsāra* merely in a change of outlook, and there is no factual change whatsoever."[69]

An important result of this view is that *mokṣa* becomes identified with the self in its true nature. The Advaitin does not, we should remember, deny the need for effort in securing freedom. Effort is necessary for putting oneself on the path leading to the realization of the truth and thereby giving scope for the self to reveal itself. Thus the Advaita conception of *mokṣa* is unique. We may say that there are two conceptions of liberation among Indian schools. It is a state of the self, according to the majority, in which the self is restored to its pristine purity. According to Advaita, it is the self itself. "The self is not valuable, but value itself. It is not a value *for* the self that is sought here as it is in the other doctrines...but value *as* the self."[70] Consequently, while for other doctrines, *mokṣa* is one of the values, though the highest, for Advaita, *mokṣa*, or the self, is the *only* value, and all other values are but partial aspects, if not distortions, of it.

The best illustration of this truth that the self is the only value is to be found in the section of the *Bṛhadāraṇyaka Upaniṣad* called Maitreyī Brāhmaṇa.[71] Its most important passage teaches that everything, like husband, wife, sons, wealth, and so on, is loved, not really for its own sake, but for the sake of the self (*ātman*) behind it, which is identical with Brahman. The lesson conveyed here is this. If a thing is valued *for* something else, it is that something that constitutes the true value; and since everything in the world is stated here to get its worth because of the self, it is the self that is the only value.

We may now refer briefly to the concept of *jīvanmukti*, which has a better appeal to the modern mind than the idea that liberation is possible only after death. Advaita, Sāṅkhya, and Buddhism believe in it in a literal sense. Connection with a finite body, according to Advaita, is not incompatible with the realization of the infinite self. Even those schools that do not formally accept *jīvanmukti* acknowledge a state equivalent to it, though actual liberation is stated to be possible only after death. The difference between the two views is in their bearing on the duration of the practical discipline meant for *mokṣa*. To the latter view, the discipline should continue till the end of life, however advanced a person may be. To the former, the discipline is superfluous after enlightenment, as there is nothing further to be achieved.

The *jīvanmukta*, it is uniformly acknowledged, is given to active sympathy for fellow beings. Only, while it is love that prompts activity according to monistic schools, it is pity, or compassion, according to dualistic and pluralistic schools. The love in the former case is born of experiencing the unity of all, and consequently it is not love for others as equals but as essentially one with oneself. It is pity in the latter case because the sense of difference is essential to such systems. In either case, the disinterested activity of the *jīvanmukta* is a natural consequence of his insight into the true nature of the universe and of man's place in it. The activity is wholly impersonal, and he responds to presented situations without relating them to himself. He does not cease from acting, and he rises above the moods of elation and discomfiture. An important service of his is imparting spiritual instruction to those who genuinely seek the truth. This is in accordance with the Indian view that only one who has himself realized the truth is fully fitted to impart it to others. In short, he serves as an example to all as to how life is to be led. That is why merit is won by merely approaching such a person.

We shall finally refer in broad outline to the means to *mokṣa*. Detachment (*vairāgya*) is regarded by all schools as the necessary preliminary to the effort for *mokṣa*. It consists in overcoming all selfish inclinations, which stand in the way of progress to liberation. The means to cultivate detachment is moral training, the modalities of which differ between the orthodox and the heterodox traditions. Another discipline which is common to all Indian schools is knowledge of the true nature of the self and its relation to the rest of reality. The content of *jñāna* depends on the conception of reality in the various schools. *Jñāna* is the positive counterpart to the negative discipline of *vairāgya*. To begin with, *jñāna* is only mediate. To convert it into the immediate form, or experience, which alone leads to release, meditation (*yoga*) is recommended by all schools. Meditation is concentrating the mind on the true nature of reality. Hence, strictly speaking, it is not an addition to knowledge but part of it. There are exercises which train the mind in the technique of meditation before it is put to constant dwelling on the nature of reality. The theistic schools prescribe also *bhakti*, or loving devotion to God, with a view to earning God's grace, which is regarded as the final condition for liberation; and here meditation merges in devotion.

The Problem of Sarva-mukti

The problem relates to whether liberation is such that it can be attained by one and all or only by some; and if it is the former, whether it is to be attained by individuals separately or by all together. There are some schools that hold the view that freedom for all is impossible. The Yoga of Patañjali and Mīmāṁsā cite the endlessness of *saṁsāra* and the infinity in the number of souls as evidence against universal freedom. The Dvaita form of Vedānta even denies the right to liberation specifically to certain types of souls. Such a view denies the equality of souls in respect of the final aim of life. Hence the majority of schools maintain that release is for all. But of them, most believe that liberation is separate for each individual in isolation from the rest. And this is the prevalent ideal in Indian philosophy on the whole. The doctrine of *karma* suggests that each person is responsible for his future. It is only a few that advocate what is called *sarva-mukti*, or universal redemption, in the sense that all souls attain liberation simultaneously. It means that "no one, whatever his qualifications and however far he may advance on the path to it, will actually attain *mokṣa* until all are qualified for it."[72] Broadly, there are three ways of conceiving the possibility of *sarva-mukti*, and they are represented by Mahāyāna Buddhism, the school of Bhartṛprapañca, and by some Advaitins.

In Mahāyāna Buddhism, *mokṣa*, or *nirvāṇa*, consists in attaining Buddhahood, or the state of the Buddha. Short of this state, is the state of the *bodhisattva*, or a person who has attained enlightenment. The *bodhisattva* is the "aspirant for perfection," or "the Buddha-to-be." The point of significance here is that a *bodhisattva* does not straightway seek Buddhahood for himself. His compassion for others who are still in suffering leads him to wait till he could take them also on the path to perfection. "Every man is a sleeping Buddha," in the sense that every one is fitted for Buddhahood. He has only to awaken himself to see it. The *bodhisattva* places his own enlightenment at the service of others in order to help them to reach the same goal. He acquires virtues not only to teach others, but also to set an example to them. Such a view directly leads to the conception of *sarva-mukti*. But it is important to note that the ideal of universal release is not inherent in the system. The system does not mean that no one can attain freedom till all are freed. It is rather a case of one who is qualified for freedom voluntarily withholding himself from it in order to help all others prepare for it.

The idea of *sarva-mukti* is built into the system of Bhartṛprapañca. The one Brahman contains within himself the variety of the world and the souls. When the variety is latent, Brahman is called *para*. And when the variety becomes manifest, he is called *apara*. There are two stages in the evolution of variety out of Brahman. In the first stage *para* Brahman becomes *apara* on the one hand and the physical world on the other. The *apara* Brahman may be described as the cosmic soul, or the universal *jīva*. In the second stage the cosmic soul further transforms itself into the individual *jīvas*. Thus the individual selves are not independent of the cosmic soul. They are only a functional divergence of the cosmic soul. The one soul functions through many centres. Strictly speaking, there is only one soul to be liberated. It follows that the so-called individual souls can only contribute to the liberation of that one soul, which will not occur until the last *jīva* is also successful. There is unity of purpose among *jīvas* in regard to *mokṣa*. Bhartṛprapañca's conception of *sarva-mukti* thus depends on the relation between *jīvas* and the cosmic soul. No one can reach his spiritual goal apart from others. Everyone who is qualified works for the perfection of all. Since evolution is in two stages, there are two stages in the path to liberation. In the first stage all finite selves realize their oneness with the cosmic soul. In the second, the selves as cosmic soul realize the oneness of all being (including matter) as Brahman. It is the first of these stages that is significant for *sarva-mukti*.

Advaitins are divided on the question of *sarva-mukti*. To begin with, we have to distinguish between those who admit only one soul (*eka-jīvavādins*) and those who admit many (*aneka-jīvavādins*). According to the former, the single soul which exists fancies that there are other souls as in a dream. The advocates of this view admit also universal release, for, when the one soul that is, is liberated, all the other so-called souls are necessarily freed. This view is not acceptable to other Advaitins, since it is sheer solipsism (*dṛṣṭi-sṛṣṭi-vāda*). If all other selves are mere appearances to one soul, by the same token, it itself will be a mere dream to other souls.

Of those who believe in many souls, it is only some that can subscribe to *sarva-mukti*. We must now identify them. In explaining the relation between *jīva* and Brahman, two broad views are taken by Advaitins. One is the *avaccheda-pakṣa*. Brahman is compared to the universal space and the *jīvas* to the space delimited by pots, jugs, etc. The other view is the *bimba-pratibimba-pakṣa*, which adopts the analogy of the original object and its reflection in a medium. Of this view, again, there are two divisions. One explains Nirguṇa Brahman as the original (*bimba*) and the *jīvas* as well as Saguṇa Brahman, or *Īśvara*, as its reflections (*pratibimba*). The other regards Saguṇa Brahman as the original and the *jīvas* alone as the reflections, the idea of Nirguṇa Brahman standing apart as the basis of both. It is those who adopt the last view that advocate *sarva-mukti*.

The analogy of reflection signifies that when the reflecting medium is destroyed, the reflection merges in the original. Let us consider the view where Nirguṇa Brahman is the original and both *jīvas* and *Īśvara* are the reflections. When the reflecting medium, viz., *avidyā*, is annulled by right knowledge, the *jīva*, so to say, merges in Brahman, i.e., realizes its non-difference with it. Simultaneously, the idea of *Īśvara*, which is also a reflection, vanishes, or merges in Brahman. There is no question of *sarva-mukti* here. According to the other view, *Īśvara* is the original and the *jīvas* are reflections of it. Hence in this case, when *avidyā* is removed, the soul merges in *Īśvara*. This is not true freedom, which consists in realizing Nirguṇa Brahman, but a state called *sarva-bhāvāpatti*.

The term means that the soul which is freed from *avidyā* realizes its oneness with all the other souls, all of them being reflections of the same *Īśvara*. He then sees all in himself and himself in all. He works for others in the form of *Īśvara*. Until all souls attain Saguṇa Brahman in the same manner, he cannot become free, i.e., attain non-difference with Nirguṇa Brahman. This is because the notion of *Īśvara* as the original, its *biṁbatva*, vanishes for this soul, but it persists for other souls. The inward perfection of no soul is completed until the whole system to which it belongs becomes perfect. When this consummation takes place, Saguṇa Brahman as such automatically disappears and endures as Nirguṇa Brahman. In other words, when the individuality of souls is eliminated, the "personality" of Saguṇa Brahman also disappears, the idea of it being relative to the idea of souls. This is final freedom. None attains it till all are qualified for it by merging with *Īśvara* in the first instance. The doctrine thus teaches that, at the last, all will come to realize the Advaita truth and win salvation. (Realizing Saguṇa Brahman as conceived here is not the same as *krama-mukti*, which does not entail waiting for others to reach the same goal.) This view of *sarva-mukti* is open to the objection that enlightenment loses its significance here, since it does not result in full freedom.

REFERENCES

1. *ICV*, p. 154.
2. Vide ibid., p. 161.
3. Ibid., p. 163.
4. Ibid., p. 166.
5. Vide ibid.
6. Vide ibid.
7. Ibid., p. 168.
8. Ibid.
9. Ibid., p. 175.
10. Vide ibid., p. 183.
11. Vide ibid.
12. Vide ibid., p. 193.
13. Ibid., p. 194.
14. Vide ibid., p. 201, n. 53.
15. Ibid., p. 219.
16. Vide ibid., pp. 223-24.
17. Vide ibid., p. 224.
18. Vide ibid., p. 221.
19. Ibid., p. 221.
20. Ibid.
21. Ibid.
22. Ibid.
23. Vide ibid., p. 222, n. 10.
24. Ibid., p. 226.
25. *pravṛttireṣā bhūtānāṁ nivṛttistu mahāphalā.* Ibid., p. 231, n. 37.
26. Ibid., p. 233.
27. Ibid.
28. Vide ibid., pp. 233-34.
29. Vide *AE*, p. 1.
30. Ibid., p. 44.
31. Ibid.
32. *QAP*, p. 31.
33. Vide ibid., p. 31.
34. *AE*, p. 44.
35. Vide *ICV*, p. 316.
36. Ibid.
37. Vide ibid., p. 321.
38. *AE*, p. 46.
39. Vide ibid., p. 31, n. 1.
40. Vide ibid., p. 31.
41. Ibid., p. 27.

42. Ibid., p. 22.
43. Vide ibid., pp. 23-24.
44. Ibid., p. 23.
45. Vide ibid., p. 18.
46. Ibid., p. 20.
47. Ibid.
48. Ibid.
49. Vide ibid., p. 28.
50. Vide *QAP*, p. 33.
51. Vide *AE*, p. 34, n. 2.
52. Ibid., p. 39.
53. Vide ibid., p. 40.
54. *ICV*, p. 343.
55. *AE*, p. 37.
56. Ibid., p. 42.
57. *QAP*, p. 32.
58. *AE*, p. 50.
59. Ibid., p. 50, n. 1.
60. Ibid., p. 51.
61. Ibid., pp. 25-26.
62. Ibid., p. 52.
63. Vide ibid.
64. Ibid., p. 53.
65. Ibid., p. 7.
66. *ICV*, p. 249.
67. *PEIP*, p. 68.
68. *QAP*, p. 87.
69. Ibid., p. 86.
70. *ICV*, p. 263.
71. II, iv. Vide also IV, iv.
72. *ICV*, p. 293.

8

Hiriyanna: An Appreciation

For a long time since the introduction of university education in India by the British, courses in philosophy in Indian universities consisted only of areas in European philosophy. The study of Indian philosophy was confined to the traditional institutions, the *pāṭhaśālās*, but these centres had already fallen into oblivion as a result of the prominence given to English education. Thus to the English-educated Indians the philosophical culture of India was gradually becoming a closed book. While this trend was on, there was a movement of an opposite kind which emanated from the voluntary effort of distinguished individuals. European scholars who were attracted to Indian thought, having learnt Sanskrit, were laboriously digging into the different aspects of traditional Indian wisdom, and bringing them to the notice of Indians and foreigners alike. Side by side with their efforts, English-educated Indian scholars who were also steeped in Sanskrit learning made their own efforts to interpret Indian philosophy in modern terminology for the benefit of scholars both in India and abroad. All together, there was, so to say, a renaissance of Indian traditional wisdom in the modern idiom in the late nineteenth and early twentieth centuries. Among the pioneers who led this movement from within the country was Mysore Hiriyanna. The list included S. Radhakrishnan, S.N. Dasgupta, G.R. Malkani, R.D. Ranade, Ganganath Jha, Jadunath Sinha, and K.C. Bhattacharya, to name but a few. Each of these thinkers had his own contribution to make in terms of both the philosophical material discovered and interpreted and also the method of exposition. While the work of some of these scholars has become widely known, Hiriyanna's contribution to the recovery of Indian philosophy still calls for fuller appreciation.

Hiriyanna's approach to Indian philosophy was perfectly balanced, and this balanced outlook stands out in three ways. First, Hiriyanna's deep commitment to Indian philosophy did not make him insular. He no doubt regarded the re-discovery and interpretation of its teachings as his mission in life. At the same time he kept his mind open to Western thought and regarded its impact on Indian thought as so much welcome for the better appreciation of our own. Secondly, his adherence to the Indian tradition in philosophy was unquestionable but not literal. He did not consider fidelity to tradition as identical with bare conformance. He took the liberty to interpret traditional thought in contemporary modes of expression while keeping the spirit of tradition intact. Thirdly, while he clearly perceived the role of religion in shaping Indian philosophical thought, he never mixed the standpoint of religion with that of philosophy. Hiriyanna recognized that without its alliance with Indian religion, Indian philosophy would have been barren and aimless like so much of Western speculative philosophy. At the same time he never succumbed to the temptation of importing uncritical faith into the justification of any philosophical position. He was thoroughly rational in his approach to philosophy while at the same time acknowledging the limits of reason as a tool of discovery. The essence of religion, according to him, was spiritual experience, and not mere faith and ritual, though these have their own value. Philosophy also, he felt, must culminate in experience, and herein lies the real bond of philosophy and religion as he saw it. Considering this poised outlook, Hiriyanna could not be easily accused of any unreasonable partiality or unaccommodative prejudice in respect of any point of view in philosophy.

Hiriyanna's contribution to Indian philosophy may be considered on two lines: with reference to its schools and with reference to its aspects, or divisions. His approach to schools of Indian philosophy is more than historical; it may be described as meta-philosophical. He does not stop with identifying the stages in the growth of Indian philosophy from early times, marking the routes of its diversification into different schools, tracing the phases in the development of each school through its successive thinkers, and assessing the impact of one school upon another in the course of history. Even in this regard his service is significant. But his more important contribution in respect of schools—though it is not easily perceivable—is that he enters into the merits of each school, and on that basis conceives of a conceptual hierarchy of doctrinal positions, which, for him, culminates in Advaita. His implied criteria for comparing one school with another on their merits may be identified as two: a larger coverage and a better organization. A system of philosophy may be considered more satisfactory than another if it takes into account a wider area of human experience than the other and if it is also comparatively free from contradiction in explaining relationships within its material.

to liberation does not accord with his own criticism of the metaphysics of the school as one involving the internal contradiction of difference-cum-non-difference. However, on the whole, Hiriyanna's leaning towards the ideal of *sarva-mukti* may be traced to his innate regard for the spirit of service and sacrifice, wherever it may manifest itself. In fact, it is this regard, we may safely surmise, that explains the admiration which he occasionally expresses for the Buddha and Gandhi, besides his abiding fidelity to Śaṅkara.

We have so far dwelt upon Hiriyanna's attention to the ultimate value. Hiriyanna is equally keen on showing that the true place of all the other values is as means to the ultimate value. It is in this spirit that in his *Indian Conception of Values* he makes the innovation of bringing epistemology under the study of values under the head "logical value," while the usual practice of writers, old and new, is to give epistemology a separate status. His contribution to the content of the logical and the ethical values is also substantial. As for his work on the aesthetic value, there is an added dimension as we shall see presently.

Hiriyanna's work was not confined to beaten tracks. He had the knack of divining resources for research in untrodden areas. He himself worked on some of these areas and produced original results. A striking instance of such contribution is Indian aesthetics. What was familiar to Indian scholars of his time was the discussion of beauty with reference to the character of art, especially literature, represented by the branch of learning known as Alaṅkāraśāstra. To that extent the study of beauty remained outside the scope of philosophy. But Hiriyanna for the first time brought it within the realm of philosophy also by drawing attention to the significance of art and, by the inclusion of nature, of beauty in general to life.

> Here is a vast field for the student of Indian antiquities to labour in and the harvest, if well garnered, will be of advantage not only for the history of Indian thought but also, it may be hoped, for universal philosophy.[5]
>
> It appears necessary in the future not only to carry research further in the departments already worked, but also to widen considerably the sphere of research itself.[6]

Hiriyanna sensed more such fields for research—Indian epistemology and formal logic, for instance. And in his works he has generously shared what he contemplated on them with future scholars and has also left for them valuable leads for investigation.[7] Love of the subject, not personal credit, was his motivation.

REFERENCES

1. *R*, p. 54.
2. *ICV*, p. 293; Vide also *QAP*, pp. 77-78.
3. Vide *ICV*, pp. 309-12.
4. Ibid., p. 305.
5. *AE*, p. 1.
6. Ibid., p. 16.
7. Vide *IPS—II*, pp. 112-18.

Bibliography

WORKS OF M. HIRIYANNA

Īśāvāsyopaniṣad with the commentary of Śrī Śaṅkarācārya, translated into English with Introduction and Notes, Sri Vani Vilas Press, Srirangam, 1911. Reprinted with the text of the Upaniṣad and the commentary, Kavyalaya Publishers, Mysore, 1972.

Kenopaniṣad with the commentary of Śrī Śaṅkarācārya, translated into English with Introduction and Notes, Sri Vani Vilas Press, Srirangam, 1912. Reprinted with the text of the Upaniṣad and the commentary, Kavyalaya Publishers, Mysore, 1974.

Kāṭhakopaniṣad with the commentary of Śrī Śaṅkarācārya, translated into English, Sri Vani Vilas Press, Srirangam, 1915.

Bṛhadāraṇyakopaniṣad, part I, sections 1-3, with the commentary of Śrī Śaṅkarācārya, translated into English, Sri Vani Vilas Press, Srirangam, 1919.

The Naiṣkarmyasiddhi of Sureśvarācārya with the *Candrikā* of Jñānottama, Introduction, and Explanatory Notes (a revised edition of the work earlier edited with Notes and Index by Colonel G.A. Jacob in 1890 and 1905), Bhandarkar Oriental Research Institute, Poona, 1925, Bombay Sanskrit and Prakrit Series no. XXXVIII.

Vedāntasāra, a work on Vedānta Philosophy by Sadānanda, edited with Introduction, Translation, and Explanatory Notes, Oriental Book Agency, Poona, 1929.

Outlines of Indian Philosophy, George Allen and Unwin, London, 1932.

Iṣṭasiddhi of Vimuktātman with extracts from the *Vivaraṇa* of Jñānottama, critically edited with Introduction and Notes, Oriental Institute, Baroda, 1933, Gaekwad's Oriental Series no. LXV.

The Essentials of Indian Philosophy, George Allen and Unwin, London, 1949.

Popular Essays in Indian Philosophy, Kavyalaya Publishers, Mysore, 1952.

The Quest After Perfection, Kavyalaya Publishers, Mysore, 1952.

Art Experience, Kavyalaya Publishers, Mysore, 1954.
Sanskrit Studies, Kavyalaya Publishers, Mysore, 1954.
Indian Philosophical Studies—I, Kavyalaya Publishers, Mysore, 1957.
The Mission of Philosophy, Kavyalaya Publishers, Mysore, 1960.
Reviews with a Foreword by Dr. V. Raghavan, Kavyalaya Publishers, Mysore, 1970.
Indian Philosophical Studies—II, Kavyalaya Publishers, Mysore, 1972.
The Indian Conception of Values, Kavyalaya Publishers, Mysore, 1975.

OTHER SOURCES CONSULTED

Professor M. Hiriyanna Commemoration Volume, Professor M. Hiriyanna Commemoration Volume Committee, Mysore, 1952.
Raghavan, V., "A Great Modest Scholar", *The Hindu,* Madras, December 1971.
Rājasudhā, Collected Papers of Dr. K. Kunjunni Raja, Dr. Kunjunni Raja Shashtiabdapurthi Celebrations Committee, Madras, 1982

Index